HISTORICAL COLLECTIONS
of the Georgia Chapters
Daughters *of the*
American Revolution
Volume V

MARRIAGE RECORDS
of
Greene County, Georgia
(1787–1875)
and
Oglethorpe County, Georgia
(1795–1852)

Compiled by
Mrs. Herschel W. Smith

CLEARFIELD

Originally published
Atlanta, Georgia, 1949

Copyright © 1949, 1977
by The Georgia Society
Daughters of the American Revolution
All Rights Reserved.

Reprinted with permission of
The Georgia State DAR.

Reprinted for
Clearfield Company, Inc. by
Genealogical Publishing Co., Inc.
Baltimore, Maryland
1995, 2001

International Standard Book Number: 0-8063-4567-5

Made in the United States of America

Preface

The Lucy Cook Peel Memorial Committee was founded by the Georgia State Conference, D. A. R., in 1923, in appreciation of her collection of valuable records and the loyal work given to the National Society, D. A. R. and to the Georgia Society, D. A. R., by Mrs. William Lawson Peel, Ex Vice President General of the National Society, Honorary State Regent of the Georgia Society, Founder and Regent of the Joseph Habersham Chapter of Atlanta, Georgia, and the First National Chairman of the Committee of Real Daughters in the National Society.

The marriage records of Oglethorpe County, Georgia (1795-1852), and Greene County, Georgia (1787-1875), were compiled by Mrs. Herschel W. Smith, Regent of the Sunbury Chapter, D. A. R., Winder, Georgia, and presented to the State Genealogical Records Committee and the Lucy Cook Peel Memorial Committee.

There are few counties in Georgia richer than Greene County and Oglethorpe County in historic names and historic places, or more important for genealogical research workers.

Greene County was created by Act of February 3, 1786, and named for General Nathaniel Greene, Revolutionary soldier. County seat, Greensboro.

Oglethorpe County was created by Act of December 19, 1793, and named for General James Edward Oglethorpe, the Founder of Georgia. County seat, Lexington.

Volume V, Historical Collections, Georgia Chapters, D. A. R., is presented as a dependable and authoritative reference book for libraries, patriotic organizations, and those interested in genealogical research work.

MARRIAGE RECORDS
Greene County, Georgia

A

AARON, Edward S. — June 24, 1860
  Martha Ann Mullins — James M. Kelly
AARON, George W. — September 6, 1860
  Mary Susan Taylor
AARON, Thomas D. — November 2, 1858
  Martha J. Mitchell — J. H. Bragg
ABEL, William A. — January 24, 1839
  Eliza Reid — James W. Godkin
ABERCROMBIE, Anderson — February 24, 1819
  Sydney Grimes — Lovick Pierce
ACREE, James M. — December 1, 1841
  Sarah Smith
ADAIR, Robert — August 28, 1800
  Babsy Reid
ADAIR, Virgil J. — March 26, 1868
  Mary F. Crawford — Thos. P. Sanford
ADAMS, John — March 5, 1804
  Patsy Johnson
ADAMS, William — November 2, 1820
  Rachel Sweeney
ADAMS, William E. — November 18, 1874
  Sallie E. Copelan — W. R. Johnson
ADERHOLD, John H. P. — June 5, 1866
  Anna N. Arnold — Hart C. Peek, O.M.
ADKINS, Booker — July 6, 1832
  Adaline Tuggle — John Armstrong
ADKINS, Joseph — October 1, 1818
  Mary Lanford — Thomas Stocks
AIKENS, William — January 25, 1821
  Betsy Ann Grigsby — O. Porter
AKERS, John — December 4, 1827
  Rebecca Turner — William Bryan
AKERS, Samuel — February 28, 1828
  Nancy Robins — William Bryan
AKIN, Edmond — October 13, 1830
  Sarah Ann Veazey — John Harris
AKINS, Elijah — February 7, 1822
  Eliza Ball — John Harris
AKINS, Henry T. — February 28, 1869
  Eliza J. Daniel — Wm. A. Overton
AKINS, James — March 17, 1800
  Nancy Ivey
AKINS, James — March 4, 1818
  Betsy Cooper
AKINS, Joseph — April 23, 1818
  Mary Rea — Lemuel Greene

AKINS, William A.   October 2, 1856
  Elizabeth Andrews   W. D. Murden
ALDRIDGE, Samuel P.   August 27, 1836
  Sarah Ann Furlow   Calb M. Key, M.G.
ALFRIEND, Benjamin   October 7, 1837
  Margaret Simonton   John G. Holtzclaw
ALFRIEND, Benjamin C.   December 22, 1863
  Eliza J. Smith   John W. McCrary, M.G.
ALFRIEND, Edward W.   January 4, 1841
  Mary E. Dunn   F. R. Golding
ALFRIEND, William L.   February 22, 1842
  Sarah Frances Dunn   F. R. Golding, M.G.
ALFORD, Bertus   October 1, 1801
  Mary Boone   W. Stocks
ALFORD, Briton   March 19, 1805
  Betsy Brassel   Thos. Crawford
ALFORD, Chinchez   January 18, 1806
  Deany Wooten
ALBRITTON, Ansel M.   January 20, 1856
  Evalina J. Macon   T. D. Martin M.G.
ALEXANDER, Rinardo B.   September 12, 1843
  Harriet C. Dolvin   Wesley P. Arnold
ALEXANDREW, Joseph K.   December 19, 1844
  Patience T. Alfriend   John Howell
ALFORD, Julius   March 14, 1821
  Eliza Cook   Lovick Pierce
ALFORD, Lodowich   May 16, 1798
  Judith Jackson
ALFORD, William H.   January 5, 1858
  Georgiana J. Mullins   T. D. Martin, M.G.
ALFORD, Zaboch   November 3, 1814
  Perrien Sherrill   Evans Myrick
ALLEN, Benjamin W.   August 15, 1860
  Martha J. Barnhart   James H. Kilpatrick
ALLEN, Dickson E.   June 7, 1859
  Nancy C. Jackson   L. B. Caldwell
ALLEN, E. M.   August 5, 1847
  Eliza Catherine Park   Francis Bowman
ALLEN, James   August 2, 1824
  Sultana Broadway
ALLEN, John   March 20, 1805
  Eliza Carleton
ALLEN, John   January 31, 1828
  Polly Jackson   Joshua Cannon
ALLEN, J. H.   December 21, 1869
  Missouri A. Hooks   L. B. Caldwell
ALLEN, Josiah   November 18, 1824
  Rachel Colclough
ALLEN, Pleasant Josiah   June 11, 1832
  Martha Pyron   Thos. W. Grimes
ALLEN, Stephen   June 14, 1830
  Martha Pyron

ALLEN, W. A.   January 2, 1872
   Martha A. Jackson   L. B. Caldwell
ALLEN, Wiley   April 19, 1821
   Penelope Powers   Francis Cummins
ALLISON, Reuben   July 7, 1836
   Louisiana King   Geo. F. Pierce
ALLISON, William   June 4, 1822
   Martha Price   Robert Booth
ALLISTON, William P.   April 16, 1848
   Martha A. Walton   Hinton Crawford
ALLRED, William   February 23, 1825
   Jane Park   John Webb
ALLRED, William H.   May 23, 1865
   Sarah F. Rowland   Jefferson Wright
ALSTON, Willis   December 18, 1828
   Eliza Howard   Lovick Pierce
ALVIS, Ashley   September 16, 1825
   Catherine McIntosh   John Dawson
AMMONS, Richard   December 9, 1830
   Rebecca Watson   George Hall
AMOSS, George M.   September 2, 1865
   Patience A. Smith
ANDERSON, Bazor   December 15, 1788
   Sarah Houghton
ANDERSON, Elijah   May 27, 1830
   Phebe Clarke   George Hall
ANDERSON, Henry   October 11, 1838
   Nancy Chapman   Ephraim Bruce
ANDERSON, John   May 26, 1831
   Elizabeth Lewis   J. P. Leveritt
ANDERSON, John M.   February 2, 1845
   Elvira O'Neal   James I. Findley
ANDERSON, Joseph   September 10, 1834
   Sarah Riley   James Anderson
ANDERSON, Noah   October 16, 1836
   Susan Mahan   Wilson S. Bishop
ANDERSON, Stewart   February 20, 1840
   Mary Watson   Thomas Stocks
ANDERSON, Thomas   July 29, 1829
   Ann Murry   William Bryan
ANDERSON, William   February 2, 1819
   Sarah Stephenson   Francis Cummins
ANDERSON, William W.   January 9, 1843
   Anna I. Whitaker
ANDERSON, William   August 5, 1857
   Adalade Tuggle   William R. Cox
ANDREWS, Adam   April 26, 1815
   Polly Brooks   C. Maddox
ANDREWS, Adam   January 28, 1847
   Martha Jane Oliver   J. L. Veazey
ANDREWS, Alexander   September 21, 1806
   Abby Atkinson   Jesse Lacey

ANDREWS, James — January 14, 1844
  Anne Greenwood — Wesley P. Arnold
ANDREWS, Lunceford M. — November 20, 1866
  Jedidah E. Moore — John O'Neal
ANDREWS, Matthew — January 12, 1837
  Susan Jones — James Moore
ANDREWS, Rohow — April 6, 1845
  Sara N. Landrum — N. Hill
ANDREWS, Rohow — July 9, 1848
  Mary Ann Hodge — J. A. Williams
ANDREWS, William R. — May 8, 1845
  Martha Ellis — D. W. McJunkin
ANDREWS, William N. — December 15, 1859
  Nancy C. Devaney — Littleton Caldwell
ANSLEY, William — December 6, 1827
  Nancy Thompson — Robert Booth
ARDIS, John — August 11, 1811
  Patsey Stallings — W. Johnson
ARKWRIGHT, James — September 18, 1823
  Sarah Pendergrass — Thomas Johnson
ARMOR, James — November 17, 1804
  Rachel Phillips
ARMOR, James N. — February 22, 1849
  Adrian W. Moore — William Bryan
ARMOR, John — November 18, 1788
  Nancy Caldwell
ARMOR, Reuben B. — July 1, 1834
  Mary S. Park
ARMOR, William — June 23, 1814
  Sarah Brown — John Armor
ARMOR, William — May 23, 1839
  Martha A. Riley — U. C. Peurifoy
ARMOR, William — November 14, 1850
  Arthanetia R. Walton — J. C. Simmons
ARMOR, William G. — February 13, 1873
  L. M. Hutcheson — J. M. Loury
ARMSTRONG, James — December 20, 1855
  Mary Edmondson — P. H. Mell
ARMSTRONG, Jesse M. — June 4, 1841
  Martha Culbreath — N. M. Lumpkin
ARMSTRONG, Jesse R. — November 30, 1866
  Olivia Baker — Henry C. Weaver
ARMSTRONG, John — November 15, 1865
  Mrs. Mary C. Armstrong — William R. Wilson
ARMSTRONG, William — January 4, 1866
  Lucy A. Crawford — John W. Tally, M.G.
ARNOLD, Martin B. — September 23, 1866
  Nancy Jane Hunter — S. I. Owens
ARNOLD, Solomon P. — May 24, 1832
  Margaret M. Brooks — A. Greene
ARTHUR, George — January 1, 1871
  Mary C. S. Johnson — B. P. Taylor

ARTHUR, Thomas J.   March 26, 1874
  C. J. Freeman   W. A. Partee
ASBERRY, Henry   November 3, 1808
  Louisa McLane   Peter Joyner
ASBURY, Jesse   April 20, 1815
  Abagail Smith   Robert Rea
ASBURY, Redman   July 29, 1841
  Mary Sophronia Norton   E. S. Hunter
ASBURY, Richard   November 12, 1817
  Martha Collier   Jesse Mercer
ASBURY, Richard   December 26, 1819
  Sarah Watts   William Cone
ASBURY, Thomas   October 31, 1822
  Nancy Lyne   Samuel Whateley
ASHLEY, Charles E.   February 18, 1841
  Lucy B. Pierce   James Moore
ASHLEY, William   November 30, 1831
  Charlotte Dorchey   Wooten O'Neal
ASHLEY, William   July 23, 1840
  Clarissa Keener   N. P. Jarrell
ASHLEY, William   December 19, 1841
  Nancy S. Wright   James Moore
ASKEW, Ezekiel P. G.   January 17, 1860
  Cornelia F. Mullins   W. G. Johnson
ASKEW, James B.   November 18, 1849
  Eliza F. Veazey   Joseph R. Parker
ASKEW, Joshua   January 23, 1862
  Elizabeth Atkinson   W. G. Johnson
ASKEW, William   January 3, 1831
  Cynthia Riley   George Hall
ASKEW, William   December 3, 1835
  Nancy Merritt   Jas. Anderson
ASTON, Robert   June 5, 1827
  Nancy Vaughn   John Harris
ASTON, William L.   May 26, 1814
  Sally Parrish   Robert Rea
ATKINS, Willis   December 31, 1815
  Priscilla D. Taylor   William Ray
ATKINSON, Isaac Parker   August 24, 1847
  Mary Rogers Moore   J. L. Rowland
ATKINSON, James C.   September 13, 1857
  Theodosia Wray   John H. M. Barton
ATKINSON, John   March 18, 1800
  Sally Moreland
ATKINSON, Lazarus   July 11, 1837
  Elizabeth Echols   Ephraim Bruce
ATKINSON, Nathan   May 28, 1813
  Polly Parker   Robert Rea
ATKINSON, Nathan L.   November 28, 1834
  Frances B. Slaughter
ATKINSON, Thomas   October 27, 1842
  Mary Merritt   H. H. Lawrence

ATKINSON, Thos. L. B. — March 2, 1848
　Elizabeth A. Bagley — James B. Nickelson
AUBREY, Lewis — June 24, 1802
　Dinah Harris
AUTRY, Jacob — May 20, 1829
　Isabeller McClane
AUTRY, O. P. — January 6, 1870
　Georgia Sanford — Philip Robinson
AVERY, Joseph — April 9, 1874
　Mary S. Haynes — John O'Neal
AWTRY, John — January 20, 1820
　Martha Moore — Malachi Murden
AWTRY, Reynolds — February 9, 1820
　Martha Carr — James Brockman
AXSON, Samuel E. — November 23, 1858
　Margaret Jane Hoyt — N. Hoyt, M.G.

B

BABB, William — January 19, 1796
　Susanna Heard
BACHELOR, Archibald — December 22, 1831
　Lucy Ann Mallory — Thomas W. Grimes
BACHELOR, Con — May 8, 1786
　(not shown)
BACHELOR, Richard — September 14, 1869
　Ella Seay — Philip Robinson
BAGBY, Charles L. — February 9, 1865
　Amanda M. Strange — J. A. Preston, M.G.
BAGBY, George E. R. — April 27, 1868
　Georgia A. P. Bowden — Jas. W. Godkin
BAILEY, Nathaniel — July 22, 1849
　Armietta Williams — J. T. Findley
BAILEY, Samuel Armstrong — May 19, 1831
　Rebecca F. Lloyd — Lovick Pierce
BAILEY, Simon — December 14, 1806
　Faithey Parker — B. Maddox
BAKER, Christopher — December 20, 1805
　Nancy Daniel
BAKER, Jonathan — October 29, 1818
　Mary Stallings — Thomas Riley
BAKER, Silas — December 29, 1830
　Mary M. Walker — S. M. Walhall
BAKER, William — September 24, 1805
　Nancy Williams
BAKER, William — July 12, 1807
　Rebkah Howell — James Holt
BALDWIN, Benjamin — January 4, 1802
　Catherine Watson
BALDWIN, Charles — August 22, 1839
　Susannah Love — Hinton Crawford, M.G.
BALDWIN, David — February 3, 1804
　Eliza Owens

BALDWIN, James Eliza White	March 13, 1804
BALDWIN, Joseph H. Harriett E. Edmondson	July 28, 1837 James Moore
BALDWIN, Robert Sarah Boning	December 22, 1788
BALDWIN, Samuel Nancy Williams	February 7, 1833 B. M. Sanders
BALDWIN, Thomas B. Ann E. Skidmore	February 14, 1837 Vincent Thornton, M.G.
BALDWIN, Thomas B. Frances I. Morris	December 10, 1840 James Jones
BALLARD, George Peggy Armour	November 9, 1801
BALLARD, John Nancy McLain	June 8, 1807 William Greer
BALLARD, William Nancy King	September 22, 1802
BARBER, Richard J. Ann Nicholson	October 29, 1840 B. M. Sanders
BAREFIELD, Arthur Sally Freeman	October 12, 1804
BARFIELD, Sampson Mary Bell	April 1, 1847
BARKER, James Eliz. Finch	April 25, 1841 James W. Godkin
BARKER, William Nancy Hackney	December 26, 1815 Leml. Greene
BARKSDALE, Greene B. Celia Connell	October 24, 1839
BARKWELL, Julius Ruth Harper	November 20, 1818 Jack Lumpkin
BARNES, Asa Mary A. Mapp	September 27, 1849 L. C. Peek
BARNES, Asa Martha Mapp	January 13, 1853 W. W. Moore
BARNES, Joshua Caroline Ledbetter	November 28, 1865 H. C. Peek, O.M.
BARNES, Samuel Elizabeth Barnhart	May 25, 1789
BARNES, William H. Martha Ann McMillan	August 5, 1841 R. F. Griffin
BARNETT, John Sally Sorrell	October 8, 1802
BARNETT, John Mary Willis	November 8, 1827 Edward Maxey
BARNETT, William Betsey Johnson	August 29, 1804
BARNHART, Bruce Christopher Smith	June 12, 1816 Thomas Snow
BARNHART, Leroy Sarah Parker	April 5, 1842 James Moore

BARNHART, Seaborn R.   December 19, 1875
  Talula E. Alford   John T. Dolvin
BARNWELL, Alexander   December 28, 1819
  Catherine Watts   Thomas Stocks
BARNWELL, Benjamin F.   July 3, 1866
  Elizabeth Ann Parrott   Philip B. Robinson
BARNWELL, Henry   January 31, 1822
  Maria Powers
BARNWELL, Henry   July 16, 1822
  Delila Booles   Thomas Stocks
BARNWELL, Jesse S.   October 6, 1858
  Rachael Nesson   James L. Tarwater
BARR, Oliver   December 10, 1873
  Margaret Freeman
BARRETT, John   February 1, 1831
  Lurany Lewis   Butt L. Cato
BARRON, Thomas   March 12, 1805
  Sally Clay
BARROW, Cyrus B.   April 19, 1851
  Frances E. Williams   Hinton Crawford
BARRY, M. M.   July 4, 1851
  Lucretia Cook   J. W. Godkin
BARTLETT, Abner   January 22, 1807
  Mary Chewning   W. McBiboney
BARTON, Thompson   November 18, 1860
  Sarah Daniel   J. W. Godkin
BASS, James A.   February 21, 1849
  Caroline McMillan   L. B. Jackson
BATCHELOR, Jesse   December 11, 1856
  Sarah A. Grant   James L. Laurence
BATES, Robert   July 13, 1821
  Patsey Campbell   John Harris
BATES, John   November 26, 1818
  Elizabeth Alford   Thomas Snow
BATES, Nathaniel   April 2, 1827
  Nancy Channell   Absalom Baugh
BATES, William   November 4, 1827
  Nancy Parker   John Harris
BATTLE, John   December 22, 1819
  Elizabeth Atkinson   Francis West
BAUCHCUM, Aaron   October 9, 1864
  Marv Camp   Wm. M. Chapman, M.G.
BAUGH, Abram   July 18, 1852
  Ridley Colley   B. Rowland
BAUGH, James E.   May 9, 1865
  Ada R. Smith
BAUGH, Richard Henry   May 12, 1858
  Marceline A. Gresham   F. F. Reynolds, M.G.
BAUGHCUM, Aaron   March 22, 1866
  Martha Holder   Ezekiel L. Williams
BAUGHCUM, Penckney   November 17, 1864
  Susan Jane Connel   Wm. M. Chapman, M.G.

BAUGHCUM, W. W. December 20, 1871
  Anna Clifton
BAXLEY, Aaron January 4, 1805
  Nancy Howell
BAXTER, William January 5, 1847
  Sarah E. Oslin H. H. Lawrence
BAYNON, Watkins January 10, 1825
  Ann Barnett
BAYS, Joseph July 27, 1823
  Edith Broadaway Nicholas Lewis
BEARDEN, Richard October 31, 1829
  Elizabeth Patrick
BEARDING, Arthur December 23, 1795
  Rebekah McClendon
BEARDS, Washington December 28, 1808
  Nancy Phillips Thomas Crawford
BEASLEY, Hiram February 1, 1851
  Lewansa Duberry
BEASLEY, William June 5, 1805
  Nancey English
BEASLEY, William December 4, 1845
  Mary Forrester E. S. Hunter
BEASLEY, William September 23, 1794
  Rachel Robinette
BEASLEY, ——— ———, 1801
  Anna Watson
BEATIE, John December 22, 1822
  Anna Todd Lovick Pierce
BEAVERS, Daniel November 19, 1799
  Nancy Pursy
BEAVERS, Nathan April 3, 1805
  Sally Blurton
BECK, T. J. December 16, 1869
  Mary L. King H. H. Tucker
BECKOM, John January 11, 1816
  Ruth Biddle Archibald Watts
BEDELL, John March 18, 1828
  Susan Perdee R. Q. Dickinson
BEDELL, Micajah October 14, 1831
  Ann Smith Vincent R. Thornton
BEEMAN, Henry February 15, 1823
  Carolyn Myrick Nathan Beeman, M.G.
BEEMAN, Samuel H. January 25, 1831
  Frances Julia Ann Cone Thos. W. Grimes
BEGNON, Cassmere J. March 16, 1871
  Mary Z. Johnson Philip Robinson
BELAND, James February 2, 1806
  Easter McElroy
BELL, A. H. December 23, 1873
  Missouri Stephen W. A. Partee
BELL, James January 28, 1812
  Sophia Woodham Robert Rea

BELL, James — September 18, 1859
  Virginia Ward — R. B. Kelly
BELL, Jarard — December 9, 1811
  Rody Smith — W. Johnson
BELL, John — March —, 1839
  Mary Beasley — John Harris, M.G.
BELL, Kendall — January 9, 1856
  Nancy Allen — G. H. Thompson
BELL, Nat. — September 8, 1787
  Elizabeth Weeks
BELL, Pierce — December 27, 1846
  Margaret Daniel — R. F. Griffen
BELL, William — December 20, 1821
  Elizabeth Hopkins
BELLAH, James W. — February 27, 1845
  Elizabeth G. McKowan — Hinton Crawford, M.G.
BENEDICT, John C. — January 27, 1850
  Susan Bates — James T. Findley
BENHAM, Lyman — November 24, 1818
  Sarah King — W. Cone
BENNETT, Charles — May 28, 1854
  Cynthia Carter — B. Rowland
BENNETT, Elias L. — September 14, 1863
  Emaliza L. Harper — E. A. Burgess
BENNETT, James — June 3, 1855
  Laura Dobbs — B. Rowland
BENNETT, James A. — October 4, 1859
  Talitha C. Brazzell — Homer Henbee, M.G.
BENNETT, Reuben — November 1, 1819
  Jane Lindsey
BENNETT, Reuben — June 19, 1845
  Sarah Forrester — E. S. Hunter
BENNETT, Reuben — October 26, 1848
  Elizabeth Mitchell — Elisha Hunter
BENNETT, Riley W. — April 3, 1864
  Louiza Cosby — A. W. Rowland, M.G.
BENNETT, William — April 23, 1804
  Peggy Hogg
BENT, John — December —, 1838
  Mary Buzby
BERGER, Seaborn — December 6, 1870
  Josephine Wood — W. C. Birchmore
BERRY, Carey W. — May 21, 1868
  Mary J. Tuggle — William A. Overton
BERRY, Charles S. — May 7, 1861
  Mary E. Booles — Vincent Thornton
BESHELL, Hezekiah G. — December 24, 1844
  Elizabeth Fambro — James T. Findley
BESSENT, Abraham W. — April 22, 1866
  Lucindia E. Wright — A. W. Rowland, M.G.
BETHUNE, Lauchlen — September 14, 1802
  Allatha Greer

BETHUNE, Lauchlin   March 8, 1815
   Sallie Fitzpatrick   James Martin
BETHUNE, William M.   June 28, 1826
   Elizabeth S. Hester
BETTIE, William H.   March 14, 1865
   Elizabeth C. Grimes   M. W. Arnold, M.G.
BICKERS, Benjamin F.   December 4, 1860
   Cordelia E. Colclough
BICKERS, Joseph   May 26, 1818
   Elizabeth Stewart
BICKERS, Lewis   February 8, 1795
   Nancy Cartwright
BICKERS, William   January 2, 1834
   Nancy Ivy   Thomas Stocks
BICKERS, William C.   October 14, 1858
   Almira Sophronia Arnold   L. B. Jackson
BIDDLE, Macajah   December 15, 1819
   Lavinia Sherrel   William Cone
BILLUPS, Thomas   January 30, 1823
   Elizabeth Victory   Lovick Pierce
BIRD, Joseph   December 11, 1828
   Lucretia Watson   James Park
BIRD, Michael   October 11, 1818
   Susannah Levine   Robert Booth
BISHOP, Asa   February 5, 1809
   Nancey Garrett   George Stovall
BISHOP, J. J.   February 19, 1847
   Amelia Red   Peter Whelan (Cath. Priest)
BISHOP, Lafayette   November 3, 1867
   Martha C. Hix   Wm. H. Thrasher
BICE, Charles   October 15, 1854
   Malissa Williams   W. S. Partee
BISHOP, Wilson S.   April 30, 1833
   Panthea T. Thompson   H. Pendergrass, M.G.
BLACK, Carwell B.   April 24, 1834
   Sarah Ann Smith   Caleb W. Key, M.G.
BLACK, George   February 16, 1840
   Mary Ralls   Francis Bowman
BLAIR, Thomas   December 23, 1795
   Polly Wall
BLANKENSHIP, John   December 24, 1833
   Mahala Caldwell   James Moore
BLANKES, Demsey   January 11, 1818
   Mary A. Hill   Robert Rea
BLANKS, William   September 25, 1799
   Jane Hill
BLANKS, William   November 8, 1819
   Narcissa Young   James Riley
BLANTON, W. M.   November 6, 1840
   Julia Thompson
BLASSINGAME, James T.   September 25, 1834
   Evaline C. Greer   Thos. W. Grimes

BLEDSOE, Aaron   July 30, 1808
  Elizabeth Stocks   William Browning
BLEDSOE, John   December 28, 1820
  Elizabeth Autrey   L. B. Johnson
BLEDSOE, Joseph   December 30, 1819
  Elizabeth Greer   James Brockman
BLEDSOE, William   October 21, 1823
  Pamely Ann Booth   John W. G. Greer
BLITCH, Joseph L.   October 5, 1863
  Martha A. Beazley   N. M. Crawford, M.G.
BLOUNT, Whitfield L.   March 5, 1876
  Della Whitehead   R. L. Burgess
BLYTHE, James   September 15, 1806
  Doly Credille
BLYTHE, Leroy   April 7, 1829
  Betsy Caroline Wars   William Bryan
BLYTHE, William H.   July 26, 1832
  Betheney Ward   J. P. Leveritt
BOGGS, Samuel   December 11, 1793
  Polly Kent
BOLES, Jackson   January 8, 1812
  Betsey Lindsey   Lemuel Greene
BOLES, Turner   October 25, 1823
  Frances Greene Robertson
BOLING, John S.   February 7, 1833
  Anne W. Nancy   Abraham Yates
BONES, John H.   June 22, 1796
  Peggy Burns
BOOKE, Samuel   November 28, 1799
  Elizabeth Stokely
BOOLES, Allen   December 12, 1815
  Averylla Broach   Lauchlin Bethune
BOOLES, Bevan   January 8, 1828
  Charity Yewen   Abraham Yeats
BOOLES, Jackson   November 16, 1845
  Nancy Brooks   Jeremiah Lindsey
BOOLES, Jeremiah   January 5, 1846
  Sarah Malone   Samuel Ely
BOOLES, John   November 12, 1822
  Mary Bennett   John Booles
BOOLES, John A.   September 13, 1849
  Rebecca Hackney   E. S. Hunter
BOOLES, William T.   November 14, 1837
  Martha Williams   B. M. Sanders
BOOLES, Willoughby   August 4, 1836
  Sarah Ann Wilson   Vincent R. Thornton
BOON, Alfred C.   August 29, 1833
  Martha Ann Barnhart   James Moore
BOON, Francis M.   August 12, 1834
  Harriett A. Greene   Abraham Perkins
BOON, Jesse   April 5, 1824
  Sarah Hicks

BOON, Sion — November 26, 1804
Gilly Hawkins
BOON, ———— — December 5, 1844
E. S. Crummer
BOONE, Allen R. — March 19, 1867
Marietta R. Hightower — William Bryan, M.G.
BOONE, Benjamin — April 22, 1810
Betsey Alford — Isaac Cook
BOONE, Benjamin — May 28, 1824
Dorothy Fay
BOONE, David L. — January 28, 1841
Mary Christopher — V. R. Thornton
BOONE, John D. — December 2, 1858
Mary Hood — Carlos W. Stephens
BOONE, Warren J. — December 2, 1841
Rebecca Runnels — E. S. Hunter
BOOTH, Beverly — July 29, 1819
Sarah Ansley — Robert Booth
BORGUST, Robert — July 12, 1821
Phoebe Fuller — Abraham Teates
BOSTWICK, Nathan — November 17, 1819
Lucy Burk — William Cone
BOSTWICK, William — March 6, 1823
Jane Smith — John Harris
BOSWELL, Reuben B. — December 16, 1869
Narcissa A. Mayo — W. A. Overton
BOSWELL, William J. — June 11, 1862
Josephine Malone — H. H. Tucker, M.G.
BOWDEN, Elliot C. — September 22, 1842
Frances Heard — James Jones, M.G.
BOWDEN, George Thomas — November 15, 1846
Cynthia W. Shirlin — William Bryan
BOWDEN, Richard — February 6, 1848
Martha Cartwright — Isaac Williams
BOWDEN, Robert C. — January 25, 1844
Elizabeth Jackson — J. W. Godkin
BOWDEN, Robert C. — November 20, 1856
Frances L. Arnold — J. P. Duncan, M.G.
BOWDEN, William — August 9, 1820
Pamelia Bell
BOWDEN, William — October 30, 1833
Sarah Jones
BOWDEN, William — December 22, 1844
Mary Broach — E. S. Hunter
BOWEN, T. J. — May 31, 1853
Lurana H. Davis — Charles M. Irwin, M.G.
BOWLES, Henry — August 4, 1835
Lucenda Bowles — Jesse H. Watson
BOWLES, Henry — September 22, 1872
Mary Farmer — W. A. Moore
BOWLES, Jesse — March 24, 1802
Sally Anderson

BOWLES, Jesse B.　　　　　　August 26, 1833
　Jane Bennett
BOWLES, John　　　　　　　　March 8, 1800
　Sally Blasingame
BOWLES, Littleberry　　　　　August 29, 1833
　Cena Cochrane　　　　　　　Nathan Hobbs
BOWLES, Thomas　　　　　　April 1, 1819
　Acintha Cothrine　　　　　　William Tuggle
BOWLES, William　　　　　　December 18, 1805
　Jincey Wade
BOWLES, William H.　　　　　August 19, 1875
　Nancy H. Cartwright　　　　A. J. S. Jackson
BOWLES, William V.　　　　　February 10, 1864
　Margaret M. Dennis　　　　V. R. Thornton
BOYCE, George　　　　　　　August 17, 1803
　Jimmy Greer
BOYCE, ——　　　　　　　　April 23, 1805
　Polly Davis
BOYKIN, Leroy H.　　　　　　February 3, 1859
　Laura E. Hunter　　　　　　T. J. Bowen, M.G.
BOZEMAN, James　　　　　　February 20, 1820
　Margaret Shelton　　　　　　Lovick Pierce
BRACK, William H.　　　　　　March 12, 1871
　Nancy Crossley　　　　　　　N. M. Jones
BRADDY, John　　　　　　　　January 7, 1847
　Aseneth Wright　　　　　　　Hinton Crawford
BRADDY, Joseph E.　　　　　December 2, 1869
　Mary E. Turner　　　　　　　C. D. Mitchell
BRADLEY, Charles A.　　　　July 7, 1859
　Emaline Harris　　　　　　　Chas. W. Launius
BRADLEY, Harrelson　　　　　October 19, 1799
　Agnes Rice
BRADLEY, John　　　　　　　August 6, 1802
　Rachel Wester
BRADSHAW, Asa　　　　　　June 30, 1803
　Polly Carrol
BRADSHAW, Elijah　　　　　　November 16, 1873
　Sarah Frances Coffield　　　W. A. Partee
BRADSHAW, Erastus　　　　　February 27, 1838
　Elizabeth Findley　　　　　　J. L. M. Porter
BRADSHAW, George　　　　　November 20, 1838
　Dulsey McCain
BRADSHAW, George　　　　　June 13, 1862
　Rhoda C. Askew　　　　　　J. W. Godkin
BRADSHAW, William　　　　　March 19, 1872
　Susan Bridges　　　　　　　Rev. J. S. Potter
BRADSHAW, William　　　　　December 30, 1873
　Letia Shields　　　　　　　　W. A. Partee
BRAGG, Mathew　　　　　　　January 6, 1804
　Anne Cheney
BRAGG, Thomas　　　　　　　December 28, 1797
　Lovinia Lunceford

BRANCH, John — January 21, 1830
  Sarah Broughton — Adeil Sherwood
BRANCH, Robert M. — May 31, 1854
  Margaret S. Wier — W. A. Florence
BRANCH, William H. H. — December 6, 1864
  Sarah Margaret Robinson — N. M. Crawford, M.G.
BRASSEL, James — April 16, 1805
  Sally Davis
BRASWELL, Isom — April 6, 1806
  Mary Morris
BREWER, David — April 21, 1804
  Polly Parker
BREWER, George Washington — December 25, 1872
  Julia Priscilla Bruce — N. M. Jones
BREWER, Henry — August 31, 1800
  Lukey Mitchell
BREWER, Wiley — April 4, 1854
  Mary Clements — Benjamin Merritt
BREWER, William — November 11, 1799
  Polly Harper
BREWER, William — December 2, 1810
  Polly Moore — Arthur Foster
BRIANT, John — March 4, 1830
  Mary Copeland
BRICE, Alfred — December 11, 1845
  Martha Williams — Ephraim Bruce
BRIDGES, Ezekiel — October 14, 1845
  Frances Slaughter — J. C. Lucas
BRIDGES, Ezekiel J. — June 24, 1849
  Elizabeth T. Smith — William Bryan
BRIDGES, Hardy — December 17, 1822
  Nancy Copelan — Henry Slaughter
BRIDGES, James — August 30, 1827
  Nancy Rowland — E. Tally
BRIDGES, James — October 27, 1831
  Susan Copeland — Lewis Parker
BRIDGES, John J. C. — February 5, 1852
  Mary Anne Credille — Hardy Bridges
BRIDGES, Robert C. — June 6, 1850
  Elizabeth F. Copelan — Hardy Bridges
BRIDGES, William — May 12, 1850
  A. H. Copelan — John Copelan
BRIMBERRY, Matthias — April 10, 1827
  Betsey Hinton
BRISCOE, John — April 22, 1858
  Elizabeth Dunn — John W. Reid, M.G.
BRISCOE, Lucius M. — May 10, 1850
  Ann Catherine Strozier
BRISCOE, Thomas — July 14, 1851
  Sarah F. Cheney — Dabney P. Jones
BRITAIN, Henry — September 6, 1825
  Louisa Booker

BRITTON, William — January 25, 1852
 Nancy Farris — H. C. Peek, M.G.
BROACH, Alexander — December 18, 1836
 Nancy Durham — John G. Holtzclaw
BROACH, James — October 28, 1824
 Lucenda Yeats
BROACH, J. E. — November 12, 1874
 Sallie Lankford — John T. Dolvin
BROACH, William — December 24, 1811
 Polly Sherrill — William Cone
BROACH, William H. — June 30, 1872
 Margaret Davidson — John R. Young
BROADDUS, Thomas — December 4, 1798
 Agnes Fielder
BROCKMAN, Moses — October 17, 1819
 Penelope Bunch — Lemuel Greene
BROOK, James — February 17, 1834
 Julia Reynolds — Nathan Hobbs
BROOK, James E. — May 20, 1844
 Eliza Anne Johnson — J. M. Davison
BROOK, John F. — January 5, 1857
 Celestia M. Sayers — Thomas Callahan
BROOK, John S. — August 1, 1860
 Nancy A. Reynolds
BROOKS, Archibald D. — October 28, 1850
 Frances D. Turnell — H. C. Peek
BROOKS, Archibald — December 1, 1859
 Mrs. Lucy A. Cremer — Hart C. Peek
BROOKS, Augustus G. — October 20, 1843
 Emeline F. Ellis — W. C. Veazey
BROOKS, Covington — May 30, 1833
 Nancy Walker — J. P. Leveritt
BROOKS, Jesse — August 15, 1823
 Elizabeth Watts
BROOKS, Peter R. — January 1, 1843
 Francina Creddille — R. F. Griffen
BROOKS, Thomas — March 26, 1815
 Polly Jackson — John Riley
BROOKS, Wilson L. — January 10, 1860
 Julia Fort — T. J. Bowen
BROOME, Alpheus — October 8, 1868
 Josephine Anderson — C. A. Mitchell
BROOME, Lucius — April 3, 1860
 Elizabeth Irby — William A. Corry
BROOX, Henry — November 20, 1824
 Sarah Broox
BROUGHTON, Edward — January 7, 1829
 Sarah Ann Lackey
BROUGHTON, Edward — May 22, 1838
 Essey Broughton — Thomas Stocks
BROUGHTON, John R. — May 8, 1833
 Genett L. Broughton — George Heard

BROUGHTON, John T. — August 26, 1843
  Anne America Perkins — Francis Bowman
BROWN, Benjamin — February 25, 1815
  Nancy Newby — Gilly Moore
BROWN, Benjamin F. — November 19, 1833
  Tennese King — Thomas W. Grimes
BROWN, Burwell — June 6, 1798
  Fanny Brown
BROWN, Charles — November 14, 1869
  Amanda Bennett — Philip Clements
BROWN, Daniel — October 10, 1858
  Adeline Wilson — James Davison
BROWN, Ezekiel — December 15, 1803
  Elizabeth Merritt
BROWN, Ezekiel — December 1, 1825
  Emily Greene
BROWN, Ezekiel — August 2, 1827
  Hannah Oslin — E. Tally
BROWN, James L. — December 19, 1843
  Julia Martin — P. H. Mell
BROWN, Jesse F. — May 18, 1865
  Lillie B. McElroy
BROWN, John — May 2, 1814
  Burchet Baxter — Joseph Tarpley
BROWN, Joseph H. — September 12, 1871
  Lavenia Smith — B. L. Hulme, M.G.
BROWN, Thomas — November 4, 1829
  Mary Foster
BROWN, Thomas — January 21, 1858
  Eliza A. Merritt — John R. Young, M.G.
BROWN, William — July 14, 1824
  Amanda Gray
BROWN, William A. — April 2, 1854
  Mary E. Littleton — J. R. Hall
BROWNING, Daniel — July 12, 1808
  Nancey Sorrell — William Browning
BROWNING, Nathan P. — July 27, 1815
  Eunice Haralson — Thomas Stocks
BRUCE, Abner W. — January 16, 1843
  Rebecca Bridges — Francis Colley
BRUCE, Anderson — December 30, 1847
  Mary A. Ward — H. H. Laurence
BRUCE, Benjamin F. — December 17, 1871
  Martha A. Allen — L. D. Caldwell
BRUCE, Edward D. — December 19, 1865
  Mrs. Patience A. Clifton — W. H. Blythe, M.G.
BRUCE, Ephriam — November 21, 1822
  Priscilla Richards — John Harris
BRUCE, Ephraim M. — April 13, 1852
  Sarah M. Moon — A. A. V. Carroll
BRUCE, Henry C. — May 12, 1872
  Mattie L. Chapman — W. C. Blythe, M.G.

BRUCE, James — May 2, 1816
  Della Richards — Walker Lewis
BRUCE, James — October 13, 1833
  Sarah Ransom — James Moon
BRUCE, James — September 13, 1866
  Mrs. Mary A. Bridges — W. H. Blythe, M.G.
BRUCE, James R. — December 19, 1844
  Jane E. Lucas — Francis S. Colley
BRUCE, James S. — December 12, 1844
  Mary Lewis
BRUCE, Joel — January 20, 1835
  Charlotte L. Lewis — Ephraim Bruce
BRUCE, John — August 28, 1827
  Tempy Sayers — John Armstrong
BRUCE, Jonathan — June 2, 1844
  Martha Shell — Ephraim Bruce
BRUCE, Seaborn M. — December 7, 1847
  Catharine Cruse — Francis S. Colley
BRUCE, Turnell — May 16, 1852
  Martha Thigpen — B. Rowland
BRUCE, Wilson — December 17, 1829
  Allah Gatlin — J. P. Leveritt
BRUNT, James — July 31, 1834
  Elizabeth Caldwell — Ephraim Bruce
BRUNT, John — January 5, 1825
  Patience Rowland
BRUNT, Williby — August 31, 1836
  Nancy Caldwell — Ephraim Bruce
BRYAN, Asbury — January 19, 1826
  Mary Ann Tarpley Ward — T. W. Slaughter, J.P.
BRYAN, James — November 18, 1830
  Mary Ann Clark — W. M. Bryan
BRYAN, James P. — February 13, 1868
  Lucenda Oliver — William Bryan, M.G.
BRYAN, Jesse M. — June 12, 1868
  Mary Ann Oliver — Alex H. Smith
BRYAN, Littleton J. — May 17, 1855
  Martha Bryan — William Bryan
BRYAN, Nathan — July 4, 1837
  Mary Ann Griggs — Ephraim Bruce
BRYAN, Richard — October 20, 1836
  Sarah Ann Oliver — Ephraim Bruce
BRYAN, Thomas M. — November 14, 1866
  Sallie F. Morris — Wm. A. Overton
BRYAN, William — January 21, 1840
  Martha Tarpley — James Jones
BRYAN, William — December 16, 1841
  Elizabeth Langford
BRYAN, William — June 28, 1855
  Sarah Tarpley — J. P. Duncan, M.G.
BRYAN, William J. — June 29, 1858
  Elizabeth Smith — William Bryan

BRYANT, Charles J. December 20, 1875
　Nancy L. Simmons 　Hart C. Peek
BRYANT, John O. April 10, 1836
　Patsy Gentry 　B. Rowland
BRYANT, Russell December 22, 1824
　Sydney Martin
BRYANT, Whit February 25, 1875
　Laura Moore 　John S. Callaway
BYCE, William C. December 21, 1874
　Emeline R. Coffield
BYNUM, James R. July 1, 1852
　Lucy A. A. Houghton 　W. A. Corry
BYRD, William June 6, 1825
　Mary Hudson
BUCKING, Peter March 26, 1820
　Sarah Furlow 　William Cone
BUCKNER, David May 8, 1802
　Betsey Findley
BUGG, Hampton C. April 24, 1845
　Martha Moore 　I. N. Glenn, M.G.
BUGG, Hampton C. November 9, 1847
　Sarah Moore 　Hinton Crawford
BUGG, William B. May 16, 1867
　Mary C. Wheeler 　A. Nelson, M.G.
BUNKLEY, Howell October 5, 1841
　Ruth Newsome 　Vincent R. Thornton
BUNN, Aldridge March 22, 1831
　Catharine Palmer 　Ephraim Bruce
BURDELE, Robert July 25, 1827
　Margaret Hays 　William Wingfield
BURFORD, John January 5, 1815
　Edna Jackson 　John Browning
BURFORD, John E. August 19, 1875
　Mary A. Bryan 　A. J. S. Jackson
BURFORD, Leonard May 12, 1795
　Polly Smith
BURGE, William January 29, 1833
　Milley Thompson 　James S. Park
BURGER, Noah January 22, 1874
　Martha Jane Coffield 　W. A. Partee
BURGESS, A. C. September 6, 1870
　Frances E. Freeman 　W. A. Colclough
BURGESS, Edward A. January 11, 1859
　Augusta E. Fambrough 　W. A. Partee
BURGESS, James D. December 22, 1857
　Satira J. Fambrough 　L. R. L. Jennings
BURGESS, Jonathan September 18, 1818
　Nancey Cone 　Thomas Stocks
BURGESS, Robert L. December 9, 1866
　Emma E. Fambrough 　John B. Young, M.G.
BURGESS, Thomas L. October 11, 1840
　Martha Wade 　I. M. Wilson

BURGESS, William   October 8, 1867
  Adaline Stephens   E. A. Burgess
BURGESS, William   December 18, 1873
  Emaline Burger   W. A. Partee
BURK, Columbus   May 16, 1850
  Elizabeth Foster   Hinton Crawford
BURK, James   October 1, 1847
  Martha A. Wynn
BURK, Seaborn   May 2, 1847
  Elizabeth Adair
BURKE, Charles I.   November 1, 1823
  Caroline Jenkins   Thomas Johnson
BURKE, James   January 28, 1844
  Martha A. King   J. W. Godkin
BURKE, Valerious J.   March 24, 1856
  Elizabeth Arnold
BURNETT, David S.   April 22, 1875
  Agnes S. Tool   P. H. McWhorter
BURNS, Owens   July 29, 1826
  Nancy Horn
BURNS, Robert   January 9, 1806
  Elizabeth Greene
BURROUGH, James   May 18, 1803
  Betsey Weathers
BURT, Dr. H. L.   July 16, 1845
  Penelope Simonton   Francis Bowman
BURTEN, William   July 20, 1826
  Martha Robertson
BUSBY, John E.   June 9, 1864
  Adaline M. O'Neal   L. D. Caldwell
BUSH, John   August 22, 1787
  Wm. Alford
BUSH, John   March 27, 1804
  Nancy King
BUSH, John L.   March 2, 1874
  Mary A. Ashe   Henry Newton
BUSH, John T.   November 4, 1875
  Mary C. Stewart   L. D. Caldwell
BUSS, William   April 19, 1810
  Betsey Maddox   John Cox
BUSSEY, James   December 21, 1814
  Elizabeth Lake   C. Maddox
BUTLER, Edward   April 9, 1788
  Fannie Garrett
BUTLER, John T.   February 11, 1869
  Adaline Wray   E. A. Burgess
BUTLER, John W.   March 15, 1824
  Elizabeth Hubbard
BUTLORD, William   November 10, 1805
  Elizabeth Dilder

C

CAGLE, Alexander	November 23, 1847
Amanda Wright	
CAIN, Thomas L.	September 4, 1833
Mary R. Swan	James Moore
CALDWELL, Augustus G.	August 9, 1849
Frances Jernigan	Wm. A. Corry
CALDWELL, Early	March 31, 1844
Jane Peek	R. H. Mapp
CALDWELL, Early J.	March 27, 1848
Nancy Jarrell	Wm. A. Corry
CALDWELL, Elisha	November 27, 1873
Susan King	J. H. Kilpatrick
CALDWELL, James	May 29, 1814
Nelly Shockley	W. M. McGiboney
CALDWELL, Jonathan E.	August 9, 1860
Martha Ann Peek	W. W. Moore
CALDWELL, Joshia	June 13, 1830
Mary Teppet	John Harris
CALDWELL, Joshua A.	January 19, 1865
Eliza Ann Wright	W. A. Partee
CALDWELL, Littleton	September 4, 1825
Cynthia McHargue	John Harris
CALDWELL, Littleton D.	November 16, 1856
Mary C. McLellan	J. A. Williams
CALDWELL, Miles	March 2, 1832
Mary Ann Caldwell	Wooten O'Neal
CALDWELL, William	October 28, 1805
Polly Parker	
CALDWELL, William	November 1, 1820
Polly Woodward	Wm. McGibony
CALDWELL, Wm. H.	July 1, 1869
Sarah T. Andrews	L. D. Caldwell
CALHOUN, Londa	August 4, 1831
Lucy Webb	George Hall
CALLAHAN, Andrew	December 1, 1838
Alice Higgins	C. D. Kinnebrew
CALLAHAN, Edward	December 20, 1815
Mary Stevens	Francis Cummins
CALLAHAN, Henry	December 6, 1849
Rhoda A. Credille	J. M. Kelly
CALLAHAN, James W.	November 2, 1869
Susan P. Brooks	L. M. Dickey, M.G.
CALLAHAN, John	October 25, 1794
Ann Stephenson	
CALLAHAN, William	March 20, 1821
Elizabeth Wilson	Jack Lumpkin
CALLAHAN, William	December 18, 1845
Frances Hall	J. W. Godkin
CALLAWAY, Lemuel L.	December 23, 1863
Anna Josephine Mullins	Nathan Crawford, M.G.

CALLAWAY, Lewis — November 1, 1824
  Mary Hunter
CALLAWAY, Willis R. — January 1, 1845
  Margarite A. Willis — Thomas Stocks
CALLOWAY, R. S. — January 22, 1846
  Sarah Ann Calloway — P. H. Mell
CALLOWAY, William — June 15, 1851
  Harriet A. Boone — S. G. Hillyer
CALLOWAY, William R. — January 17, 1838
  Rhoda Ann Cheney — Reuben Owen, M.G.
CALWAY, Night — December 31, 1799
  Mary Connell
CAMERON, Henry C. — February 28, 1872
  Mary E. Ware
CAMPBELL, James — July 18, 1807
  Scintha Hill — Claborn Maddox
CAMPBELL, Obediah — April 17, 1825
  Luria Norris
CAMPBELL, Samuel — May 28, 1801
  Charity Edwards
CANE, Joseph C. — December 22, 1859
  Maria Louisa Compton — R. B. Kelly
CANE, William C. — June 14, 1860
  Mary J. Bennet — R. B. Kelly
CANNON, John — November 3, 1831
  Anne Pyron — John Park
CANNON, Joshua — June 24, 1819
  Elizabeth Harris — John Wilson
CAREY, James — January 20, 1853
  Martha Ann Littleton — J. L. Billingslea
CARGILL, John — April 14, 1800
  Tabitha Babb
CARLETON, James M. — December 17, 1838
  Mary Jane Wagnon — Walter Branham
CARLETON, James — September 10, 1843
  Lucienda Broach — John Robins
CARLETON, John W. — October 31, 1834
  Nancy Durham — Thomas W. Grimes
CARLETON, Larkin — February 20, 1812
  Eliza Boothe — Lovick Pierce
CARLETON, Larkin — May 25, 1822
  Rachel Munfort — Lovick Pierce
CARLISLE, Brantlet — August 4, 1854
  Martha Higginbotham
CARLTON, Archibald — January 26, 1825
  Emily Ann Crutchfield
CARLTON, B. F. — June 8, 1854
  Frances B. Tuggle — S. G. Hillyer
CARLTON, James S. — August 23, 1854
  Martha C. Jones — James S. Key, M.G.
CARLTON, John T. — October 13, 1859
  Margaret Daniel — George C. Clarke

CARMICHAEL, Arden Evans January 15, 1806
  (?) Thomas Crawford
CARMICHAEL, John July 9, 1855
  Adeline Seymour
CARMICHAEL, Oswell E. October 22, 1868
  Georgiana Hicks E. W. Speer, M.G.
CARMICHAEL, Reuben September 12, 1847
  Sidney Frances Parker J. L. Rowland
CARR, Elijah W. December 19, 1860
  Anna E. Macon N. M. Crawford, M.G.
CARR, Elisha February 16, 1832
  Nancy Taylor Nathan Walker
CARR, James December 10, 1849
  Frances O'Neal
CARREL, Starling September 15, 1806
  Anna Richards John Mapp
CARROLL, Allison J. April 30, 1840
  Elizabeth Mapp James Moore
CARROLL, Allison J. December 5, 1848
  Sarah Veazey J. J. Loudermilk
CARROLL, Charley April 3, 1804
  Sally Johnson
CARROLL, David March 21, 1804
  Barbary Richards
CARROLL, Harwell October 10, 1803
  Elizabeth Parker
CARROLL, John September 19, 1800
  Nancy Gatling
CARROLL, John D. August 12, 1833
  Emoline Humphrey James Moore
CARROLL, John D. May 6, 1857
  Frances Hardeman L. D. Caldwell
CARTER, Benjamin F. October 27, 1868
  Martha F. Wilson E. A. Burgess
CARTER, Benowne August 29, 1818
  Elizabeth Bryant Robert Booth
CARTER, Hezekiah September 30, 1839
  Margaret Brunt Ephraim Bruce
CARTER, John January 7, 1819
  Sarah Stevens Robert Moore
CARTER, John B. May 21, 1851
  Georgiana L. Gresham Francis Bowman
CARTER, Joseph April 28, 1820
  Lucy Jones George Watkins
CARTER, Joseph W. March 29, 1827
  Dicey White E. Tally
CARTER, Joseph September 8, 1829
  Mary Smith John Chew
CARTER, Josiah Anthony June 17, 1851
  Louisa A. Northern E. G. Hillyer
CARTER, William May 11, 1824
  Sarah Jones

CARTWRIGHT, James M.　　　　　　October 6, 1850
　Adeline Copeland　　　　　　　　John C. Merritt
CARTWRIGHT, John　　　　　　　　June 23, 1800
　Martha Hay
CARTWRIGHT, John A.　　　　　　　November 16, 1837
　Emeline W. Lewis　　　　　　　　James Moore
CARTWRIGHT, John B.　　　　　　　December 19, 1836
　Margaret Burford　　　　　　　　William Rowland
CARTWRIGHT, John B.　　　　　　　December 16, 1844
　Mary E. Lawrence　　　　　　　　Ephraim Bruce
CARTWRIGHT, Jonas　　　　　　　　April 19, 1804
　Jinny Bickers
CARTWRIGHT, Joseph　　　　　　　August 28, 1838
　Terrissa Richards　　　　　　　　James W. Godkin
CARTWRIGHT, Miles　　　　　　　　November 25, 1829
　Maria Carr　　　　　　　　　　　John Harris
CARTWRIGHT, Peter, Jr.　　　　　　April 22, 1801
　Betsy Shaw
CARTWRIGHT, William B.　　　　　January 22, 1843
　Elizabeth Jane Barker　　　　　　John Veazey
CARSON, William E.　　　　　　　　December 24, 1835
　Caroline F. Broughton　　　　　　Thomas Stocks
CASH, Elbert L.　　　　　　　　　　November 6, 1834
　Caroline Foster　　　　　　　　　Wm. E. Adams
CASSEUS, William Bass　　　　　　July 25, 1854
　Ann Octavia Nickelson　　　　　　G. F. Pierce
CATCHINGS, Jo　　　　　　　　　　November 8, 1802
　Parmelia Stephens
CATCHINGS, J. W. T.　　　　　　　October 10, 1850
　Matilda Jane Thompson　　　　　Hinton Crawford
CATCHINGS, John W. T.　　　　　　February 11, 1847
　Elizabeth W. Sanders　　　　　　Hinton Crawford
CATCHINGS, Joseph　　　　　　　　March 8, 1825
　Loveny Duncan
CATCHINGS, Joseph　　　　　　　　December 29, 1836
　Julia L. Cone　　　　　　　　　　J. T. Crawford
CATLIN, Abejah　　　　　　　　　　July 5, 1838
　Mary Simonton　　　　　　　　　Francis Bowman, M.G.
CATO, George F.　　　　　　　　　March 6, 1864
　Sarah F. M. Head　　　　　　　　E. S. Williams
CATO, William　　　　　　　　　　June 14, 1863
　Ariadne Kinney　　　　　　　　　E. S. Williams
CATO, Wyche　　　　　　　　　　　January 26, 1803
　Patsy Peoples
CATREHEAD, John　　　　　　　　　December 2, 1807
　Phebe Foster　　　　　　　　　　William Johnson
CAUSEY, Phillips　　　　　　　　　September 3, 1822
　Sarah Laws　　　　　　　　　　　William Winfield
CAWTHON, John W.　　　　　　　　December 1, 1858
　Mary A. E. Barnhardt　　　　　　George C. Clarke
CAWTHON, J. W.　　　　　　　　　December 17, 1868
　Nannie Barnhardt　　　　　　　　J. J. Jones

CHAFIN, Thomas — December 27, 1824
 Sarah G. Taylor
CHAMBER, John Finch — March 7, 1835
 Emily Adalene Hall — James H. Taylor
CHAMBERLAIN, Elliot R. — April 10, 1854
 Mary K. Watson — Samuel K. Talmadge
CHAMPION, Henry W. — September 9, 1852
 Lucinda P. King — T. W. Wilkes, M.G.
CHAMPION, James D. — May 19, 1864
 Mary S. Janes — N. M. Crawford
CHAMPION, Jesse — November 8, 1827
 Louisa Jackson — William Austin
CHAMPION, Jesse W. — July 20, 1870
 Mary V. Champion — R. A. Johnson, M.G.
CHANDLER, Daniel B. — April 5, 1866
 Georgia A. Moss — James Davison
CHANDLER, Walton — August 27, 1845
 Martha Hamilton — W. A. Florence, M.G.
CHANNELL, Isham — May 2, 1830
 Nancy Howell — T. Wright
CHANNELL, Littleton — November 29, 1804
 Sally Skinner
CHANNELL, Littleton — March 24, 1832
 Nancy Tolver — John Copeland
CHANNELL, Michael — May 16, 1831
 Tibathy Marchman — Butt L. Cato
CHANNELL, Michael — July 18, 1833
 Sarah Westbrook
CHANNELL, Thomas — January 17, 1835
 Elizabeth Montgomery
CHANNELL, William — September 19, 1826
 Elizabeth Wilson — Butt L. Cato
CHANNELL, William H. — January 21, 1868
 Georgia Ruarke — John C. Merritt
CHAPMAN, John M. — January 1, 1838
 Martha Crews — Ephraim Bruce
CHAPMAN, John M. — May 27, 1855
 Sarah E. Jones — Benjamin Merritt
CHAPMAN, John — February 12, 1860
 Sarah Ann Everett — James W. Wragg
CHAPMAN, Miles — March 4, 1864
 Margaret Harper
CHAPMAN, Randle — July 23, 1822
 Elizabeth Tally — Stephen Hightower
CHAPMAN, Randol — May 30, 1833
 Nancy Perkins — J. P. Leaverett
CHAPMAN, Thomas — May 25, 1848
 Catherine Bruce — Ephraim Bruce
CHAPMAN, William M. — December 14, 1837
 Sarah C. Lewis — Ephraim Bruce
CHAPMAN, William M. — May 10, 1857
 Jeannett Norris — Hart C. Peek

CHAPMAN, William — September 30, 1859
  Amanda Allen — R. B. Kelly
CHAPPELL, John — April 12, 1820
  Anne Forrester — William Cone
CHAPPELL, Robert — January 8, 1854
  Martha Frances Quill — W. A. Florence
CHATMAN, Miles — March 1, 1868
  Mary C. Wiggins — A. H. Smith
CHEATHAM, Lovera B. — June 15, 1875
  Emma A. Printup — E. W. Speer, M.G.
CHEEK, Asbill — January 6, 1848
  Elizabeth R. Bennett — Wm. F. Gaston
CHENEY, Enoch R. — October 5, 1852
  Sarah H. English — P. H. Mell, M.G.
CHENEY, John F. — January 8, 1867
  Martha E. Wilson — P. H. Mell, M.G.
CHENEY, William O. — April 7, 1857
  Mary F. English — J. R. Young
CHESTER, Francis — January 17, 1832
  Ann G. Neal — Raleigh Greene
CHEVES, Adoniram J. — December 15, 1863
  Anna M. Sanford — N. M. Crawford, M.G.
CHEVES, Grief — November 8, 1808
  Betsy Parker — W. M. McGiboney
CHEVES, Joseph — October 15, 1846
  Mary E. Stubblefield — Wm. I. Parks
CHEW, John — December 15, 1814
  Ann Montford — Thomas Stocks
CHEW, Thomas J. — December 9, 1852
  Mary Jane Fountain — Jas. M. Kelly
CHEWNING, William I. — February 28, 1826
  Parmelia Adams
CHINN, Charles C. — December 5, 1867
  Sarah E. Strozier
CHRISTOPHER, Henry — December 22, 1872
  Mary Bugg — B. P. Taylor
CHRISTOPHER, Seaborn — August 22, 1822
  Ollie Mayhan — Robert Newsome
CHRISTOPHER, William — December 29, 1829
  Nancy Parker — John Copeland
CHRISTOPHER, William H. — December 4, 1868
  Martha H. Johnson
CHRISWELL, John — April 26, 1866
  Martha J. Norris — Wm. Chapman, M.G.
CHRISWELL, William — August 22, 1866
  Nancy Bennett — E. T. Williams
CLARK, Arthur — July 18, 1799
  Agnes Hall
CLARK, Benjamin — October 28, 1847
  Mary I. Woodard — Hinton Crawford
CLARK, James — October 26, 1810
  Sally Robinson — Robert Rea

CLARK, J. S.	August 2, 1803
Betsey Prince	
CLARK, William J.	February 16, 1847
Martha A. Lawrence	William Bryan
CLARKE, Francis A.	December 16, 1875
Sarah E. West	C. C. Davison
CLARKE, William	December 20, 1827
Frances Penny	E. Talley
CLAY, Samuel	February 7, 1803
Elizabeth Fitzpatrick	
CLAYTON, Phillip	May 2, 1837
Leonora Harper	George F. Pierce
CLEMANCE, Ellis	December 7, 1871
Martha Merritt	W. H. Wright
CLEMENTS, Aaron	June 20, 1796
Hannah Clements	
CLEMENTS, Anderson	December 19, 1834
Lucy Burford	Francis West
CLEMENTS, Anderson	December 11, 1862
Eliza Rhodes	James M. Kelly
CLEMENTS, Franklin	October 30, 1866
Louiza Channel	John C. Merritt
CLEMENTS, Jesse	September 24, 1851
Jane Rhodes	
CLEMENTS, Peyton	December 1, 1808
Polly Ward	Francis P. Martin
CLEMENTS, Peyton	September 2, 1824
Mary Tyler	
CLEMENTS, Peyton	January 16, 1845
Elizabeth Wright	Ephraim Bruce
CLEMENTS, Phillip	October 8, 1803
Elizabeth Howell	
CLEMENTS, Phillip	October 5, 1841
Sara Blythe	
CLEMENTS, William B.	February 5, 1867
Malissa Jackson	William Bryan
CLEPBON, Daniel	July 4, 1826
Eliza Ledbetter	
CLEVELAND, Larkin	September 16, 1802
Sally Buchanan	
CLIFTON, Alanson	March 4, 1847
Nancy Marchman	R. L. Clifton
CLIFTON, Charles	January 10, 1849
Winney Kinney	W. T. Gaston
CLIFTON, John R.	January 20, 1873
Sarah Ruarks	L. D. Caldwell
CLIFTON, William	October 13, 1824
Martha Watson	
CLIFTON, William	January 27, 1848
Patience Kinney	W. F. Gaston
COATS, James	August 31, 1831
Elizabeth Laws	Matthew Winfield

COBB, John	December 2, 1819
Mary Grimes	F. Cummins, M.G.
COCHRAN, James M.	February 8, 1853
Elizabeth Hutchinson	J. W. Yarbrough
COCHRAN, John	November 10, 1803
Peggy Dorough	
COCHRAN, John	January 22, 1852
Martha Bridges	L. B. Jackson
COCHRAN, Samuel	March 23, 1802
Sally Furlow	
COCHRAN, Samuel	September 26, 1841
Judith Gentry	J. M. Wilson
COCRAFT, James	November 9, 1833
Caroline B. Lewis	Wm. S. Parks, M.G.
COFER, Lewis C.	May 15, 1842
Elizabeth Mills	James Davidson
COGEN, Jacob H.	January 15, 1837
Harriet Cook	James Moore
COLBERT, Frederick	January 3, 1816
Tempey Powers	Archibald Watts
COLCLOUGH, John M.	February 5, 1874
Fannie J. Boswell	Henry Newton
COLCLOUGH, William A.	November 12, 1854
Matilda J. Moore	W. H. C. Cone
COLE, Thomas	August 12, 1801
Elizabeth Talley	
COLEMAN, Daniel	January 7, 1824
Clarendia A. R. Randle	Adiel Sherwood
COLEMAN, Samuel	July 4, 1805
Sally Evans	
COLEMAN, Thomas	April 2, 1805
Jane Trimble	
COLEY, John	June 1, 1835
Eliza Ann Swan	
COLEY, John C.	December 1, 1837
Catharine Marchman	
COLEY, John	January 24, 1869
Catherine Bruce	W. H. Blythe
COLEY, William	January 13, 1828
Mary Bivins Wood	J. P. Leveritt
COLLIER, Edwin	July 7, 1829
Henrietta Brown	James Osgood Andrews
COLLIER, James	June 14, 1820
Frances Brown	David White
COLLIER, Thomas	January 9, 1811
Mary Williams	Josiah Randle
COLLIER, Williamson	November 27, 1822
Sarah Denson	John W. Grier
COLLINS, James	December 21, 1826
Rebecca Carr	Joseph Wright
COLLINS, Jones	May 3, 1819
Sophronia Wright	John Wilson

COLLINS, Nathaniel — November 25, 1818
  Elizabeth Coleman — John Wilson
COLLINS, Richard — January 23, 1859
  Elizabeth M. Porter — J. M. Kelly
COLON, James — January 22, 1825
  Elizabeth P. Furlow
COLWELL, Edward — September 22, 1812
  Polly Payne — Elias Bell
CONDON, William D. — March 26, 1856
  Anna A. Statham — Francis Bowman
CONE, Ezekiel — January 25, 1810
  Margaret Bethune — W. McGiboney
CONE, Francis — January 8, 1829
  Jane W. Cook — Francis Cummins
CONE, James T. — December 23, 1833
  Martha A. Boon — Elijah E. Jones
CONE, Rich — October 29, 1794
  Patsey Perkins
CONE, Robert — September 20, 1872
  Barby Ann Kinnebrew — N. R. Polk
CONINE, Richard — April 20, 1804
  Patsey Boon
CONINE, William — December 26, 1839
  Eliza Swindall — Hinton Crawford
CONLEY, S. W. — December 4, 1873
  Mary F. Cochran — P. H. McWhorter
CONNELL, Daniel — October 28, 1849
  Nancy Hammond — John C. Merritt
CONNELL, Hartwell — February 18, 1865
  Sarah Ann Kinney — E. S. Williams
CONNELL, John — January 30, 1801
  Sarah Awsby
CONNER, Abel C. — September 28, 1843
  Maria D. Hightower — Ephraim Bruce
CONNER, Burill — February 16, 1848
  Lucinda Ivey — L. B. Jackson
COOK, Emory — October 19, 1815
  Nancy Keaton — Walker Lewis
COOK, James — September 11, 1808
  Elizabeth Ransom — Francis Ross, M.G.
COOK, Jasper T. — June 25, 1874
  Henrietta Porter — John R. Young
COOK, John — January 16, 1823
  Lucy McCain — George Watkins
COOK, John R. — February 11, 1873
  Cornelia Sayers — H. C. Peek
COOK, Joseph — October 11, 1818
  Anne Curtis — Hinton Crawford
COOK, Joshua — March 15, 1831
  Mary Figgs — Ephraim Bruce
COOK, Joshua — August 4, 1831
  Martha Bruce — Ephraim Bruce

COOK, Thomas — November 30, 1809
  Elizabeth Stone — H. Ransom
COOK, Thomas — August 25, 1819
  Mary Colquitt — Lovick Pierce
COOK, William — October 17, 1844
  Frances Anne Walker — E. R. Thornton
COOPER, Amos — January 21, 1821
  Gedida Bradshaw — Davy Perrill
COOPER, Thomas B. — May 20, 1856
  Carrie A. Stow — P. H. Mell
COOPER, William — December 20, 1811
  Betsey Rhodes — William Janes
COPELAN, A. H. — April 8, 1875
  A. M. Maddox — John T. Dolvin
COPELAN, Daniel E. — February 27, 1873
  Elizabeth J. Lundy — John D. Copelan
COPELAN, Elias D. — July 21, 1834
  Juday Sanders
COPELAN, John — December 22, 1822
  Elizabeth Wood — Stephen Hightower
COPELAN, John — May 17, 1827
  Nancy Williams — John Harris
COPELAN, John B. — December 1, 1867
  Annie V. Copelan — Philip B. Robinson
COPELAN, John D. — November 3, 1865
  Sarah E. Wynn — Thos. F. Pierce
COPELAN, Major — December 29, 1782
  Adeline Alfriend — John T. Dolvin
COPELAN, Miles G. — March 14, 1867
  Ellen J. O'Rear — William Bryan, M.G.
COPELAN, Obadiah — December 16, 1830
  Sarah R. Credille — W. Alexander
COPELAN, Obadiah G. — January 21, 1864
  Sarah Elizabeth Lundy — William Bryan
COPELAN, Obadiah G. — October 10, 1867
  Mary J. Lundy — W. H. Blythe, M.G.
COPELAN, Rowan — December 4, 1872
  Parmelia Winslett — J. W. Godkin
COPELAN, Thomas M. — April 30, 1848
  Mary A. E. Walker — W. F. Gaston
COPELAN, Wiley R. — January 17, 1871
  Antoinette W. Downing — J. H. Kilpatrick
COPELAND, Alexander — April 18, 1837
  Julia A. Tuggle — Vincent R. Thornton
COPELAND, Archibald H. — May 1, 1826
  Agathy Ledbetter
COPELAND, Coalson — July 1, 1826
  Martha Richards
COPELAND, Jasper — November 28, 1834
  Mary E. Furlow — A. Hutcheson
COPELAND, Jasper N. — February 15, 1872
  Patience C. Zachary — Geo. W. Yarbrough

COPELAND, John — March 27, 1828
  Betsey Ann Credille — William Bryan
COPELAND, Peter — November 24, 1825
  Mary Tuggle
COPELAND, William — January 2, 1816
  Nancy Tally — Thomas M. Bush
COPELAND, William, Jr. — December 15, 1839
  Mary Dunn — William Tuggle
COPELAND, William D. — January 20, 1859
  Elizabeth D. Hailes — George C. Clarke
CORE, Richard — March 12, 1808
  Eliza Mead — Peter Early
CORRY, Daniel — January 3, 1830
  Addie Forrester — Robert Newsom
CORRY, G. T. — November 24, 1852
  Jane E. Harris — Thomas Stocks
CORRY, James Thomas — December 15, 1872
  Irwia Rhodes — Henry Newton
CORRY, John — November 22, 1822
  Elizabeth Carter
CORRY, John A. — May 12, 1864
  Mary A. Reynolds — R. A. Houston, M.G.
CORRY, William A. — May 19, 1838
  Martha M. Brinley
COTHRUM, Thomas — March 17, 1868
  Lottie Brown — Jas. W. Godkin
COTTON, Henry — May 28, 1825
  Maria Jenkins
COWLES, Samuel — April 11, 1820
  Judith Harroway — Lovick Pierce
COX, James M. — May 4, 1852
  Sarah A. Rawls — Vincent R. Thornton
COX, John T. — April 29, 1847
  Sarah T. Houghton — E. S. Hunter
CRABB, Benjamin R. — August 6, 1861
  Fannie A. Bryan — Albert Gray
CRAFT, Hugh — September 9, 1830
  Eliza Collier — Francis Cummins
CRANE, William H. — May 31, 1859
  Henrietta W. Statham — R. A. Houston, M.G.
CRAWFORD, Bennet — December 6, 1808
  Nancey Crawford — Isaac Cook
CRAWFORD, Fitus — May 8, 1814
  Nancy Powers — A. Bledsoe
CRAWFORD, George — August 12, 1847
  Louisa Burk — J. F. Billingslea
CRAWFORD, James Thomas — November 24, 1853
  Beatrice H. Rosser — Hinton Crawford
CRAWFORD, James — September 13, 1855
  Harriet C. Ballard
CRAWFORD, James Thomas — December 18, 1855
  S. E. R. Peoples — Hinton Crawford

CRAWFORD, Josiah H.   December 20, 1855
  Mary Howze   Hinton Crawford
CRAWFORD, Nowel   December 1, 1829
  Jane Finley   John Park
CRAWFORD, William   October 27, 1801
  Nancy Hemphill
CRAWFORD, William H.   July 25, 1867
  Harriet L. McGwier   Thos. P. Safford
CREDILLE, Cullen S.   December 19, 1833
  Jane Phillips   Hinton Crawford
CREDILLE, Gray   September 27, 1804
  Polly Smith
CREDILLE, Henry   October 27, 1804
  Sarah Smith
CREDILLE, Henry R.   January 20, 1839
  Sarah P. Jones   John Copelan
CREDILLE, Jesse   April 15, 1819
  Sarah Shockley   Wm. McGiboney
CREDILLE, Reuben A.   November 27, 1852
  Mary A. Hines   William Owen
CREDILLE, William   December 22, 1814
  Lina Smith   James Baldwin
CREDILLE, William G.   December 11, 1845
  Mary Ann Smith   William Bryan
CREDILLE, William H.   January 31, 1865
  Fannie L. Blythe
CREDILLE, William S.   September 15, 1842
  May Rosser   William Arnold
CRENSHAW, William H.   May 6, 1873
  M. E. Newsom   Henry Newton
CRENSHAW, William L.   December 14, 1844
  Mary E. Craddock
CRITTENDEN, Isaiah   December 20, 1865
  Toletha E. Tolbert   Lorenzo D. Carlton
CROCKETT, Augustus C.   November 1, 1855
  Harriet A. Skidmore   G. L. McCluskey
CROSS, Fetherhanx   April 13, 1820
  Mary Tucker   William Cone
CROSLEY, C. M.   January 28, 1847
  Marv Veazey   James Jones
CROSSLEY, Columbus M.   April 25, 1871
  Annie Luckie   J. M. Loury, M.G.
CROSSLEY, Edward   December 1, 1840
  Parmelia Linch   Reuben B. Armor
CROSSLEY, Edward   November 19, 1842
  Harriet Drake   John Howell
CROSSLEY, Edwin   June 24, 1824
  Nancy Wright
CROSSLEY, Josiah   April 30, 1843
  Rena Channell   Reuben Armor
CROSSLEY, Lemuel   December 14, 1826 '
  Sally Shipp   Thomas Whalev

CROSSLEY, Wiley A. — October 10, 1859
  Cynthia A. E. Leslie — W. G. Johnson
CROUCH, Joseph — December 20, 1821
  Elizabeth Joiner — Thomas Riley
CROW, Stephen — December 30, 1870
  Rebecca Kinnie
CROW, Stephen — August 20, 1871
  Rebecca Kinney — Rev. J. S. Patten
CROWDER, Richard P. — May 17, 1843
  Lucy Ann Thompson — John L. Oliver
CROWLEY, Thomas — March 5, 1828
  Lurania R. Ward — Roger Dickinson
CRUTCHFIELD, George — November 18, 1836
  Martha Matilda Moore — William Cone
CRUTCHFIELD, John — January 9, 1806
  Jinney W. Jelk
CRUTCHFIELD, John — October 27, 1842
  Jane E. Stephen — E. Sparks Hunter
CRUTCHFIELD, John W. — April 13, 1871
  Alice J. Harris — J. M. Loury, M.G.
CRUTCHFIELD, Robert F. — September 28, 1856
  Martha J. Turnell — I. A. Williams
CULBERTSON, David — December 24, 1818
  Lucy Wilkinson — John Browning
CULBERSON, David — June 15, 1819
  Sarah Stovall — L. Bethune
CULBERSON, Jeremiah F. — March 27, 1827
  Nancy Macon — Jas. Culberson
CULBERSON, William B. — June 8, 1852
  Margaret Carter — J. T. Findley
CULP, Peter — September 30, 1835
  Martha Bennett — John I. Holtzclaw
CULVER, Alfred — December 22, 1842
  Arena Credille — R. F. Griffen
CULVER, George P. — March 19, 1872
  Emma P. Arnold — James L. Pierce
CULVER, John P. — December 23, 1871
  Martha F. Strozier — J. H. Kilpatrick
CULVER, Joshua I. — June 20, 1843
  Mary Figgs — E. P. Jarrell
CUMBIE, Peter — February 6, 1853
  Lucinda Williams — Ephraim Bruce
CUNNINGHAM, Cornelius — July 8, 1844
  Sarah Elizabeth Cessena — Francis Bowman
CUNNINGHAM, Thomas T. — October 6, 1836
  Jane Fereba Gastin — James Anderson
CUNNINGHAM, William — July 15, 1830
  Ann Eliza Early — H. Reid
CUNNINGHAM, William H. — November 30, 1873
  Ella F. Knowles — J. Knowles
CURETON, William — November 4, 1789
  Margaret Crawl

CURRY, James   October 7, 1828
  Mary Forrester   Robert Newsom
CURRY, William H.   May 1, 1864
  Sarah E. Wright   J. R. Parker
CURTIS, Johnson   May 3, 1815
  Isabella Smith   Francis Cummins
CURTIS, Robert   January 30, 1811
  Margaret Taylor   Francis Cummins
CURTIS, Robert   January 27, 1820
  Sara Johnson   William Cone
CURTIS, William   January 10, 1821
  Sarah Grier
CURTWRIGHT, John   January 7, 1833
  Isena Warde   Thomas W. Grimes
CURTWRIGHT, Samuel   March 4, 1827
  Barbara Howell   James Woodham

D

DALE, Archibald Buchanan   October 24, 1832
  Margaret Ritchie   Thomas W. Grimes
DANIEL, Charles S.   April 8, 1852
  Adeline Jones   W. A. Corry
DANIEL, Charles W.   December 22, 1835
  Elizabeth Ann Jenkins
DANIEL, Cordial   April 17, 1824
  Anne Eliza Watts
DANIEL, Dana B.   February 16, 1865
  Julia F. Hunter   J. A. Preston, M.G.
DANIEL, Denton   February 10, 1806
  Saddy Jones
DANIEL, Henry F.   August 1, 1832
  Martha S. Moore
DANIEL, Ire A. M.   August 20, 1835
  Rebecca I. Walker   William Choice
DANIEL, James   December 7, 1819
  Eca Woodham   James Holt
DANIEL, James   December 21, 1789
  Grezil Clemonts
DANIEL, John   June 11, 1808
  Polly Fuller   Thomas Crawford
DANIEL, John   January 31, 1822
  Mary McLain   John Leftwich
DANIEL, Oliver P.   June 13, 1848
  Fanny M. Clark   Francis Bowman
DANIEL, Oliver T.   November 3, 1858
  Jane Victoria Cone   Samuel K. Talmadge
DANIEL, Samuel B.   January 12, 1843
  Mary E. Morgan   John Reid, M.G.
DANIEL, William   March 9, 1789
  Mary King
DANIEL, William   November 15, 1827
  Adaline Moore   Francis Cummins

DANIEL, William   December 20, 1853
   Sarah J. Watts   John Scott
DANIEL, William   December 7, 1856
   Rebecca A. House   N. M. Crawford
DANIEL, William T.   January 11, 1859
   Letitia M. Branch   John W. Reid, M.G.
DANLEY, William L.   January 19, 1866
   Lucy G. Shaffer
DARNELL, Zachariah   October 20, 1811
   Jenny Hopkins   O. Porter
DARROCOTT, William   October 17, 1804
   Sally Beckley
DAVANT, James   March 26, 1843
   Rebecca F. Matthews   B. M. Sanders
DAVANT, P. E.   January 8, 1856
   Hortense Moore   N. M. Crawford, M.G.
DAVANT, Samuel   March 15, 1829
   Agnes Ledbetter   William Rowland
DAVANT, William F.   October 28, 1856
   Anna Cocroft   J. P. Duncan
DAVENPORT, Burkett   May 12, 1824
   Sophiah Park
DAVENPORT, Henry   March 9, 1824
   Elizabeth Hubbard
DAVIES, John O.   October 29, 1854
   Mary Jane Eden   G. H. Thompson
DAVIES, William   February 28, 1801
   Nancy Rutledge
DAVIES, Capt. William   October 31, 1808
   Susannah Barnett
DAVIS, Aaron L. B.   August 9, 1853
   Elizabeth Hancock
DAVIS, Abner   December 11, 1817
   Elizabeth Parrish   Thomas Rhodes
DAVIS, Augustus V.   December 9, 1873
   Frances L. Saggus   Henry Newton
DAVIS, C. A.   February 27, 1849
   A. B. Swift   P. H. Mell
DAVIS, David   May 11, 1809
   Rebecha Woodwin   Wm. McGiboney
DAVIS, Genge C.   January 16, 1875
   Emma J. Reynolds   Henry Newton
DAVIS, George   July 31, 1819
   Patsy Gellum Price
DAVIS, John   March 11, 1830
   Elizabeth Downey   James Burton
DAVIS, John W.   December 4, 1873
   Lizzie Bass   W. H. Chapman
DAVIS, Leroy W.   December 11, 1855
   Martha O'Neal   H. D. Murden
DAVIS, Martin   December 4, 1806
   Frances Harper   Thomas Crawford

DAVIS, Reuben		February 23, 1847
Elizabeth Glaze		William Bryan
DAVIS, Reynolds		December 20, 1823
Catherine Tuggle		
DAVIS, Thomas		May 18, 1801
Patsy Woodwin		
DAVIS, Thomas W.		December 25, 1859
Adaline H. Jackson		T. J. Bowen
DAVIS, William		February 9, 1802
Hannah Cochran		
DAVIS, William G.		November 15, 1863
M. A. E. Grant		
DAVIS, William L.		March 15, 1863
Elizabeth Forte Foster		J. M. Stillwell
DAVIS, William M.		August 29, 1860
Virginia A. Ely		Jas. H. Kilpatrick
DAVIS, William S.		October 27, 1853
Ann S. Kimbro		J. W. Yarbrough
DAVISON, James		March 26, 1843
Rebecca F. Matthews		B. M. Sanders
DAVISON, James		December 8, 1872
Ella M. Tiller		W. A. Overton, M.G.
DAVISON, James M.		January 14, 1833
Mary Ann Southerland		Abraham Yeats
DAVISON, James M.		July 6, 1852
Margaret Moore		J. T. Findley
DAVISON, Reuben		February 18, 1841
Elizabeth Wilson Jones		Vincent R. Thornton
DAVISON, Robert E.		December 22, 1875
Hattie Armstrong		P. H. Mell, M.G.
DAWSEY, Daniel		November 13, 1808
Unity Coplan		F. T. Martin
DAWSON, George, Jr.		June 17, 1818
Sarah Branch		Lovick Pierce
DAWSON, George M.		March 21, 1839
Mary D. Riley		Thomas Stocks
DAWSON, James I.		August 5, 1847
Missouri S. Martin		J. L. Dagg
DAWSON, John T.		September 20, 1865
Betsy A. Park		William C. Bass, M.G.
DAWSON, William Crosby		January 28, 1819
Henrietta Wingfield		Lovick Pierce
DAY, John		April 30, 1848
Frances Harris		R. B. Kelly
DAY, Wiley		October 15, 1850
Sarah Jane Gaston		James M. Kelly
DEFOUR, William		January 2, 1848
Nancy Jane House		Wm. F. Gaston
DEFUR, Joseph		March 30, 1856
Martha Ray		B. Rowland
DEJARNET, Reuben		December 26, 1795
Nancy Reid		

DELANEY, Drury W.
  Laura Elliot
DENNARD, Jarred
  Emma H. Macon
DENNING, George A.
  Sarah G. Tunison
DENNIS, George W.
  Sarah Ann Jackson
DEVANEY, John Thomas
  Emily Harris
DEVANEY, William
  Mary Ann Palmer
DEVANT, James M.
  Celina Cocroft
DEVINEY, Thomas
  Tempy Riley
DICK, William
  Polly Price
DICKENS, Tillman
  Sarah Jane Pickett
DICKERSON, William
  Elizabeth Credille
DICKINSON, Francis
  Elizabeth Garrett
DICKINSON, John T.
  Ella Lindsey
DICKINSON, Roger
  Catherine Atkinson
DICKINSON, William
  Cornelia Daniel
DICKS, George
  Nancy Elton
DILLARD, George
  Martha Wall
DILLON, John
  Lethea Thigpen
DIX, John W. K.
  Sarah Elizabeth Martin
DIXON, David
  Martha Aubrey
DIXON, Hugh
  Rickah Alford
DIXON, Joel
  Nancy Watson
DOBLE, Joshua M.
  Ellen V. Wilson
DOLVIN, James
  Nancy Boone
DOLVIN, James
  Peggy Ann McHargue
DOLVIN, James
  Bede McMillan

July 16, 1857
Littleton D. Caldwell
January 26, 1858

February 4, 1863
R. A. Houston, M.G.
November 21, 1865
Lorenzo D. Carlton
April 20, 1857
Daniel Owens
November 10, 1871
J. H. Kilpatrick
November 15, 1860
J. J. Wallace, M.G.
December 4, 1821
A. Hutchinson
January 3, 1811
H. Gatlin
April 3, 1852
Hart C. Peek
November 5, 1819

November 9, 1826
A. H. Scott
May 3, 1869
Wm. A. Overton
February 11, 1825

June 22, 1859

April 8, 1800

July 29, 1822
Lovick Pierce
April 16, 1848
W. F. Gaston
July 23, 1851
P. H. Mell, M.G.
March 10, 1788

October 3, 1807
George Stovall
January 10, 1800
O. Porter
February 16, 1869
P. H. Mell, M.G.
February 7, 1821
William Cone
December 18, 1823
Thomas Johnson
December 7, 1835
John H. Steele

DOLVIN, James H.	June 17, 1856
Sarah E. E. Turnell	I. A. Williams
DOLVIN, William B.	February 8, 1855
Sarah C. Boswell	J. W. Reid
DOOLEY, L. J.	November 11, 1852
Martha W. Smith	William Bryan
DOSSEY, John	January 25, 1815
Nancy Smith	James Baldwin
DOSTER, Jonathan	August 27, 1854
Amanda Edge	Absalom Rhodes
DOSTER, William T.	January 8, 1852
Sarah C. Hale	Homer Hendel
DOUGHTER, William	September 3, 1803
Martha Norsworthy	Jesse Lacey
DOWELL, James W.	December 9, 1790
Elizabeth Carson	
DOWNING, Thomas	December 28, 1826
Adaline Gatlin	
DOWNS, William A.	December 18, 1856
Mary A. Moore	William Williams
DRAKE, James W.	February 6, 1837
Caroline F. Boswell	Vincent R. Thornton
DRAKE, James V.	September 6, 1856
Mrs. Sarah A. Callaway	
DRAKE, John	December 7, 1869
Ellen Bough	W. C. Birchmore
DRAKE, Patrick Henry	April 24, 1826
Martha Billbrath	
DRAKE, Thomas R.	February 23, 1864
Laura R. Carlton	W. R. Foote, M.G.
DUKE, Green	August 5, 1830
Ann Robinson	Francis West
DUKE, Isham	October 1, 1806
Elizabeth Sherrel	
DUKE, Robert	February 19, 1800
Patty Holloway	
DUNAWAY, John	September 20, 1821
Elizabeth Mayhay	Francis West
DUNCAN, Daniel	December 7, 1806
Paty Johnson	Thomas Crawford
DUNCAN, Daniel	January 16, 1844
Millie Williams	Thomas Stocks
DUNCAN, James	July 22, 1805
Sally Sinsdel	
DUNN, Hiram	February 5, 1821
Letitia Grier	
DUNN, Ishmael	January 8, 1833
Martha Darlington	J. P. Leveritt
DUNN, William	December 15, 1788
Anne Thompson	
DUPREE, James	February 6, 1872
Susan Jones	N. M. Jones, M.G.

DUPREE, James M. December 7, 1867
  Jane Shedd Columbus Heard
DURHAM, Abram February 4, 1845
  Elizabeth Durham Samuel Ely
DURHAM, Columbus December 5, 1871
  Catherine Reynolds
DURHAM, George W. December 18, 1859
  Hattie M. Hendon J. M. Stillwell
DURHAM, Henry H. June 27, 1865
  Fannie C. Edwards John R. Young, M.G.
DURHAM, James August 10, 1837
  Rebeccah Norris John G. Holtzclaw
DURHAM, J. D. May 20, 1875
  Cordelia West John S. Callaway
DURHAM, John C. November 17, 1831
  Sarah Bowles Augustine Evans
DURHAM, Jonathan D. January 31, 1867
  Eliza Ann Parham William Britain, M.G.
DURHAM, Joseph V. April 22, 1875
  Hattie A. Tool P. H. McWhorter
DURHAM, Samuel D. July 5, 1835
  Rebecca Armstrong Jack Lumpkin, M.G.
DURHAM, Samuel D. January 24, 1839
  Alzira E. Watson B. M. Sanders
DURHAM, Samuel D. December 12, 1858
  Henrietta Morgan P. H. Mell
DURHAM, Samuel J. October 9, 1866
  Nancy Harrison E. B. Moody
DURHAM, Silas December 4, 1827
  Alvina Booles
DURHAM, William January 5, 1805
  Reba Reynolds
DURHAM, William J. November 27, 1866
  Virginia A. Moss P. H. Mell
DURST, Adolphus F. February 28, 1861
  Henrietta W. Crane R. W. Houston
DUVVAL, Ezekial July 3, 1838
  Luriah Hunt James M. Godkin
DYER, John December 7, 1817
  Frances Pendergrass Hinton Crawford

E

EADES, William M. September 2, 1860
  Lucy E. Heath Hart C. Peek
EARLY, Clement January 8, 1810
  Frances Terrell A. Gresham
EARLY, Jeremiah October 15, 1806
  Eliza Cunningham Thomas Crawford
EARLY, Seaborn November 8, 1819
  Nancy Porter
EASLIN, James M. October 20, 1841
  Sara Anne Turner Ephraim Bruce

EASON, Thomas T.   August 2, 1857
   Mary A. Hightower   Joseph R. Parker
ECHOLS, Robert   April 22, 1824
   Polly Freeman
ECHOLS, Silas M.   January 4, 1838
   Sarah C. Hammonds   Vincent R. Thornton
EDMONDS, Reuben B.   December 21, 1837
   Miriam Kennedy   Nathan Hobbs
EDMONDS, William   October 19, 1856
   Frances G. Greer   William English
EDMONDSON, Augustus   June 26, 1842
   Mary Ann Jones   N. M. Lumpkin
EDMONDSON, John   April 8, 1859
   Martha Freeman   George A. Mathews
EDMONDSON, Joseph   December 29, 1846
   Rebecca Ann Wilson   W. H. Cone
EDMUNDSON, James   March 28, 1817
   Elizabeth Humphrey   James Greer
EDWARDS, Ambrose   May 12, 1807
   Betsey Kimbrough   William Johnson
EDWARDS, Ethelbred   December 9, 1823
   Julie Ogletree
EDWARDS, Gresham   October 23, 1840
   Emily Armstrong
EDWARDS, Jacob   December 14, 1815
   Matilda Acre   Thomas Lyne
EDWARDS, John   December 23, 1848
   Susan McBride
EDWARDS, Leroy   January 8, 1824
   Polly Allen   Chesley Bristow
EDWARDS, Pitman R.   August 24, 1845
   Elizabeth I. Malone   R. L. McWhorter
EDWARDS, Thomas   December 18, 1848
   Angeline Chain
EIDSON, Ellis   July 12, 1821
   Celia Fuller   Abraham Teates
EIDSON, John R.   December 23, 1835
   Mary Harris   John Wilson
EIDSON, Thomas   December 5, 1827
   Mary Hodges
EIDSON, Willis   August 30, 1840
   Mary Richardson   James M. Porter
ELDER, John   November 25, 1823
   Susan Barnett
ELDER, William H.   June 23, 1806
   Catherine Jackson
ELEY, Samuel   February 13, 1828
   Sarah Brooks   Sylvanus Gibson, M.G.
ELEY, Wilborn   June 3, 1829
   Mary Newsom
ELLINGTON, Enoch   February 12, 1816
   Nancy C. Blankenship   R. Baugh

ELLINGTON, Hekekiah — January 5, 1809
  Lucy A. G. Green — Francis Ross, M.G.
ELLINGTON, Richard — December 24, 1825
  Eliza White
ELLIOTT, Benjamin — December 27, 1860
  Elizabeth Williams — John O'Neal
ELLIOTT, David — November 6, 1818
  Dionia Findley — L. Bethune
ELLIOTT, George — October 7, 1819
  Mary Malone — William Cone
ELLIS, James H. — June 29, 1843
  Lucienda Hendricks — James W. Godkin
ELLIS, John W. — December 9, 1847
  Elizabeth Ellerbee — J. J. Loudermilk
ELLIS, Mathew — July 8, 1819
  Martha McHargue — Thomas Johnson
ELMORE, John William — August 30, 1824
  Martha Sims
ELMORE, Matthew — September 15, 1824
  Lucy Tait
ELY, James J., Jr. — November 15, 1873
  Menlo Rucker
ELY, John — January 12, 1843
  Frances Jernigan — James Jones, M.G.
ENGLISH, Henry — May 10, 1807
  Nancy Middleton — J. Mapp
ENGLISH, James N. — October 17, 1865
  Sallie M. Greer — John B. Young
ENGLISH, J. H. — December 18, 1855
  Elizah Holtzclaw — P. H. Mell
ENGLISH, John — January 2, 1847
  Ann Holtzclaw
ENGLISH, John H. — November 26, 1868
  Mary V. Beazley — Wm. A. Overton
ENGLISH, Stephen — December 13, 1849
  Martha Cheney — Enoch Calloway
ENGLISH, William — November 28, 1851
  Mary Durham — B. L. Ward
EPPS, Alexander — June 10, 1869
  Louisa Hunter — W. H. Brimberry
EPPS, Alexander W. — June 6, 1868
  Melissa Jane Butler
EPPS, Chesley — March 4, 1858
  Elizabeth T. Mitchell — J. H. Wragg
EPPS, William C. — December 27, 1868
  Emaline Barnes — E. A. Burgess
EPPS, William — October 9, 1875
  Amanda Roberts — R. A. Credelle
ERRICK, Charles C. — March 26, 1866
  Martha Ann Elizabeth Williams — W. G. Johnson
ESPRY, Robert — September 21, 1799
  Mary Barnette

ETHRIDGE, Henry C.   August 5, 1868
   Sarah E. Sharp   H. H. Tucker, M.G.
EVANS, Arden   January 15, 1805
   Elizabeth Carmichael
EVANS, Ardin B. C.   September 15, 1842
   Josephine McMichael   James McKenzie
EVANS, Benjamin F.   February 7, 1867
   Emma F. Littleton   A. J. S. Jackson
EVANS, Elijah   December 24, 1811
   Polly Reed   Malachi Murden
EVANS, Nicholas H.   November 16, 1860
   Catherine C. White   T. R. Swanson
EVANS, Winston   May 14, 1823
   Elizabeth Jackson   John Park
EVANS, Winston   July 3, 1827
   Sarah Park   Julius Alford
EZELL, Henry Clay   January 14, 1869
   Olive M. Arnold   Hart C. Peek
EZELL, James M.   February 9, 1865
   Martha H. Arnold   Hart C. Peek
EZELL, James M.   October 28, 1870
   Frances L. Bowden

F

FLOYD, George F.   June 15, 1833
   Maranda Copeland   William Bryan
FLOYD, John   January 29, 1833
   Ruth Grimes   A. Hutcheson
FLUKER, John C.   October 12, 1837
   Mary Ann Culbreth   John B. Cassels
FLUKER, Jesse M.   February 14, 1872
   Julia Holtzclaw   W. A. Overton
FLUKER, Oscar S.   January 12, 1869
   Mollie Sanford   Philip H. Robinson
FOLIS, Turner P.   June 3, 1802
   Nell Ledbetter
FOLLY, William   March 9, 1816
   Elizabeth Ellis   C. Maddox
FORCE, Albert W.   December 22, 1870
   Irene Howell   Homer Hendee, M.G.
FORCE, Benjamin W.   October 21, 1841
   Julia Ann Harper   F. R. Golding
FORD, John S.   April 14, 1840
   Sarah Ann May   John G. Holtzclaw
FORD, William   April 27, 1852
   Sarah Wyatt   B. Rowland
FORD, William   April 21, 1853
   Virginia Bennett   B. Rowland
FORD, William   September 30, 1855
   Winnie Thigpen   B. Rowland
FORREST, James N.   January 30, 1864
   Sarah Chapple   M. W. Arnold, M.G.

FORRESTER, Gresham — March 14, 1831
  Jane Waddell
FORRESTER, Jesse M. — December 17, 1840
  Sarah Ann Mitchell — Vincent R. Thornton
FORRESTER, Joel — October 24, 1799
  Sarah Tatum
FORRESTER, Joel — September 26, 1833
  Elizabeth Newsom — Jesse H. Watson
FORRESTER, Redman — June 19, 1858
  Martha E. Holtzclaw
FORRESTER, William — March 5, 1804
  Sarah Hunt
FORRESTER, William — May 9, 1822
  Nancy Payne — Robert Newsom
FORRESTER, Willie — January 9, 1812
  Polly Boles — Lemuel Greene
FOSTER, Anderson — November 29, 1801
  Salley Billingsby
FORT, Fernch S. — July 8, 1835
  Lena Chambers — James H. Taylor
FOSTER, Arthur — February 12, 1790
  Elizabeth Glenn
FOSTER, Arthur — October 5, 1819
  Harriet Crawford — Thomas Stocks
FOSTER, Arthur R. — November 1, 1874
  Mrs. Harriet T. Leverett — Albert Gray
FOSTER, James F. — June 18, 1815
  Matilda Houghton — Lovick Pierce
FOSTER, John — November 3, 1808
  Nancey Mallory — William Johnston
FOSTER, Joseph — January 13, 1819
  Charlotte Daniel — William Robinson
FOSTER, Robert — July 18, 1833
  Nancy Ellis — Hartwell H. Laurence
FOSTER, Robert M. — June 22, 1852
  Nancy Watts — Vincent R. Thornton
FOSTER, Samuel — March 13, 1827
  Jane Watkins
FOSTER, Seaborn — August 8, 1842
  Clementine P. Simmons — Ephraim Bruce
FOSTER, Thomas F. — May 14, 1851
  Mary Higginbotham — S. I. Pinkerton
FOSTER, William — September 10, 1833
  Mary Tally — Hartwell H. Laurence
FOUNTAIN, Elias G. — May 15, 1859
  Rachael A. Duncan — Reuben Kelly
FRAZIER, John V. — November 18, 1841
  Martha Irby — John Howell
FREEMAN, Beasley — August 2, 1840
  Polly Cummins — J. M. Wilson
FREEMAN, George A. — December 23, 1858
  Catherine S. Edmonds — James Davison

FREEMAN, James   December 19, 1822
  Anny Thurmon   Abraham Teats
FREEMAN, John G.   October 7, 1852
  Martha J. Durham   William Tuggle
FREEMAN, Valentine   March 20, 1805
  Nancy Legett
FREEMAN, Zacharia   July 3, 1842
  Margaret Findley   John H. Zuber
FRENCH, Lewis   April 10, 1823
  Julia Ann Newton   Hugh Smith, M.G.
FRETWELL, Micajah H.   November 11, 1804
  Jane L. Harper
FULLER, David   January 19, 1817
  Lucy Bedford   William Cone
FULLER, Elijah   October 25, 1811
  Elizabeth Boggis   A. Veazey
FULLER, Elijah   January 31, 1825
  Nancy Bowles
FULLER, Frederick C.   June 20, 1860
  Julia M. Nickelson   Homer Hendee, M.G.
FULLER, Greene   March 18, 1812
  Susannah Burford   A. Veazey
FULLER, Jesse   November 25, 1807
  Polly Jackson   William Browning
FULLER, Simon   January 4, 1842
  Nancy Hall   James Hutchinson
FULLER, William S.   December 13, 1836
  Celea White   James Moore
FULLWOOD, John Thomas   September 30, 1846
  Rebecca Lamar   B. M. Sanders
FURLOUGH, Charles   February 1, 1820
  Elizabeth Tucker
FURLOW, David   March 20, 1804
  Sally Dawson
FURLOW, George W.   November 21, 1850
  Lucy J. Dickens   J. T. Billingslea
FURLOW, James   February 5, 1803
  Peggy Pague
FURLOW, James T.   February 28, 1839
  Sarah Ann Hutchinson   Wm. L. Strain
FURLOW, Osborn   January 14, 1831
  Sarah Anne Brinckley   William Cone
FUTRAL, Benjamin   October 17, 1811
  Nancy Smith   Robert Rea
FAMBROUGH, James   December 10, 1854
  Elizabeth Le Wood   W. A. Partee
FAMBROUGH, Jesse M.   January 24, 1856
  Delilah Jane Freeman   W. A. Partee
FAMBROUGH, Thomas M.   November 30, 1840
  Jane Freeman   James Porter
FAMBROUGH, William   March 10, 1814
  Sally Bradshaw

FAMBROUGH, Zachariah   September 10, 1838
  Elizabeth Jane Jackson   James M. Porter
FANNIN, Isham   September 1, 1809
  Peggy Porter   Samuel Harper
FANNIN, Jepthah   May 10, 1814
  Catherine Porter   Jack Lampkin
FANNIN, William   January 13, 1800
  Nancy Pierce
FANNIN, William   January 18, 1807
  Catherine Martin   J. Mapp
FARMER, William Thomas   December 22, 1871
  Mary Jane Bowles   Wm. A. Overton
FARRAR, William J.   June 11, 1848
  Louisa Bailey   T. M. Fambrough
FARRIS, James   June 26, 1856
  Nancy Aurena Bennett   Isaac R. Hall
FARROW, Nathaniel   December 8, 1850
  Jane Williams   Joseph W. Drennan
FASSETT, Early P.   September 29, 1842
  Martha Brunt   Robert F. Griffen
FARWATER, James L.   October 9, 1840
  Mary Ann Hall   Wm. I. Heard
FAUCH, Jonas   October 20, 1793
  Polly Daniell
FAULKNER, Zachariah   December 2, 1866
  Sarah A. D. Thompson   E. L. Williams
FAUNTLEROY, George L.   November 10, 1831
  Aphiah F. B. Todd   Lovick Pierce, M.G.
FAY, Frank   January 25, 1821
  Dorothy Hicks   Francis Cummins
FEARS, Ezekiel   June 9, 1803
  Alisey Stringfellow
FEARS, James P.   December 13, 1864
  Elizabeth Bowden   N. M. Arnold, M.G.
FEARS, Jesse W.   September 6, 1864
  Mary E. Perkins   E. W. Warren, M.G.
FERREL, Archelaus   August 28, 1797
  Sally Parker
FEW, Joseph   July 23, 1804
  Fanny Fields
FIELDS, Joseph W.   July 24, 1851
  Emily Foster   M. G. Foster
FIELDS, Lewis   December 27, 1827
  Eliza Fitten   Francis Cummins
FIELDS, Thomas   December 19, 1791
  Sally Kilgoar
FILLINGHAM, Counsel   August 23, 1814
  Nancy Williams   Archibald Watts
FILLINGHAM, Henry C.   December 14, 1865
  Angeline C. O'Neal   L. C. Caldwell
FILLINGHAM, Jarvis W.   December 14, 1843
  Nancy A. Veazey   John L. Veazey

FILLINGHAM, Jarvis W.   December 14, 1868
  Eliza Stanley   L. D. Caldwell
FINCH, George W.   October 22, 1837
  Martha Ann Pierce   Nathan Hobbs
FINCH, John E.   November 12, 1840
  Almira Moody   James Davidson
FINCH, John E.   December 12, 1866
  Mary R. A. Patrick   Lucius C. Broome
FINCH, William   August 25, 1831
  Elizabeth Stallings   George Hall
FINLEY, John   May 3, 1804
  Mary Ray
FINLEY, Leroy I.   January 23, 1840
  Hannah Woodham   John Hutchinson
FINLEY, Norwood H.   January 1, 1835
  Cynthia Caldwell   Abraham Jenkins
FINLEY, Robert   November 26, 1802
  Janie Finley
FINLEY, Robert   August 18, 1803
  Lucendia Finley
FINLEY, Thomas   February 5, 1801
  Margaret Allen
FINLEY, Thomas   November 9, 1823
  Anna Waggoner
FINLEY, Thomas   August 3, 1846
  Nancy Gregory   W. D. Maddox
FINLEY, Thomas L.   August 19, 1869
  C. A. Crawford   W. R. Foote
FINLEY, William   June 29, 1805
  Polly Sharpe
FISHER, Joseph   May 10, 1865
  Mrs. Georgia Ann White   W. G. Johnston
FITZGERALD, Bird   December 20, 1825
  Eliza B. Springer
FITZPATRICK, Joseph   July 12, 1823
  Ruth Hodge   Hinton Crawford
FITZPATRICK, Rene   January 15, 1816
  Polly Watts   Jack Lumpkin
FITZSIMMONS, Henry   April 22, 1819
  Elmira Burk
FLANAGAN, Edward   September 4, 1864
  Frances R. Moose   Ezekiel S. Williams
FLANAGAN, William   February 10, 1867
  Marietta Holder   E. S. Williams
FLEETWOOD, Littleberry   October 15, 1857
  Tillitha J. Evans   L. B. Jackson
FLEETWOOD, William   April 17, 1832
  Mary Ann Jackson   J. P. Leveritt
FLEMING, William   July 31, 1836
  Delila Kennedy   Jas. H. McWhorter
FLINT, William T.   February 18, 1874
  Lilla W. Moore   J. H. Kilpatrick

FLORENCE, Frank S. L.   April 17, 1860
  Sarah Eldecia Winfield   A. Gray
FLORENCE, William A.   June 7, 1859
  Betsy Ann Park   George C. Clarke
FLOURNEY, Gibson   September 8, 1802
  Huldy Williams
FLOW, Guilford   February 23, 1809
  Elizabeth Coleman

G

GAFFORD, Thomas   May 1, 1801
  Polly Whatley
GAISERT, John Mathew   August 22, 1844
  Delacy Hughes
GAILSFIELD, Thomas   February 28, 1801
  Polly Tarby
GANN, John   January 5, 1856
  Susan Johnson   B. Rowland
GANN, Marion   January 29, 1852
  Sarah Z. Wright   Alfred L. Willis
GANN, Samuel   April 24, 1788
  Mary Hambrion
GANTT, Eli   June 28, 1856
  Elizah Dunn   J. W. Reid, M.G.
GARDNER, Samuel   December 7, 1869
  Sarah E. H. Bowles
GARDNER, S. A.   December 8, 1870
  Selina S. Durham   W. R. Wilson
GARLINGTON, James   July 17, 1820
  Martha Colquitt   William Tally, M.G.
GARLINGTON, Thomas C.   December 10, 1835
  Elizabeth Edmondson   Vincent R. Thornton
GARNER, John J.   February 14, 1856
  Mary Cumbie   B. Rowland
GARNER, Thomas   September 6, 1821
  Martha Webb   Thomas Riley
GARNER, William   January 28, 1819
  Elizabeth Webb   Thomas Riley
GARNER, William D.   July 29, 1855
  Elizabeth Cheek   B. Rowland
GARRD, William W.   August 4, 1840
  Mary M. Urquhart
GARRET, John   April 4, 1816
  Jean Greer   Miller Hunter
GARRETT, Thomas B.   December 17, 1818
  Betsey Ann Cole   John Park
GARROT, John   June 24, 1818
  Anny Cole   L. Bethune
GARROTT, Robert   October 5, 1818
  Mary Hale
GARTRELLE, John O.   December 19, 1848
  Mary A. W. Randle   L. G. Hillyer

GARTRELLE, William J.   December 30, 1849
   Eliza A. Scott   Hinton Crawford
GASTIN, Alex   December 9, 1802
   Sally Garner
GASTON, John   January 8, 1826
   Martha Blanks
GASTON, Matthew   December 13, 1793
   Rebekah Harden
GASTON, Matthew   April 11, 1827
   Phereba Brown
GASTON, William   March 16, 1839
   Louisa A. Fosett   Robert F. Griffin
GASTON, William   January 19, 1843
   Sarah Matthews   R. F. Griffin
GASTON, William   August 2, 1849
   Mary Ann Wilson   J. M. Kelly
GATEWOOD, Phillip   October 7, 1821
   Sarah Colquitt   C. Maddox
GATLIN, Alpheus   May 1, 1826
   Mariah, Gatlin
GATLIN, Churchwell   May 1, 1802
   Patsey Moore
GATLIN, Lemuel M.   March 8, 1829
   Elizabeth H. Jackson   Ephraim Bruce
GATLIN, Major   September 21, 1808
   Darkes Gatlin   S. Gatlin
GATLIN, Radford   June 5, 1818
   Elizabeth Daniel
GAYLORD, Giles   January 26, 1811
   Ferriby Jones   Arthur Foster
GENTRY, Burgess   March 29, 1825
   Polly Parrish
GENTRY, John D.   April 25, 1850
   Nancy Copelan   William Bryan
GENTRY, Seaborn   August 6, 1839
   Malinda Shirley
GENTRY, Samuel   February 1, 1820
   Cynthia Connell   Wm. McGiboney
GENTRY, William   October 17, 1848
   Mary Gilmer   W. T. Gaston
GENTRY, William H.   December 28, 1871
   Laura Tunnell   R. P. Perdue, M.G.
GEORGE, John R.   February 1, 1859
   Lucy C. Anderson   George C. Clarke
GEORGE, William   October 10, 1821
   Elizabeth Grimes   Thomas Johnson
GERDINE, George Augustus L. J.   December 20, 1871
   Anne Fleming Cartwright   Geo. W. Yarbrough
GERMANY, John   March 7, 1806
   Elizabeth Brown
GETTATHEWS, George   February 5, 1816
   Cassandra Wells   N. Lewis

GIBBS, Miles	October 3, 1803
Martha Shephard	
GIBBS, Thomas	June 2, 1819
Nancy Maddox	Thomas Johnson
GIBBS, Thomas	May 26, 1842
Julia Cornelia Ralls	W. M. I. Hard
GIBSON, Henry A.	November 10, 1842
Sarah A. Jones	B. M. Sanders
GIBSON, Isaiah	November 24, 1804
Lydia White	
GIBSON, Isaiah	September 1, 1808
Lydia White	Thomas Carleton
GIBSON, Thomas C.	November 23, 1869
Clementina J. Reid	J. M. Dickey
GILBREATH, Daniel	August 26, 1819
Martha Gwinn	Wm. McGiboney
GILBERT, Robert	July 8, 1831
Eliza Turner	J. P. Leveritt
GILES, Thomas	January 7, 1804
Mary Whatley	
GILES, William	April 11, 1805
Nancy Daniel	
GILLEN, John	May 9, 1839
Jane Caldwell	James M. Davison
GILLEN, Samuel T.	December 21, 1875
Margaret J. Freeman	M. M. Landrum, M.G.
GILMER, Joseph	February 13, 1853
Susan Divine	W. H. Blythe
GILMORE, John	January 8, 1802
Betsey Cartwright	
GIRDING, Charles	April 17, 1854
Ann H. G. Green	S. G. Hillyer
GLASS, B.	August 20, 1803
Sally White	
GLASS, Elias	November 26, 1804
Sally Wilson	
GLASS, James	June 25, 1805
Penny Pace	
GLASS, Jonathan	June 22, 1814
Milly Fullar	John Browning
GLASS, William	October 7, 1799
Mary Baker	
GLASS, Z., Jr.	December 18, 1799
Sally Wilson	
GLAWSON, Eli	October 15, 1849
Mary Ann Divine	R. F. Griffen
GLAZE, Samuel	July 27, 1848
Elizabeth Glosson	W. T. Gaston
GLAZIER, Hyram	September 24, 1804
Nancy Lasseter	
GLOVER, L. L.	July 27, 1873
Romelia N. Wheeler	M. M. Landrum

GODKIN, James W.	March 18, 1827
Harriet A. Patrick	N. H. Harris
GOOCH, Nathan	August 19, 1819
Polly Jenkins	L. Bethune
GOODWIN, David W.	December 15, 1859
Lucretia C. Littleton	James W. Godkin
GORE, Thomas	November 26, 1818
Mary Alford	Thomas Snow
GORLEY, Jonathan	March 31, 1825
Mary Beckom	
GOUGER, Stephen	November 4, 1819
Julia Veazey	
GRAHAM, Joseph	December 18, 1803
Nancy Catchings	
GRAHAM, Joseph	December 20, 1808
Winney Gooch	John Dingler
GRANT, Allen	January 4, 1855
Mary Ann Barnhart	W. J. Hanley
GRANT, Cullen E.	December 8, 1850
Robelia H. Bates	Daniel Hightower
GRANT, Daniel	June 20, 1810
Lucy Crutchfield	Josia Randle
GRANT, James	January 4, 1848
Eliza Wright	James Moore
GRANT, James T.	July 4, 1872
Frances Hester	J. H. Kilpatrick
GRANT, John G.	December 10, 1861
Sarah F. Coley	Joseph R. Parker
GRANT, John C.	October 14, 1870
Texana Howell	
GRANT, Joseph	May 16, 1851
Eliza L. Grant	Daniel Hightower
GRANT, J. T.	April 6, 1841
Mary S. Chew	Thomas Stocks
GRANT, Thomas	January 4, 1826
Mary P. Baird	Lovick Pierce, M.G.
GRANT, William S.	October 10, 1847
Nancy R. Lundy	Francis Bowman
GRAVES, Joseph	February 12, 1822
Mary Shorter	James Woodberry
GRAVES, Young W.	November 12, 1857
Martha E. Holtzclaw	
GRAY, Archibald	January 29, 1807
Cynthia Arnold	Robert M. Cunningham
GREENE, Augustus F.	January 27, 1840
Amanda Jane Robertson	
GREENE, Benjamin F.	November 24, 1846
Susan Amorette Greene	Francis Bowman
GREENE, Farnafold	July 8, 1818
Ruth Dawson	Lovick Pierce
GREENE, James H.	January 27, 1853
Ann Raden	J. R. Hall

GREENE, James H.   October 2, 1864
  Permelia D. Criswell   E. S. Williams
GREENE, John   May 20, 1821
  Patsey Curtis   William Moore
GREENE, Joseph   December 14, 1804
  Tabitha Whatley
GREENE, Lemuel   October 22, 1806
  Nancy Merritt   Jesse Lacey
GREENE, Lemuel   May 6, 1824
  Eliza Palmer   Jack Lumpkin
GREENE, Lemuel   February 22, 1842
  Sarah Clements
GREENE, Lemuel H.   August 21, 1843
  Frances King   John W. Reid
GREENE, Lemuel   August 4, 1850
  Pharibee Jane Hall   James M. Kelly
GREENE, Walter   January 4, 1825
  Nancy W. Maddox
GREENE, William   July 3, 1822
  Frances Tucker   Robert Newsome
GREENWOOD, Thomas   April 25, 1805
  Nancey Mitchell
GREENWOOD, Thomas   March 9, 1819
  Leonora Ann Mounger   Lovick Pierce
GREENWOOD, Thomas E.   March 31, 1833
  Emaline D. Baird   Thos. P. C. Shelman
GREER, Aquila   August 11, 1814
  Thene Yates   Thomas Johnson
GREER, Aquilla   November 29, 1821
  Sarah Sayers   Abraham Yates
GREER, Archibald   June 10, 1828
  Elizabeth King   William Cone
GREER, David   December 19, 1822
  Sarah Grier   Jeremiah Ragan
GREER, D. L.   November 1, 1873
  Annie Durham
GREER, Henry   May 12, 1818
  Nancy Hoobes
GREER, Henry F.   December 9, 1830
  Ann A. Ragan   Jack Lumpkin
GREER, Henry   March 2, 1845
  Polly Nichols   Robert McWhorter
GREER, Isaac   March 25, 1800
  Ione Hays
GREER, James   February 3, 1802
  Pansey Merritt
GREER, John   April 1, 1805
  Elizabeth Greer
GREER, John   March 20, 1822
  Emma Crawford   Thomas Stocks
GREER, John   June 23, 1830
  Emily Talbot   W. B. Barnett

GREER, John   June 24, 1823
  Jane Pinkard   A. B. Longstreet
GREER, Richard   November 5, 1824
  Lucy Greer
GREER, Robert   January 31, 1822
  Caroline McCoy
GREER, Thomas G.   December 20, 1831
  Catherine Stephens   Williamson Bird
GREER, Thomas L.   June 16, 1831
  Elizabeth White   William Bird
GREER, William   January 15, 1794
  Delilah Haynes
GREGORY, Benjamin F.   December 18, 1856
  Ann C. Ray   John W. M. Barton
GRESHAM, Albert   May 10, 1827
  Mary Wells   Jacob King, M.G.
GRESHAM, Albert W.   January 9, 1866
  Emma E. Lindsey   R. A. Houston, M.G.
GRESHAM, John H.   January 26, 1865
  Susan E. Rhymens   H. H. Fitzpatrick
GRESHAM, Sterling A.   June 5, 1849
  Sarah E. Stokes   Francis Bowman
GRESHAM, Young   June 10, 1803
  Henson Harrison
GRESHAM, Young Felix   June 15, 1858
  Sarah Jane Baugh   F. F. Reynolds
GRIFFEN, John A.   May 4, 1871
  Anna L. Scudder   C. W. Lane, M.G.
GRIFFEN, Walter   June 18, 1846
  Rosina Willis   Francis Bowman
GRIFFETH, Nathan   November 3, 1828
  Judith Booles
GRIFFEY, John   December 19, 1825
  Frances Rainey
GRIFFIN, Andrew J.   December 30, 1835
  Adaline Sanders   John F. Hillyer
GRIFFIN, Matthew   January 6, 1824
  Harriet Carrell
GRIFFIN, Robert   September 8, 1824
  Susanna Brooks
GRIFFITH, Jedekiah   June 20, 1848
  Jane Johnson   T. D. Martin, M.G.
GRIFFITH, Thomas   November 17, 1824
  Becky Akins
GRIFFITH, William P.   December 21, 1856
  Sarah A. Eidson   J. G. Holtzclaw
GRIFFITH, William V.   December 16, 1860
  Martha L. Dickson   J. M. Stillwell
GRIMES, Henry   February 24, 1831
  Mary W. King   Francis Cummins
GRIMES, James   January 29, 1833
  Lucenda King   James H. Taylor

GRIMES, Jesse — October 2, 1832
  Rhoda Bates — Dickerson Jones
GRIMES, Joseph — October 21, 1824
  Eliza Cunningham
GRIMES, Joseph — December 11, 1833
  Harriott Bouden — William Park, M.G.
GRIMES, R. M. — February 10, 1870
  Leila M. Jernigan — C. P. Beeman
GRIMES, Robert M. — April 6, 1874
  Lucy M. Jernigan
GRIMES, Sterling F. — May 5, 1841
  Sarah Bowdre — George Pierce
GRIMES, Thomas — June 29, 1843
  Frances Meriwether — Francis Bowman
GRIMES, Thomas W. — January 11, 1844
  Anne Coleman — Otis Smith
GRIMES, William P. — January 28, 1858
  Martha A. Sayers — Charles W. Launius
GRIMETT, Robert — July 10, 1788
  (widow)
GUILL, William B. — March 26, 1856
  Virginia Moody — John G. Holtzclaw
GUISE, Isaac N. — October 26, 1831
  Nancy Corry — C. T. Beeman
GUNTER, William M. — September 2, 1870
  Sarah Harper
GUR, John L. — December 1, 1838
  Mary Wright — James M. Porter
GWYNN, Thomas — April 12, 1846
  Emily Crossley — L. B. Jackson

H

HACKNEY, John — October 25, 1815
  Nancy Musgrove — Evans Myrick
HACKNEY, Samuel — November 1, 1868
  Cornelia C. Dorsey — James Davison
HACKNEY, William — October 5, 1818
  Patsey Barker
HAGABY, Joshua — February 11, 1801
  Sally Wester
HAGERTY, Abel — December 30, 1803
  Anna Buckhannon
HAILES, Henry J. — April 29, 1852
  Margaret Findley — J. T. Findley
HAILES, John T. — January 30, 1868
  Amanda A. Hall — William Bryan
HAILEY, James A. — April 20, 1852
  Mary E. Crenshaw — John R. Young
HAISTEN, James — August 12, 1819
  Margaret Cartwright — John Harris
HALL, Dickson — November 3, 1818
  Priscilla Baugh

HALL, Edihugh   September 21, 1825
  Elizabeth Kelly
HALL, George   May 5, 1822
  Malenda Dunn   Thomas Riley
HALL, George   April 17, 1824
  Nancy Slaughter
HALL, Hugh   March 2, 1803
  Sally Hall
HALL, Hugh   November 10, 1824
  Mary Brown
HALL, Hugh A.   August 17, 1848
  Susan Ann Jackson   L. B. Jackson
HALL, Isaac R.   May 14, 1863
  Sarah E. Hall   L. B. Jackson
HALL, James D.   October 15, 1861
  Sarah Pyron   Hinton Crawford
HALL, James F.   February 26, 1857
  Missouri A. Corry   J. S. K. Axson
HALL, John   August 27, 1811
  Polly Little   Josiah Randle
HALL, John   March 17, 1834
  Nancy E. Leverett   A. Hutcheson
HALL, John L.   November 5, 1863
  Emma A. Zimmerman   R. A. Houston, M.G.
HALL, Josiah T.   October 3, 1855
  Elizabeth Taylor   W. H. C. Cone, M.G.
HALL, Samuel   February 26, 1806
  Nancy Smith
HALL, Samuel   February 7, 1840
  Nancy Malone   Jas. C. Hutchinson
HALL, Vincent S.   September 3, 1872
  Mary E. Hall   W. D. Atkinson
HALL, Young   September 7, 1825
  Mariah Ann Howell   Thos. Slaughter
HAMES, A. Baker   September 21, 1871
  Macon Hester   W. R. Foote, M.G.
HAMMETT, James   June 13, 1816
  Elizabeth Brooker   George Owen
HAMMOND, Robert   April 5, 1810
  Lovy Hines   Robert Rea
HAMMOND, William   April 2, 1816
  Mary Johnson   Francis Cummins
HAMMOND, William   September 22, 1835
  Nancy Clark   J. P. Leverett
HANCOCK, George   November 7, 1847
  Elizabeth O'Neal   John W. Reid
HANCOCK, George P.   October 29, 1874
  Nannie E. Stewart   C. H. Strickland
HANCOCK, Henry L.   July 14, 1864
  Katharine Elizabeth Stewart   John O'Neal
HANCOCK, Henry W.   March 26, 1874
  Elva Emma Saggus   W. A. Overton

HANCOCK, James A.   May 23, 1872
  Mattie Simpson   Henry Newton
HAND, Richard   June 25, 1842
  Unity Medley (Uny)
HARALSON, Braddy B.   December 21, 1848
  Martha Ann Chambers   W. H. C. Cone
HARALSON, Hugh   November 27, 1828
  Caroline M. Lewis   Lovick Pierce
HARALSON, Jesse B.   March 22, 1827
  Elizabeth R. Conyers   James Culberson
HARALSON, Kenchin L.   February 28, 1833
  Jane W. Lewis   Sam J. Cassels
HARALSON, Vincent   January 10, 1809
  Lucy English   William Greer
HARBIN, James T.   December 24, 1872
  Fanny Pitman   H. C. Peek
HARDEN, Henry   March 17, 1829
  Mary Ann Watson   Ephraim Bruce
HARDIN, James   March 27, 1821
  Matilda Richards   John Harris
HARDWICK, James   May 10, 1806
  Violet Elder
HARDY, W. J.   December 10, 1804
  Hannah Rimes
HARGIN, Alex   November 28, 1796
  Gressy Bonon
HARGROOVES, Sanford   April 27, 1833
  Frances Bickers   Lovick Pierce, M.G.
HARLBERT, Roswell   July 11, 1871
  Frances Ella Davis
HARLOW, James B.   February 16, 1874
  Ella Geer
HARP, Samuel   September 23, 1810
  J. Clemens   W. Johnson
HARP, William   December 23, 1799
  Polly Brewer
HARPER, Allen   February 28, 1801
  Lucy Smith
HARPER, Axamins   January 3, 1805
  E. Ward
HARPER, George A.   May 6, 1858
  Sophy J. Perkins   J. M. Wragg
HARREN, James H.   January 1, 1837
  Rosamonds A. Caldwell   Thomas W. Grimes
HARRIS, Benjamin   November (?), 1829
  Susan Pyron
HARRIS, Charles   December 20, 1820
  Tabitha Gibbs   Lovick Pierce
HARRIS, Charles F.   December 7, 1831
  Rachael James   Joshua Cannon
HARRIS, Elios   May 10, 1800
  Nancy W. Hudson

HARRIS, Henry C. June 16, 1848
  Mary H. Taylor John B. Chappell
HARRIS, James November 10, 1817
  Lucretia Jones Francis Cummins
HARRIS, James July 5, 1833
  Abigail Fambrough John H. Ray
HARRIS, Jesse January 12, 1789
  Rachael Pendleton
HARRIS, Jesse December 1, 1838
  Louisa Rainwater
HARRIS, John March 19, 1816
  Betsey Wilkinson Robert Rea
HARRIS, John April 29, 1846
  Henrietta Jackson Francis Cowman
HARRIS, John M. June 10, 1819
  Olive Stevens Thomas Johnson
HARRIS, John T. February 1, 1852
  Frances C. Leslie Hart C. Peek
HARRIS, J. P. January 6, 1878
  Mary Elizabeth Allen J. F. Hester
HARRIS, Myles G. April 2, 1845
  Lucy Elizabeth Seymor Francis Bowman, M.G.
HARRIS, Nathaniel N. December 14, 1826
  Ellen N. Victory Lovick Pierce, M.G.
HARRIS, Robert July 13, 1818
  Mary Freeman Jesse Mercer
HARRIS, Robert L. August 3, 1875
  Susan L. Head F. G. Hughes
HARRIS, Capt. S. B. December 9, 1794
  Patience Williams
HARRIS, Seaborn December 19, 1823
  Polly Shaw
HARRIS, Singleton December 23, 1822
  Maria Acree Horatio A. B. Nunnally
HARRIS, Thomas McCall August 27, 1804
  Margaret Baldwin
HARRIS, Thomas August 8, 1829
  Sarah Hall George Hall
HARRIS, Thomas April 12, 1836
  Elizabeth Bunkley William Cone
HARRIS, Thomas March 3, 1840
  Catherine Baldwin James Jones
HARRIS, Thomas July 22, 1852
  Burget Ann Burford
HARRIS, William August 23, 1787
  Hannah Hogg
HARRIS, William October 5, 1818
  Matilda Blanks
HARRIS, William February 19, 1846
  Chrisaline Bruce H. Lawrence
HARRIS, William L. M. December 3, 1850
  Sementha D. Johnson P. H. Mell, M.G.

HARRIS, William L. U.   October 13, 1856
  Sarah F. Johnson
HARRISON, Benjamin   December 11, 1814
  Jane Matthews   Thomas Stocks
HARRISON, James   July 31, 1801
  Mary Harrison
HARRISON, James W.   February 10, 1831
  Elender T. Evans   Leveritt V. Dee
HARRISON, Robert   May 6, 1821
  Isabel Pattillo   William Tally
HARRUP, James   August 14, 1816
  Ridley Harrup   Arch McCoy
HARRUP, Warren   February 11, 1849
  Anzelina T. Taylor   L. B. Jackson
HART, Isaac   September 20, 1855
  Polly Merritt   W. W. Moore
HART, John S.   September 10, 1857
  Martha J. Leveret   W. W. Moore
HART, Thomas   January 18, 1810
  Ann Barnett   Clayborn Maddox
HART, William M.   January 12, 1869
  Mary E. Nave   Philip H. Robinson
HARVELL, Daniel   November 11, 1801
  Mary Cosal
HARVILL, Thomas   September 4, 1818
  Mary Chatham   Lovick Pierce
HARWELL, James M.   April 14, 1857
  Sarah Lou Smith Moore   G. Bright, M.G.
HARWELL, William   March 21, 1816
  Polly Hobbs   John Browning
HATCHETT, John   December 18, 1820
  Eliza Tuggle   Lemuel Greene
HATTON, Thomas   March 15, 1810
  Nancey Lacey   William Cone
HAWKE, John   July 4, 1830
  Mary Head   Matthew Winfield
HAWKES, Peter   January 4, 1806
  Polly Roberts
HAYES, Ezekeil   May 2, 1874
  Rebecca Shelton
HAYES, Robert   May 2, 1820
  Susan Beckham   Lovick Pierce
HAYES, William   October 26, 1801
  Polly Herd
HAYNES, Jasper   January 15, 1846
  Elizabeth Armstrong   S. G. Hillyer
HAYNES, John   September 3, 1829
  Elizabeth McKnight   Robert Newsom
HAYNES, Parmenas   October 10, 1843
  Mary Anne Tuggle   P. H. Mell, M.G.
HAYNES, Robert   May 16, 1825
  Elizabeth Reid

HAYS, Howard	April 19, 1853
Sarah A. V. Walker	J. W. Yarbrough
HAYS, William	March 29, 1805
Nell Luckey	
HAZEL, John	August 4, 1816
Leonard Levine	Thomas Bush
HAZLETT, Wilson	September 14, 1873
Nancy Mullins	D. H. Moncrief
HEARD, Franklin	February 22, 1820
Anne Bozeman	
HEARD, James T.	July 5, 1866
Amorette Greene	Philip B. Robinson
HEARD, John	January 26, 1805
Nancy Wallis	
HEARD, John T.	January 12, 1860
Margaret F. Mitchell	H. H. Tucker, M.G.
HEARD, Stephen I.	November 30, 1840
Lucy S. Foster	
HEARD, Thomas	January 7, 1830
Ann Richards	Peter Johnson
HEARD, Woodrow	May 29, 1805
Polly Peoples	
HEARD, W. T.	November 9, 1875
Lula W. Moore	J. H. Kilpatrick
HEARD, Clem Freena	October 31, 1858
Martha L. Hester	John Calvin Johnson
HEARN, William T.	May 22, 1867
Betsey Ann Armor	John W. Talley, M.G.
HEATH, Matthew	November 28, 1831
Elizabeth Clements	Ephraim Bruce
HEATH, Rylan	April 26, 1808
Ann Gilbert	C. Maddox
HECK, Thomas	August 17, 1818
Elizabeth Sturdivant	William Cone
WHITFIELD, Hedge	December 10, 1817
Elizabeth Greene	William Cone
HEFLIN, James	February 19, 1802
Sarah Winn	
HEFLIN, James	December 30, 1805
Nancy Thurmon	
HEFLIN, James	December 31, 1806
Nancy Thurmon	William Browning
HEMPHILL, Hiram	December 22, 1840
Jane Moore	Francis Bowman
HEMPHILL, Thompson	January 21, 1808
Rhoda Baggett	John Dingler, M.G.
HEMPHILL, William	October 10, 1800
Nancy Hughes	
HENDEL, Homer	June 1, 1847
Frances King	Francis Cowman
HENDERSON, Joseph M.	February 18, 1864
Emma H. J. Dawson	P. H. Mell, M.G.

HENDRICKS, James A.   December 28, 1865
   Frances V. Pollard   William R. Wilson
HENDRY, C. M.   January 5, 1873
   L. A. Blackman   W. A. Moore
HENRY, Thomas Wyatt   January 13, 1852
   Mary Francis Cunningham
HENSON, Louden   November 8, 1829
   Nancy Robinson   John Chew
HERMON, William   November 10, 1802
   Betsey R. Nolton
HERN, William   September 4, 1825
   Peggy Haynes   James Culberson
HERN, Zabad   July 21, 1818
   Lydia Rumsey
HESTER, Francis   August (?), 1837
   Mary Ann McCowen
HESTER, Robert A.   July 6, 1837
   Roxanah Martin   John Hendricks, M.G.
HESTER, Simeon   November 27, 1866
   Ann Elizabeth Tuggle   William A. Overton
HARMON, Hete   September 9, 1819
   Elizabeth West   Robert Booth
HEWSTON, John   December 17, 1807
   Nancey Harris   George Stovall
HICKEY, William   September 12, 1844
   Mary Connell   J. J. Howell
HIEAR, Cornelius   March 25, 1873
   Amanda Fisher   Jas. W. Godkin
HIGGINBOTHAM, Riley N.   March 8, 1868
   Martha Little   Jas. H. McWhorter
HIGHTOWER, Daniel   May 24, 1801
   Betset Johnson
HIGHTOWER, Daniel Lee   May 19, 1843
   Mary A. Credille   Wesley Arnold, M.G.
HIGHTOWER, Elisha   December 31, 1816
   Polly Olling   Gilly Moore
HIGHTOWER, Jacob   February 18, 1799
   Nancy Colbert
HIGHTOWER, Matthew   October 2, 1821
   Mary Copeland   H. G. Slaughter
HIGHTOWER, Oscar T.   January 13, 1870
   Mary R. Tunnison   Albert Gray, M.G.
HIGHTOWER, Pressly   September 3, 1805
   Polly Ann Woodson
HIGHTOWER, Stephen   December 21, 1815
   Sally Coplan   Gilly Moore
HIGHTOWER, Thomas   December 18, 1838
   Minny Credille   Hinton Crawford
HIGHTOWER, William   December 10, 1807
   Becka Dawsey   J. Mapp
HIGHTOWER, William   August 29, 1838
   Nancy Parrott

HILL, Abner R.   April 27, 1844
  Mary Anne Fitzpatrick   E. S. Hunter
HILL, James   September 15, 1806
  Christian Laseter
HILL, James   March 14, 1825
  Elizabeth Smith   Horatio Nunnally
HILL, James   January 10, 1830
  Lucy Baldwin   S. W. Michael
HILL, Joseph   July 11, 1849
  Henrietta W. Dawson   Francis Bowman
HILL, Robert   October 2, 1825
  Elvina Bledsoe   Jack Lumpkin
HILL, William   June 14, 1820
  Lucy Purdue   Lovick Pierce
HILL, William G.   April 25, 1861
  Ella F. Poulain   R. A. Houston
HILLSMAN, Jeffre E.   September 12, 1841
  Martha Alexander   John Howell
HILLSMAN, Micajah   July 15, 1823
  Nancy Barnett
HILLYER, S. G.   May 12, 1846
  Elizabeth T. Dagg   P. H. Mell
HINES, Nathaniel   July 26, 1815
  Martha Lewis   Walker Lewis
HINES, Nathaniel   September 16, 1824
  Elizabeth Lewis
HINES, Sabury R.   September 29, 1850
  Susan Anderson   William Bryan
HINTON, L. H.   July 5, 1852
  Nancy L. Broom   W. W. Moore
HITCHCOCK, Samuel Chewer   December 21, 1851
  Louisa Marion Walker   Francis Bowman
HIXON, E. C.   June 22, 1865
  Ezenomia A. Thornton   John R. Young, M.G.
HIX, Ephraim   October 25, 1804
  Edith Lucas
HOBBS, Isham   May 6, 1821
  Martha Lankford   Abraham Yates
HOBBS, James   September 27, 1810
  Jurasha Adkinson   Thomas Stocks
HOBBS, Joseph   January 25, 1807
  Peggy Summerland   Jon Cox
HOBBS, Nathan   November 16, 1812
  Mary Lankeford   Ebenezer Torrence
HODGE, Alston   November 9, 1827
  Phaney Barker
HODGE, Alston   February 25, 1841
  Mary Jane Dunson   E. P. Jarrell
HODGE, James   October 31, 1820
  Louisa Coleman   George Watkins
HODGES, James   July 23, 1818
  Polly Price

HODGES, John, Jr. — March 26, 1818
 Ruthy Hodges — L. Bethune
HOGG, Henry T. — September 4, 1851
 Sarah Ann Burgess — James Geer
HOGG, Hugh — February 8, 1818
 Margaret Ray
HOGG, Isaac — October 20, 1833
 Mary Caldwell — Nathan Hobbs
HOGG, John — January 20, 1825
 Susan Johnson
HOGG, Mathew — August 11, 1807
 Lucy Read — J. Mapp
HOGG, William — December 22, 1835
 Mary Forrester — Vincent R. Thornton
HOGG, William D. — September 4, 1845
 Nancy Ann Johnson — W. H. C. Cone
HODNETTE, James — November 2, 1820
 Sarah Greer — James Brockman
HOLCOMB, H. L. — November 23, 1845
 L. A. Devereaux — I. W. Simmons
HOLLAND, Harrison — December 2, 1802
 Elizabeth Rowland
HOLLAND, Tobias — August 10, 1872
 Mary A. Watson — J. H. Kilpatrick
HOLLAND, Thomas — September 24, 1821
 Elizabeth Wall — Hermon Mercer
HOLLIDAY, John — April 20, 1809
 Kittey Colleman — Josias Randle
HOLLIDAY, William — August 13, 1789
 Elizabeth Neel
HOLLOWAY, David — December 15, 1807
 Polee Hardeys — O. Porter
HOLMES, George P. — August 25, 1831
 Mary Jane Swindall — Wm. Rowland
HOLNS, John — October 17, 1807
 Nancy East — A. Gresham
HOLT, David S. — August 26, 1847
 S. Catherine Godkin — Francis Bowman
HOLT, Robert — December 15, 1829
 Emily Moore — Thomas Darley
HOLT, Thomas — April 27, 1830
 Charity Slaughter — J. P. Leverett
HOLTSCLAW, John G. — December 14, 1825
 Lucy M. Nusum (Newcom)
HORN, Edward — February 9, 1810
 Sally Butler — Ben. Crawford
HORN, John — September 10, 1828
 Elizabeth Allen — Joshua Cannon
HORN, Preston A. — September 30, 1835
 Mary Ann Purdue — George Heard
HORTON, James W. — February 12, 1852
 Georgianna A. Hart — Alfred T. Mann

HOUSE, John H. — August 14, 1840
  Armenia H. Medley — J. M. Wilson
HOUSE, John — November 17, 1849
  Mary Bell
HOUSE, Lion S. — March 8, 1842
  Elizabeth Shirley — I. M. Wilson
HOUGHTON, Alex — November 19, 1799
  Tabitha Cheatham
HOUGHTON, Alexander — May 15, 1815
  Rebecah Finley — John Armor
HOUGHTON, Henry W. — April 4, 1837
  Martha Ann Rebecca Dolvin — W. R. H. Mosely
HOUGHTON, James — August 11, 1788
  Sarah Burke
HOUGHTON, James — December 19, 1822
  Lourena Thornton — Lovick Pierce
HOUGHTON, James R. — December 18, 1866
  Ophelia T. Gentry — Thos. F. Pierce
HOUGHTON, Josiah — November 26, 1804
  Elizabeth Crawford
HOUGHTON, Matthew — December 12, 1827
  Elizabeth King — William Cone
HOUGHTON, Seaborn — February 21, 1822
  Ann Newsom — Abraham Yeates
HOUGHTON, William — March 3, 1788
  Elizabeth Burke
HOUGHTON, William M. — January 18, 1842
  Mary S. Smith — James Jones, M.G.
HOWARD, James — August 24, 1822
  Nancy Wells — Abraham Yeats
HOWELL, Allen — August 19, 1805
  S. Thompson
HOWELL, Alonzo — January 18, 1860
  Annett Parrott
HOWELL, Clark — March 26, 1863
  Margaret A. Park — W. J. Cotter, M.G.
HOWELL, Daniel — April 7, 1824
  Mary Oslin
HOWELL, David — November 21, 1865
  Mrs. Bettie A. Florence — R. A. Houston, M.G.
HOWELL, Matthew C. — March 31, 1831
  Sarah M. Simonton — C. P. Beeman
HOWELL, Nathaniel — March 27, 1804
  Elizabeth Wagner
HOWELL, William J. — November 21, 1871
  Anna Jernigan — J. H. Kilpatrick
HOWELL, Wyly — November 9, 1803
  Sally Wiggins
HUBBARD, Andrew Jackson — September 29, 1836
  Elizabeth Gatlin — James W. Godkin
HUBBARD, Augustus — March 9, 1847
  Martha Jones — N. M. Crawford

HUBBARD, James — January 5, 1826
　Sarah Tippett
HUBBARD, Larkin — November 11, 1830
　Elizabeth Yates — John Armstrong
HUBBARD, Thomas — October 25, 1831
　Sarah Jackson — Benjamin F. Martin
HUBBARD, William H. — June 5, 1826
　Irene Jackson
HUCKABY, James — February 18, 1828
　Mary Griffen
HUDSON, Garrett — April 5, 1802
　Polly Parker
HUDSON, John — March 15, 1807
　Martha Patrick — Adam Hays
HUDSON, Thomas — October 25, 1810
　Elizabeth Patrick — Jon Heard
HUDSON, Ward — February 19, 1805
　Jimmy Haynes
HUFF, John — December 25, 1818
　Malinda Martin — Thomas Riley
HUFF, Ralph — December 4, 1817
　Polly Palmore
HUGHES, John — January 22, 1800
　Nancy Holloway
HUGHES, John — December 15, 1803
　Alis Dixon
HUGHES, John — December 2, 1855
　Francis Bryant — B. Rowland
HUGHES, William M. — May 31, 1864
　Mary A. Cant — J. F. Zimmerman
HUGHEY, Thomas — January 24, 1827
　Sam B. Fielder
HUMPHRIES, Noel M. — October 23, 1870
　Frances E. Rainwater — J. H. Kilpatrick
HUNNICUTT, Matthew R. — October 20, 1850
　Martha L. McGraw — A. L. Willis
HUNT, Anderson — September 29, 1818
　Archy Tyler — L. Bethune
HUNT, George — February 22, 1816
　Susannah Ware — William Cone
HUNT, James — March 8, 1800
　Agnes Hunt
HUNT, James T. — October 23, 1834
　Rebecca May — Nathan Hobbs
HUNT, John — —— 4, 1807
　Elizabeth Sorrell — Henry English
HUNT, Timothy — November 26, 1815
　Letitia Mayfield — James Martin
HUNTER, Edward — October 19, 1820
　Sarah Davis — John Harris
HUNTER, Elisha S. — October 4, 1836
　Ann E. Rally — Thomas Stocks

HUNTER, Henry M.   December 10, 1833
  Ann J. King   James Donnelly
HUNTER, Phillip   April 6, 1806
  Mary Jackson   Jesse Lacey
HUNTER, Samuel   February 7, 1800
  Charity Whatley
HUNTER, William A.   April 8, 1826
  Sophronia A. Heard
HUNTER, William C.   August 4, 1835
  Lucinda Bowles
HUNTER, William C.   October 9, 1837
  Elizabeth Scoggins
HURLBERT, Roswell   September 20, 1812
  Casandria Corlew   J. W. Godkin
HURLBERT, Roswell   April 29, 1828
  Eliza Hamilton   J. P. Leveritt
HURT, George   December 25, 1827
  Lucy Wilkins   Abraham Yeats
HUTCHESON, Albert M.   November 27, 1866
  Henrietta L. Champion   B. F. Breedlove
HUTCHESON, John   May 12, 1831
  Evelina A. Greene   J. N. Gleen
HUTCHINSON, Albert S.   November 28, 1839
  Harriet A. Lawrence
HUTCHINSON, Ambrose   March 30, 1815
  Rachael Robins   John Turner
HUTCHINSON, Charles R.   October 23, 1856
  Mary Kimbrough   J. P. Duncan, M.G.
HUTCHINSON, James   December 22, 1829
  Jane Walker   J. P. Leveritt
HUTCHINSON, Richard   December 23, 1841
  Harriet Furlow   Thomas Stocks
HUTCHINSON, Seaborn L.   June 2, 1859
  Martha J. Champion   J. H. Kilpatrick

I

IDSON, John   October 25, 1821
  Mary Corry   Robert Booth
INGRAM, Abraham   February 28, 1801
  Nancy Greer
INGRAM, James G.   October 6, 1859
  Rebecca McGibony   Jos. R. Parker
IRBY, Abraham   December 6, 1821
  Tabitha Evans   Wm. Robertson
IRBY, Eli   February 27, 1850
  Mary A. Tunnell   W. A. Corry
IRBY, Elisha   July 17, 1842
  Elizabeth Satterwhite   E. P. Jarrell
IRBY, Thomas F.   November 15, 1849
  Martha M. Peek   J. J. Loudermilk
IRVING, Carnell   December 5, 1855
  Catherine E. Keith   J. P. Duncan

IRWIN, James   March 8, 1816
  Amanda Nisbet   Francis Cummins
IVEY, Jerrey   April 4, 1801
  Fanny Williams
IVEY, John   February 27, 1823
  Nancy Evans   John Harris
IVY, James   October 4, 1838
  Lucinda Rowland   Robert T. Griffin
IVY, Jeremiah   August 27, 1811
  Milly Shockley   W. McGiboney
IVY, Jordan   December 8, 1817
  Polly Smith
IVY, Jordan   March 29, 1827
  Patience Woods   Wm. L. Austin
IVY, Josiah   August 11, 1803
  Patience Williams

J

JACKS, John W.   December 11, 1873
  Anna Carson   C. H. Strickland
JACKSON, Aldridge   April 15, 1824
  Celia Pendergrass
JACKSON, Alexander J. S.   December 4, 1860
  Sarah F. Hudson
JACKSON, Alfred   March 31, 1844
  Martha Wright   J. J. Howell
JACKSON, Alfred H.   October 10, 1850
  Julia E. Parrott   W. W. Moore
JACKSON, Allen   November 15, 1830
  Elizabeth Short   Lewis Pyron
JACKSON, Andrew F.   April 4, 1867
  Adaline M. O'Neal   L. D. Caldwell
JACKSON, Arthur M.   February 12, 1867
  Sarah Elizabeth Hester   John Calvin Johnson
JACKSON, Daniel   January 15, 1805
  Sally Bowen
JACKSON, Daniel   November 20, 1806
  Mary Phillips   Thomas Crawford
JACKSON, Daniel   January 14, 1823
  Cassandra Maddox   Thomas Stanley, M.G.
JACKSON, David   November 30, 1796
  Rachel Lewis
JACKSON, David   August 2, 1824
  Elizabeth Bickers
JACKSON, Edmond   December 23, 1806
  Abbe Jackson   O. Porter
JACKSON, Edmund   December 19, 1823
  Sally Shaw
JACKSON, Floyd
  Mary Fambrough
JACKSON, George A.   May 29, 1866
  Fanny V. Baker   J. W. Tally, M.G.

JACKSON, Henry	December 20, 1809
Delilah Gorden	William Watson
JACKSON, Isaac	January 25, 1821
Elizabeth Perkins	Jo Roberts
JACKSON, Isaac	July 12, 1825
Louisa Caldwell	John Harris
JACKSON, Isaac M.	September 13, 1866
Sarah F. Smith	Hart C. Peek, M.G.
JACKSON, Israel	December 21, 1845
Amy W. Callahan	S. G. Hillyer
JACKSON, Jacob	November 19, 1807
Patsey Simes	Frances S. Martin
JACKSON, James	December 2, 1827
Mary Underwood	William Cone
JACKSON, James	April 10, 1828
Nancy Lewis	John Harris
JACKSON, James	April 2, 1846
Electra Ann Bird	William Parks
JACKSON, James A.	November 27, 1856
Martha Fullingham	William T. Merritt
JACKSON, James W.	February 5, 1840
Catherine M. Butler	Francis Bowman
JACKSON, James W.	September 9, 1852
Martha Ann Broom	Daniel Hightower
JACKSON, Job	October 7, 1819
Mary Heard	John Harris
JACKSON, John	April 15, 1800
Jane Richards	
JACKSON, John	February 18, 1818
Mary Webb	Thomas Riley
JACKSON, John E.	April 16, 1833
Martha Ann Eliza Davis	Albert R. Jackson
JACKSON, John E.	January 1, 1862
Julia A. Hudson	
Jackson, John H.	November 2, 1872
Eliza J. Moore	J. H. Kilpatrick
JACKSON, John S.	July 6, 1856
Artimisa Hall	L. R. L. Jennings
JACKSON, John S.	March 2, 1865
Alice G. Jones	
JACKSON, Jesse W.	March 15, 1863
Julia C. Tunnell	W. G. Johnson
JACKSON, Littleberry	July 4, 1827
Patience Harris	
JACKSON, Littleberry	January 11, 1840
Frances Parmelia Ivy	Thomas Stocks
JACKSON, Luther R.	May 11, 1875
Emma A. Carlton	F. G. Hughes, M.G.
JACKSON, Mark	December 17, 1828
Elizabeth R. Pyron	Joshua Cannon
JACKSON, Martin	September 13, 1826
Rachael Martindale	

JACKSON, Martin	October 11, 1832
Frances Hendricks	William Moncrief
JACKSON, Martin	April 19, 1853
Mary E. Harris	A. L. Willis
JACKSON, Moody	September 9, 1833
Patience T. Bishop	Thos. W. Grimes
JACKSON, Peter	March 16, 1796
Mary Lindall	
JACKSON, R. H.	January 14, 1847
Mary E. Hall	L. B. Jackson
JACKSON, Robert B.	December 13, 1874
Lilly V. Jones	J. H. Kilpatrick
JACKSON, Robert Hausen	March 12, 1844
Mary M. Ely	J. J. Howell
JACKSON, Roling	September 20, 1807
Susannah Richards	J. Mapp
JACKSON, Stephen	July 9, 1805
Jimmy Brooks	
JACKSON, Thomas	August 28, 1807
Pearly Bullwood	John Robertson
JACKSON, Thomas	December 5, 1826
Mary Smith	
JACKSON, William	March 9, 1816
Holly Harwell	John Browning
JACKSON, William	March 23, 1830
Martha Foster	J. P. Leveritt
JACKSON, William N.	November 26, 1824
June Daniel	
JACKSON, Wm. T.	February 23, 1869
Mary A. E. Brooks	J. M. Dickey
JAMES, Henry	March 7, 1825
Mary Grier	
JAMES, John	January 9, 1823
Priscilla Greer	Jeremiah Ragan
JAMES, Thomas G.	July 26, 1839
Elizabeth P. Sanford	Shales G. Hillyer
JAMES, Williamson	October 6, 1828
Rachel Martindale	
JANES, Thomas	January 30, 1821
Malinda West	Jesse Mercer
JANES, Thomas G.	July 28, 1839
Elizabeth P. Sanford	S. H. Hillyer, M.G.
JARRELL, (Giles) Jacob	December 28, 1820
Millie Chandler	Francis West
JARRELL, Jacob	May 8, 1828
Frances Williams	Francis West
JARRELL, Redden	July 15, 1836
Elizabeth Johnson	James Moore
JARRELL, Willis	December 27, 1818
Mary Campbell	Thomas Snow
JARROLD, Ruben	December 24, 1868
Ann Gentry	J. H. Kilpatrick

JEFFERSON, Francis M.   November 17, 1859
  Elizabeth Chappell   Geo. C. Clarke
JEFFERSON, William M.   October 15, 1857
  Mary Chapple   G. Bright, M.G.
JEFFREY, Thomas   December 23, 1803
  Elizabeth Morris
JEFFRIES, William   October 24, 1806
  Nancy Tuggle   Jesse Lacey
JENKINS, Elijah   February 13, 1797
  Amy Daniel
JENKINS, Harmond   April 16, 1834
  Julia Ann Simpkins
JENKINS, James R.   April 19, 1807
  Milly Gresham   William Browning
JENKINS, James   July 5, 1810
  Betsey Duncan   Bennett Crawford
JENKINS, James A. T.   October 5, 1838
  Francis B. Sanders   James W. Godkin
JENKINS, John   September 13, 1845
  Meron L. Hobbs
JENKINS, Jesse   February 24, 1805
  Anne Martin
JENKINS, Mass   October 28, 1875
  Ophelia E. Jenkins   Philip Robinson
JENKINS, Pleasant C.   November 9, 1831
  Harriet A. Daniel   William Jones
JENKINS, Robert   April 3, 1806
  Sarah B. Johnson   Thos. Crawford
JENKINS, Waites   May 25, 1843
  Jane H. McHargue   John W. Reid
JENNINGS, Giles   January 11, 1820
  Mary Hague   Lemuel Greene
JENNINGS, Henry   February 13, 1866
  Elizabeth J. McWhorter   J. M. Stillwell, M.G.
JERNIGAN, Albert   December 23, 1822
  Lucy Perkins
JERNIGAN, Albert   January 14, 1861
  Henrietta M. Shaffer   A. Gray, M.G.
JERNIGAN, Albert A.   October 15, 1850
  Rebecca A. Parrott   L. C. Peek
JERNIGAN, Hardy E.   December 2, 1862
  Margaret A. Alexander   Hart C. Peek, M.G.
JERNIGAN, John E.   December 9, 1830
  Margaret Rankin   Francis Cummins
JERNIGAN, John R.   February 2, 1868
  Sideria D. Mann   C. A. Mitchell, M.G.
JERNIGAN, Petolemy   January 8, 1822
  Sarah Jarrell   James Woodberry
JERNIGAN, Seaborn J.   March 13, 1838
  Evelina B. Williams
JETER, Samuel   October 1, 1822
  Winney Cone   Anderson Ray, M.G.

JETER, William P.   November 25, 1872
   Lou Anna McCarty   W. A. Overton
JETT, Francis   July 26, 1818
   Elizabeth Lee   C. Para, M.G.
JEWELL, James, Jr.   December 1, 1859
   Eliza C. Colclough   John G. Holtzclaw
JONES, Andrew J.   January 15, 1866
   Ellen A. Johnson
JONES, B. F.   January 15, 1874
   M. E. O'Neal
JONES, Charles P.   December 17, 1873
   Mary V. Overton   J. H. Kilpatrick
JONES, Dickinson   October 28, 1829
   Martha Harris   Francis Cummins
JONES, Hezekiah   January 10, 1837
   Hulda Simmons   Ephraim Bruce
JONES, Hezekiah   June 14, 1868
   Nancy L. Norris   W. M. Chapman
JONES, Isaac   January 22, 1825
   Temperance Akins
JONES, James A.   January 5, 1875
   Mary A. Price   L. D. Caldwell
JONES, James   January 6, 1802
   Elvey Rowland
JONES, James   September 14, 1810
   Sally Harper   H. Davenport
JONES, James J.   October 28, 1847
   Louisa M. Hightower   John C. Lucas
JONES, John   October 7, 1847
   Emily W. Sims
JONES, John   May 8, 1857
   Mrs. Martha Bruce   A. L. Willis
JONES, John P.   September 12, 1849
   Sarah A. Veazey   Wm. A. Corry
JONES, Joseph   December 18, 1796
   Sarah Heard
JONES, Joseph   January 29, 1824
   Penelope S. Pullen
JONES, Joseph A.   May 30, 1843
   Lucy M. Manley   James T. Findley
JONES, L. N.   December 18, 1853
   Adalade Jackson   I. A. Williams
JONES, Nathan   June 21, 1818
   Sarah Jett   Lovick Pierce
JONES, Nicholas M.   December 8, 1847
   Emeline Veazey   J. J. Loudermilk
JONES, Nicholas M.   October 26, 1851
   Martha Jackson   Hart C. Peek, M.G.
JONES, Robert   October 6, 1825
   Harriet Macon   Lovick Pierce
JONES, Robert   February 22, 1827
   Sarah Conyers   James Culberson

JONES, Robert S.   January 15, 1841
  Julia Amanda Peek   James Jones
JONES, Robert W.   March 25, 1841
  Pharabee Cunningham   Reuben Armor
JONES, Russell   November 25, 1801
  Mary Tuggles
JONES, Sanders   February 2, 1875
  Virginia Stewart
JONES, Sterling W.   April 29, 1847
  Martha Swinney   Hinton Crawford
JONES, Thomas   January 17, 1828
  Emily West   Jonathon Davis
JONES, Thomas   June 8, 1831
  Matilda Maria Caldwell   Peter C. Johnson
JONES, Thomas D.   June 12, 1808
  Mary D. Harper   I. Porter
JONES, Wiley   April 15, 1821
  Sarah Ball   Thomas Slaughter
JONES, William   January 5, 1808
  Emelia Paterson   A. Hays
JONES, William   July 19, 1832
  Rebecca Baldwin   A. Perkins
JONES, W. T.   November 13, 1872
  Sallie Wilson
JONES, Zachariah   November 12, 1831
  Sarah R. Morris   J. P. Leveritt
JOHNSON, Allen   June 12, 1820
  Nelly Finley
JOHNSON, Allen   July 2, 1843
  Elizabeth Eidson   James P. Findley
JOHNSON, Amos   November 9, 1843
  Priscilla Marchman   Ephraim Bruce
JOHNSON, Amos   November 6, 1860
  Catherine Moon
JOHNSON, Barnard   December 1, 1814
  Sally Taylor   Francis Cummins
JOHNSON, Frederick   November 9, 1809
  Patience Knowles   William Johnson
JOHNSON, George W.   July 21, 1859
  Sarah H. V. Bickers   L. B. Jackson
JOHNSON, Gilbert   June 29, 1850
  Susan Smallwood   I. A. Williams
JOHNSON, James T.   August 9, 1838
  Corcyra E. Matthews   Francis Bowman
JOHNSON, James   December 13, 1817
  Liza Harrison   Lovick Pierce
JOHNSON, James W.   October 4, 1864
  Mary Anne Franklin   G. G. Norman, M.G.
JOHNSON, James W.   June 17, 1875
  Sarah J. Rankin   Henry Newton
JOHNSON, Jesse   February 20, 1816
  Nancy Johnson   Francis Cummins

JOHNSON, Jesse — November 14, 1817
  Lucy Barnett
JOHNSON, John — January 25, 1802
  Anne Butt
JOHNSON, John — September 4, 1804
  Prudence Farley
JOHNSON, John — November 26, 1815
  Nancy Williams — Alex. Johnson
JOHNSON, John — May 24, 1823
  Joice Fears
JOHNSON, John — December 18, 1845
  Martha Smith — William Bryan
JOHNSON, John — November 25, 1858
  Cornelia J. Ledbetter — George C. Clarke
JOHNSON, John — January 18, 1866
  Corrinne C. Moore — J. H. Kilpatrick
JOHNSON, John R. — January 25, 1836
  Mary Ann Bristoe — Abraham Jenkins
JOHNSON, John S. — January 3, 1854
  Coroline E. Hogg — William English
JOHNSON, Kinchen — December 28, 1856
  Matilda McGiboney — Wm. W. Moore
JOHNSON, Laban Scott — October 7, 1830
  Susannah Walker — J. P. Leveritt
JOHNSON, Leonidas B. — December 22, 1857
  Mary A. Raden — T. D. Martin
JOHNSON, Littleberry — July 27, 1819
  Mary Robinson — Robert Booth
JOHNSON, O. B. — March 31, 1869
  Martha E. McLaurin — J. J. Brantley
JOHNSON, Peter — May 18, 1820
  Clarissa Bedell — Thomas Johnson
JOHNSON, Peter G. — May 18, 1835
  Susan Bedell — Thos. W. Grimes
JOHNSON, Robert — March 4, 1800
  Nancy Dolvin
JOHNSON, Robert G. — November 23, 1838
  Eleanor Johnson — Thos. W. Grimes
JOHNSON, Samuel — September 11, 1804
  Patsey Hightower
JOHNSON, Silvester A. — December 10, 1874
  Louisa Underwood — H. C. Peek
JOHNSON, Terry — December 1, 1838
  Rebeccah Fleming — C. D. Kennebrew
JOHNSON, Thomas — June 21, 1818
  Terza Greene — Thomas Johnson
JOHNSON, Thomas — December 25, 1825
  Nancy Tippett — E. Talley, J.P.
JOHNSON, William — October 1, 1846
  Martha Ann Hall — V. R. Thornton
JOHNSON, William B. — April 20, 1864
  Mary P. Brown — R. A. Houston, M.G.

JOHNSON, William Daniel — January 13, 1870
  Manissa R. Channell
JOHNSON, William H. — December 22, 1859
  Martha English — R. A. Houston
JOHNSON, W. G. — April 26, 1844
  Mary Statham — Francis Cummins
JOHNSON, W. T. — February 28, 1871
  Mattie J. Fillingim — H. C. Peek, M.G.
JOINER, Henry — July 20, 1828
  Elizabeth Taylor — George Hall
JOHNSTON, George — July 13, 1808
  Tibitha Johnston — Thomas Crawford
JORDAN, Edward — March 5, 1807
  Nancy Moore — W. McGiboney
JORDAN, Zachariah — July 7, 1819
  Betsey Reed — Wm. McGiboney
JOURDAN, Elijah — April 13, 1814
  Cynthia King — Isaac Moore
JUNE, John Houghton — November 23, 1824
  Mary McDowell

K

KEARNEY, Richard B. — March 29, 1827
  Elizabeth Buchanan — James Blassingame
KEATON, James K. P. — September 12, 1867
  Dora Copeland — H. H. Tucker, M.G.
KELLER, David C. — February 22, 1855
  Mary E. Carlton — J. P. Duncan, M.G.
KELLEY, James — January 20, 1808
  Polly Wyatt — James Holt
KELLEY, Reuben B. — December 20, 1840
  Bellina Linch — Matthew Oliver
KELLY, Charles — October 17, 1810
  Betsey Wiley — James Holt
KELLY, Hugh P. — April 18, 1848
  Margaret S. Young — W. H. Cone
KELLY, James M. — November 10, 1836
  Holly Ann Sayers — A. Hutcheson
KENDALL, Thomas K. — July 15, 1841
  Mary Mapp — John I. Howell
KENDALL, Thomas — February 20, 1843
  Asenith W. Mapp — John Howell
KENDRICK, Robert — March 30, 1823
  Elizabeth Park
KENNEBREW, C. D. — January 22, 1849
  Nancy J. Wilson
KINNEBREW, Marcus B. — May 9, 1862
  Julia M. Edmondson — John R. Young, M.G.
KENNEDY, James — March 5, 1846
  Sarah Eidson — T. D. Martin
KENNEDY, John — April 28, 1804
  Agnes Sanders

KENNEDY, John — July 6, 1808
  Sally Price — William Browning
KENNEDY, John E. — February 21, 1869
  Mary Ann McCarty — H. H. Tucker
KENNEY, James — April 1, 1866
  Vernecey Baughcum — Wm. Chapman, M.G.
KENNEY, Jesse — September 17, 1816
  Polly Smith — Robert Rea
KENNEY, Joshia — November 25, 1789
  Catherine Langston
KENNEY, Seaborn — April 26, 1837
  Jane H. Clifton — Lemuel T. Crossley
KEOUGH, William L. — April 26, 1870
  Josephine Echols — Thomas F. Pierce, M.G.
KICKER, William G. — December 12, 1841
  Elizabeth S. Lee — William C. Veazey
KICKLIGHTER, Spencer C. — January 30, 1873
  Mary M. Jean — H. C. Peek
KILGOAR, William — December 19, 1791
  A. Higginbotham
KILLPATRICK, James H. — May 9, 1856
  Cornelia Hall — H. C. Peek
KIMBALL, David — June 23, 1827
  Susannah Anderson — Miller Bledsoe
KIMBRO, Isaac — August 3, 1856
  Bessie Anne Hall — L. R. L. Jennings
KIMBROUGH, Alexander — December 8, 1870
  Sarah A. Smith
KIMBROUGH, Asbury — December 13, 1838
  Eliza Rowland — James W. Godkin
KIMBROUGH, Augustus L. — December 10, 1860
  Mary A. E. Champion — Jas. H. Killpatrick
KIMBROUGH, Bradley — February 9, 1820
  Martha Wingfield
KIMBROUGH, Bradley — June 22, 1830
  Lucinda Clark — William Bryan
KIMBROUGH, Jesse — August 24, 1848
  Sarah E. Creddille — W. T. Gaston
KIMBROUGH, John — December 12, 1815
  Esther Winslett — Gilly Moore
KIMBROUGH, John P. — January 7, 1875
  Mary A. Copelan — W. H. Blythe, M.G.
KIMBROUGH, Locket M. — April 15, 1862
  Mary E. Credille
KIMBROUGH, Stephen T. — August 31, 1837
  Agathy N. Peek — L. O. Peek, M.G.
KIMBROUGH, Thomas — June 27, 1806
  Sally Stallings
KIMBROUGH, William — April 28, 1830
  Mary Rowland
KIMBROUGH, William A. — July 4, 1875
  Emma M. Simpkins — J. Knowles

KIMBROUGH, William G.   August 8, 1848
  Sarah H. Credille   W. T. Gaston
KING, Charles M.   October 7, 1874
  Josephine Gray
KING, Drury   July 2, 1823
  Elizabeth Taylor   Thomas Johnson
KING, Drury   April 11, 1830
  Martha Taylor   S. M. Michael
KING, Edwin D.   May 10, 1814
  Nancy Hunter   Jack Lampkin
KING, Elisha   August 12, 1832
  Margaret Champion   J. P. Leveritt
KING, Ezekiel   December 8, 1842
  Lorena McGee   James McKenzie
KING, Henry   January 29, 1846
  Caroline Greenwood   J. O. Andrew
KING, Hugh Moore   November 20, 1852
  Virginia C. Todd
KING, James   June 6, 1798
  Fanny Perkins
KING, James   September 6, 1825
  Elizabeth Moore   Francis Cummins
KING, James R.   November 5, 1867
  Susan F. Wright   Thos. F. Pierce
KING, James William   October 4, 1843
  Nancy Jane Swindall   R. F. Griffin
KING, James W.   September 11, 1843
  Frances B. Slaughter
KING, Jesse   February 18, 1837
  Sarah L. Rankin   Thomas Stocks
KING, John, Jr.   February 16, 1796
  Patsey Lacey
KING, John   February 20, 1866
  Irene P. Moore   J. W. Talley, M.G.
KING, Joseph   March 5, 1816
  Elizabeth Cone   William Cone
KING, Joseph   January 4, 1831
  Sarah Ballard   A. Perkins
KING, Ulysses B.   May 11, 1857
  Celest C. Swinney
KING, William   May 6, 1822
  Elizabeth Davis   John Harris
KING, Dr. William   May 1, 1834
  Margaret Barnett   William Cone
KING, William C.   July 23, 1835
  Martha Wright   James Moore
KINMAN, John   August 22, 1804
  Elizabeth Lewis
KINMORE, Robert   February 29, 1844
  Eliza Catherine Tribble   I. M. Wilson
KINNEY, James   December 29, 1846
  Mary Ann Clifton

KINNEY, James — January 9, 1849
 Jemiah J. Compton — W. T. Gaston
KINNEY, William R. — December 5, 1865
 Martha A. E. Ruark — W. H. Blythe, M.G.
KINNION, James — January 15, 1805
 Sally Williams
KIRK, John — August 14, 1820
 Barsheba Tyler — L. Bethune
KLOTZ, John
 Maria Clark
KNIGHT, Coffield — June 23, 1802
 Edey Murphey
KNIGHT, Joel — November 21, 1815
 Elizabeth Pollard — Edwin D. King
KNIGHT, Robert B. — July 21, 1802
 Kitty Bailey
KNOWLES, Benjamin — November 9, 1820
 Joanna Thomas — Wm. McGibony, J.P.
KNOWLES, Brittain — August 12, 1826
 Rebeccah Ransom
KNOWLES, Edmond — February 24, 1820
 Christian Thomas — Wm. McGiboney
KNOWLES, Isaac — March 25, 1824
 Mary H. Owen
KNOWLES, James, Jr. — January 3, 1806
 Amy Read — W. M. Johnson
KNOWLES, James — April 25, 1821
 Anna Thomas
KNOWLES, James — February 9, 1823
 Lucy Thomas — Thomas Slaughter
KNOWLES, John — October 2, 1855
 Martha Grubbs — B. H. Thompson
KNOWLES, Pretty — August 3, 1802
 Patsey Greer
KNOWLES, Richard P. — May 13, 1806
 Dell Martin
KNOWLES, Thomas — November 11, 1819
 Matilda McGiboney — William Cone
KNOWLES, Thomas B. — November 4, 1833
 Adaline Wheatt — Ephraim Bruce
KOCH, Henry I. — January 14, 1846
 Lucy Borach — J. M. Davison

L

LAFFOLD, Seaborn — January 6, 1818
 Julia Heard — E. Torrence
LAMBKIN, William — July 4, 1841
 Eleanor Fambrough — I. M. Wilson
LANCASTER, Samuel — September 17, 1822
 Rebecca Bowden — Whitman Hill
LANDRUM, Alsey L. — August 29, 1833
 Margaret Arthur — John W. Cox

LANDRUM, James N.	December 5, 1840
Sarah M. Underwood	E. S. Hunter
LANGFORD, James M.	December 1, 1844
Caroline B. Hobbs	Jeremiah Lindsey
LANIER, Manson E.	December 31, 1838
Elizabeth Fitzpatrick	
LANKFORD, Daniel, Jr.	April 25, 1833
Betsy Tolly	Alvin Perkins
LANKFORD, James C.	January 5, 1868
Mary A. Wilson	Lucius C. Broome
LANKFORD, Robert	January 4, 1842
Elizabeth C. Burton	P. W. Farabee
LANKFORD, Robert C.	March 4, 1860
Elizabeth Bennett	Thomas B. Cooper
LANKFORD, Willis J.	August 28, 1856
Mildred A. S. Black	John G. Holtzclaw
LANSDALE, William S.	October 23, 1855
Lizzie Zimmerman	J. P. Duncan, M.G.
LASLEY, David	April 24, 1832
Patience Winfield	J. P. Leveritt
LASSETER, Brown	January 1, 1802
Anne Stewart	
LASSETER, Elisha	January 1, 1802
Nancy Baker	
LASSETER, Jesse	January 28, 1806
Deppe McClendon	
LASSETER, John	December 10, 1804
Nancey Griffen	
LAURENCE, E. C.	January 18, 1844
C. A. Hubbard	B. M. Sanders
LAURENCE, Hartwell	August 28, 1821
Elizabeth Wingfield	Wm. Tally
LAURENCE, Hartwell	November 10, 1830
Sarah Rowland	W. M. Bryan
LAURENCE, John	February 27, 1823
Harriett Ward	W. H. Sledge
LAURENCE, Orson	February 2, 1823
Arabella Allen	A. Hutchinson
LAWRENCE, Enoch C.	January 30, 1837
Mary H. Daniel	Vincent R. Thornton
LAWRENCE, James	May 2, 1795
Ginney Lawson	
LAWRENCE, James	March 29, 1810
Mary Simonton	Wm. McGiboney
LAWRENCE, Thomas	October 15, 1796
Polly Moreland	
LAWS, Bennett	January 20, 1836
Sarah Thornton	John T. Holtzclaw
LAWS, Isarn	July 21, 1806
Rhody Chhings	A. Hays
LAWSON, John T.	January 2, 1849
Matilda Broach	E. S. Hunter

LAWSON, Sheltin December 11, 1818
  Polly Bird Philemon Ogletree
LAYERS, William February 22, 1816
  Rachael Ward Gilly Moore
LEACH, John B. March 14, 1858
  Caroline Nash James M. Kelly
LEACH, John W. May 22, 1873
  Bertha Lynch W. H. Blythe
LEDBETTER, James January 11, 1849
  Rebecca Furge W. T. Gaston
LEDBETTER, James C. October 5, 1875
  Irena C. Coffield W. H. Blythe
LEDBETTER, Littleberry August 26, 1842
  Sarah Ann Kinney Reuben Armor
LEDBETTER, Malden S. January 28, 1841
  Patience Smith Ephraim Bruce
LEDBETTER, William T. January 9, 1875
  Sallie Callahan Joel F. Thornton
LEE, Charles October 21, 1828
  Elizabeth Broughton James Park
LEE, Elijah December 13, 1821
  Malinda Phillips Jo Fitzpatrick
LEE, James August 31, 1814
  Elizabeth Phillips Lemuel Greene
LEE, Nathan December 20, 1824
  Olivia Heard
LEE, William December 31, 1817
  Sarah West Walter Lewis
LEFTWICH, John February 20, 1822
  Mary Brooker Hermon Mercer
LEONARD, Coleman September 1, 1837
  Eliza Johnson Ledbetter
LEONARD, Irbane February 2, 1815
  Rebekah Collier Thomas Stocks
LEONARD, Thomas November 30, 1836
  Martha Ann Harris Copelan
LEONARD, William August 13, 1829
  Penelope Massingille William Bryan
LeREBOUR, B. A. November 20, 1853
  E. E. Heard J. W. Yarbrough
LESLIE, Julius W. November 25, 1858
  Mary F. Ashley W. G. Johnson
LESTER, Benjamin April 22, 1801
  Betsy Hill
LESTER, Josiah August 30, 1818
  Leleta Johnson Isom Goss
LETBETTER, Washington June 21, 1801
  Lucy Bostwick
LEVERETT, Francis M. May 28, 1836
  Susan Cartwright Thomas Stocks
LEVERETT, George December 8, 1831
  Delila Cook Ephraim Bruce

LEVERETT, Joel	November 18, 1827
Mary Bishop	John Harris
LEVERETT, William	May 27, 1837
Nancy Woodham	Robert F. Griffin
LEVERITT, L. D.	May 23, 1870
Hattie Pennington	
LEWIS, Cyphas	November 14, 1834
Sarah Ellis	James Moore
LEWIS, Cephas	January 30, 1843
Emily Chambers	James Moore
LEWIS, Curtis	March 12, 1826
Jane Collier	N. H. Harris, M.G.
LEWIS, Fields	September 6, 1796
Hannah Hall	
LEWIS, Frisman	February 26, 1831
Aseneth Connell	J. P. Leverett
LEWIS, Gabriel	February 7, 1828
Mary Hightower	R. White
LEWIS, George	March 6, 1820
Charlotte Baugh	
LEWIS, Henry	January 1, 1807
Nancy Edwards	J. Holt
LEWIS, Ira	January 3, 1820
Lourina Cook	
LEWIS, John	August 17, 1819
Jenny Moore	John Turner
LEWIS, Miles W., Jr.	October 20, 1873
Amorette C. Champion	Albert Gray, M.G.
LEWIS, Richard	February 23, 1802
Susannah Hightower	
LEWIS, Theophilus	May 31, 1827
Rebecca Ship	John Harris
LEWIS, Thomas S.	November 9, 1852
Leah Williams	Benjamin Merritt
LEWIS, Thomas W. S.	December —, 1838
Margaret Sullivan	James Moore
LEWIS, Walker	June 1, 1798
Polly Graham	
LEWIS, William	December 1, 1818
Mary Woods	
LEWIS, William	July 6, 1820
Temperance Lewis	R. White
LEWIS, William	June 21, 1827
Sarah Cartwright	Nat. Harris
LEWIS, William	January 4, 1861
Margaret Beasley	
LEWIS, William, Jr.	October 27, 1853
Mary T. Moody	William T. Doster
LEWIS, William W.	April 4, 1856
Priscilla Marchman	
LIGON, John	February 29, 1816
Sarah Barker	George Owen

LIGON, Thomas — May 30, 1805
  Betsey C. Daniel — A. Gresham
LILY, John E. — January 22, 1841
  Malinda Bryan — Reuben B. Arnold
LINCH, Elihu — September 25, 1842
  Nancy Kinney — Reuben Armor
LINCH, James C. — January 16, 1866
  Martha A. F. Bryan — C. R. Hutcheson
LINCH, William — December 27, 1869
  Lucienda Bryan
LINDSEY, Clabourn — January 8, 1812
  Nancey Therman — Lemuel Greene
LINDSEY, Jeremiah — May 18, 1837
  Julian Edmondson — W. R. N. Mosely, M.G.
LINDSEY, John — November 21, 1817
  Nancey Houghton — Lovick Pierce
LINDSEY, William — August 4, 1840
  Mary Whitaker — Jas. M. Davidson
LINDSEY, William T. — October 13, 1870
  Mrs. Martha Beans — W. A. Overton
LINTON, Alexander — November 21, 1811
  Jean Daniel — Jesse Mercer
LINTON, Samuel D. — September 21, 1847
  Mary Cunningham — Francis Bowman
LINTON, William — August 5, 1847
  Martha Inorana Grimes — Francis Bowman
LISTER, Edwin — February 28, 1826
  Mehaney Martin
LITTLE, Anderson — November 22, 1846
  Sarah Ann Gwill — P. H. Mell
LITTLE, Charles E. — February 22, 1870
  Winnie F. Copelan — J. M. Louney, M.G.
LITTLE, James F. — September 5, 1860
  Martha J. Seals — H. H. Tucker
LITTLE, John W. — December 5, 1875
  Mary Mason — W. T. Foster
LITTLE, Walter G. — December 17, 1874
  Mary E. Gresham — Henry Newton
LITTLE, William — August 15, 1867
  Mary A. Callahan — Philip Robinson
LITTLEJOHN, Thomas — November 11, 1804
  Elizabeth Hall
LIVINGSTONE, Aaron — March 8, 1821
  Respy Ship — Wm. McGiboney
LOCKE, Josiah — September 21, 1841
  Sarah Johnson — Wooten O'Neal
LOFTON, Van — January 27, 1795
  Rebekah Walls
LOVE, David — April 12, 1810
  Elizabeth King — Wm. McGiboney
LOVE, Henry Chappel — March 3, 1836
  Rebecca S. Houghton — J. W. F. Pierce

LOVETT, Robert W.   October 24, 1865
  Marietta A. Smith   Albert Gray, M.G.
LOWREY, Benjamin   April 20, 1790
  Mary Hogg
LOYD, Alfred   July 3, 1818
  Jemima Connell
LOYD, James T.   August 17, 1862
  Lorena H. Brook   W. R. Wilson
LUCAS, John   December 11, 1845
  Elizabeth Kimbrough   Francis Colly
LUCKIE, William F.   April 19, 1853
  Frances Delaney Sayers   J. W. Yarbrough
LUDEWIG, Leiman Kohl   November 11, 1853
  Nancy Susan Kennedy   T. D. Martin
LUKE, David   August 28, 1837
  Elizabeth Scoggins
LUMPKIN, Edmund   May 24, 1825
  Lucy Dillard
LUMPKIN, James   October 24, 1850
  Mary E. Porter   J. W. Godkin
LUMPKIN, Leroy   January 16, 1848
  Elizabeth Bryan   James Findley
LUMPKIN, William   March 14, 1816
  Rebekah Moon   L. Bethune
LUMPKIN, William   June 30, 1818
  Elizabeth Bowden   Lovick Pierce
LUNDY, Alexander S.   February 22, 1870
  Matilda M. Lee   J. M. Louney, M.G.
LUNDY, Archibald P.   April 20, 1854
  Martha Jane Grimes   Hinton Crawford
LUNDY, Lewis W.   July 19, 1832
  Jane K. Turner   Lewis Parker
LUNDY, Wm. C. D.   March 16, 1869
  Martha C. Parrott   Wm. Bryant, M.G.
LUPO, James M.   September 19, 1848
  Elizabeth Bowden   J. W. Godkin
LYLE, Charles V.   January 25, 1854
  Francis S. E. Parker   J. S. Key, M.G.
LYNCH, Edlow   September 21, 1820
  Elizabeth Thomas

M

MABRY, Alfred   December 30, 1826
  Sarah Curry
MABRY, Hinchia   October 22, 1818
  Lynnea Stallings   Thomas Riley
MABRY, John   January 3, 1821
  Elizabeth Irby   W. Robertson
MABRY, Thomas   January 8, 1824
  Sarah Irby   Thomas Johnson
MADDOX, Clayborn   September 4, 1818
  Betsey Weaver

MADDOX, William James
  Elizabeth W. Tally
MADDOX, John D.
  Nancy F. Fisher
MADDOX, Joe C.
  Sarah Morrow
MADDOX, Joseph D.
  Eliza Copelan
MADDOX, Robert T.
  Margaret S. Mahaffey
MADDOX, William D.
  Elizabeth E. Davenport
MAGUE, Laban
  Rebekah Whatley
MAISEY, William
  Sarah Anna Randle
MALLORY, Irvin
  Caroline Hubbard
MALLORY, John
  Nancy Brown
MALLORY, Joseph
  Elizabeth Mitchell
MALLORY, Rollin D.
  M. J. Dagg
MALLORY, Thomas
  Patsey Moore
MALONE, Drury
  Elizabeth Delouch
MALONE, John
  Susannah Boring
MALONE, John
  Harriett Tranum
MALONE, John
  Margaret Jane Bowles
MALONE, Thompson
  Laura Williams
MALONE, Washington
  Frances Deloach
MALONE, William B.
  Lucy Hicks
MALONE, Young
  Mary Price
MANLEY, William
  M. F. Garner
MANN, David
  Polly Nelson
MANN, Jesse
  Annie Nelson
MANN, Joseph B.
  Saphrone Channell
MANNING, Michael
  Elizabeth Watson

December 1, 1835
James Moore
June 23, 1870

December 31, 1788

November 2, 1875
W. H. Wright
January 1, 1854
J. R. Hall
December 26, 1836
Thomas W. Grimes
January 9, 1806

May 20, 1869
Thos. F. Pierce
May 30, 1833
William Bryan
October 8, 1813
Robert Mapp
January 13, 1818
E. Torrence
July 28, 1853
C. D. Mallory, M.G.
August 21, 1818

October 18, 1829
George Hall
November 10, 1811
A. Gresham
October 16, 1834
John F. Hillyer, M.G.
November 24, 1836
John G. Holtzclaw
November 5, 1839
B. M. Sanders
September 6, 1829
George Hall
November 21, 1823

December 17, 1829
William James
October 24, 1845

January 15, 1818
George Dillard
January 15, 1818
George Dillard
July 10, 1853
B. Rowland
December 18, 1824

MAPP, Almarion / Susan Copelan — September 25, 1847 / Francis Bowman
MAPP, Archibald P. / Rebecca Lundy — December 10, 1874 / J. H. Kilpatrick
MAPP, E. J. / Antoinette Snellings — September 30, 1872
MAPP, R. Hanson / Hannah Jackson — September 27, 1794
MAPP, Henry S. / Havilah Howell — February 8, 1864 / J. H. Kilpatrick
MAPP, James H. / Sarah Jane Moore — September 22, 1857 / William W. Moore
MAPP, James H. / Austria Howell — November 22, 1859 / James H. Kilpatrick
MAPP, James / Mary Wright — November 25, 1800 / John W. Harris
MAPP, J. F. / Elizabeth D. Chapman — December 22, 1870 / J. R. Parker
MAPP, Littleton / Lucretia McGiboney — July 23, 1818 / John Harris
MAPP, Moore / Lucy R. Jetter — February 6, 1822 / Lovick Pierce, M.G.
MAPP, Robert H. / Fatha Taylor — November 12, 1857 / W. W. Moore
MAPP, Robert H. / Teresa Pittman — June 5, 1859 / Carlos W. Stephens
MAPP, William / Marietta Jernigan — October 20, 1846 / Wm. I. Parks
MAPP, William B. / Mattie J. Mathews — November 27, 1875 / W. H. Blythe
MAPP, William J. / Patience C. Alexander — December 8, 1859 / James H. Kilpatrick
MARABLE, Augustus / Mary W. Hester — June 17, 1847 / Hinton Crawford
MARABLE, Champion / Julia A. Wagnon — August 19, 1866 / L. D. Carlton
MARABLE, John / Elizabeth Shelton — November 24, 1803
MARABLE, John / Fanny Lawson — December 13, 1804
MARCHMAN, Cicero S. / Margaret Watson — September 18, 1842 / Thomas Stocks
MARCHMAN, James / Emily Bruce — December 26, 1843 / Francis S. Coley
MARCHMAN, John M. / Virginia Barnhart — August 23, 1857 / James J. Laurence
MARCHMAN, Levi / Adaline Montgomery — January 26, 1831 / Ephraim Bruce
MARCHMAN, Nathan / Sarah Ransom — December 10, 1835 / Ephraim Bruce
MARCHMAN, Risdon / Martha Johnson — March 5, 1848 / James Moore

MARK, Samuel — May 31, 1805
  Susannah Brewer
MARKWALTER, Martin — March 10, 1864
  Mary Ann E. Winter — J. W. Godkin
MARTIN, Archabald — December 17, 1803
  Nancy Houghton
MARTIN, Baily G. — January 19, 1864
  Eliza Jane Boon — J. R. Parker
MARTIN, Elijah — November 18, 1819
  Jane McDoal — John Harris
MARTIN, Francis — December 29, 1807
  Bethish McClendon — J. Mapp
MARTIN, John — March 27, 1873
  Amanda E. McCarty — W. A. Overton
MARTIN, Joseph John — January 3, 1800
  Polly Jenkins
MARTIN, Robert — April 6, 1802
  Betsey Jones
MARTIN, Robert — May 10, 1820
  Edna Sanford — Lovick Pierce
MARTIN, Thomas D. — December 21, 1843
  Sarah A. M. Northern — P. H. Mell
MARTIN, William — November 27, 1828
  Jane Copeland
MARTIN, William M. — July 2, 1835
  Julia E. Nickelson — G. A. Chappell, M.G.
MARTIN, Zadah — November 9, 1802
  Peggy Robertson
MARTINDALE, Westley — December 1, 1838
  Elizabeth Southerland — Nathan Hobbs
MASON, Charles B. — November 6, 1867
  Sarah M. Carson — Philip B. Robinson
MASON, Edwin — November 1, 1821
  Amanda Grimes — Lovick Pierce
MASON, Wiley — October 21, 1824
  Martha Cunningham
MASSEY, James — August 9, 1818
  Nancy Miller
MASSEY, John W. — December 23, 1875
  Mattie J. Harris — R. L. Burgess
MASSINGALE, John — May 30, 1826
  Polly Moore
MASSINGALE, Jordan — July 8, 1830
  Mary Prince — William Bryan
MASSINGALE, Nathan — December 27, 1821
  Cynthia Jarrel — A. Hutchinson
MASTERS, James — September 4, 1851
  Martha O'Neal — Joseph W. Drennan
MATHEWS, Charles L. — January 31, 1807
  Lucy Early
MATHEWS, Charles L. — September 15, 1831
  Emeline T. Strain — Lovick Pierce

MATTHEWS, James T. — December 3, 1842
  Martha Ann Kimbrough — R. F. Griffen
MAULL, James — June 18, 1829
  Rebecca Alford
MAXEY, Barnabus A. — December 4, 1867
  Sarah F. Powell — M. M. Landrum, M.G.
MAXEY, Booze — December 21, 1823
  Sarah Landman — J. Ragan
MAXEY, Jeremiah — August 3, 1830
  Jane Finley
MAXEY, George W. — December 13, 1866
  Virginia E. Burgess — E. A. Burgess
MAXEY, Joseph W. — December 15, 1825
  Mary Peek
MAXEY, William — June 9, 1815
  —— DeGraffenreid — A. S. Johnson
MAY, Isaac — June 15, 1820
  Sara Shelton — Thomas Johnson
MAY, John — December 31, 1850
  Emily Jackson — Hart C. Peek
MAY, Major W. — December 30, 1828
  Rebecca Hunt — James Park
MAY, Thomas — October 1, 1828
  Mary McLane — Robert Newsom
MAYS, William — May 1, 1836
  Elizabeth Gentry — Nathan Hobbs
MAYNE, James P. — April 24, 1866
  Emma B. Stovall — John Calvin Johnson
McALPIN, Andrew — December 13, 1827
  Nancy Hubbard — Alexander McAlpin
McCAIN, Robert Patrick — May 29, 1835
  Nancy Dickson
McCALL, James P. — December 15, 1868
  Claud M. Weaver — Luther M. Smith
McCARTHUR, James — August 10, 1837
  Elizabeth Harriett Mabry — John Wilson
McCARTY, Walker — February 9, 1874
  Rosa Landrum
McCARTY, William — July 8, 1860
  Marion L. Jenkins — Wm. A. Colclough
McCLAIN, Bennett — September 9, 1828
  Juriah Freeman
McCLAIN, Elisha — August 5, 1852
  Nancy Wyatt — B. Rowland
McCLAIN, Elizah — August 1, 1822
  Rosa Ray — Abraham Yeats
McCLAIN, John — September 19, 1822
  Mary Williams — Abraham Yeats
McCLELLAN, James — January 16, 1825
  Sarah Sturdivant
McCLENDON, Jeremiah — December 23, 1795
  Elizabeth Sheffel

Georgia Society, Daughters of the American Revolution   91

McCLENDON, Marvel   November 24, 1803
  Phebe Williams
McCLUSKEY, Thomas   June 14, 1820
  Julia Ann Dillard   Lovick Pierce
McCOMMON, James H.   November 3, 1864
  Helen Mary Geer   John R. Young, M.G.
McCOWEN, John W.   September 11, 1817
  Ann Perkins   Robert Gilbert
McCOY, Ewell   January 25, 1821
  Rebecca Boone   William Cone
McCOY, John   February 18, 1823
  Lucy Fitzpatrick   John Park
McCRARY, John W.   August 11, 1853
  Elizabeth Anderson   J. W. Yarbrough
McCREA, Wiley B.   January 5, 1871
  Laura A. McWhorter   J. C. Calvin
McDONALD, Daniel   April 11, 1858
  Susan A. Bridges   T. J. Bowen
McDONALD, Marion   February 7, 1851
  Sarah Alfriend   L. C. Peek
McGAN, William Henry   September 1, 1835
  Rachel Copeland
McGIBONEY, William R.   September 1, 1865
  Lodusca Irby   J. R. Parker
McGRAY, Richard T.   June 2, 1850
  Mary Ann Warner   J. W. Drennan
McGruder, Bryan   November 23, 1838
  Martha Bryan   Thos. W. Grimes
McGUIRE, A.   November 10, 1818
  Patsey Aldmon
McGUIRE, Thomas   April 22, 1795
  Peggy Hays
McGUIRE, ———   April 22, 1795
  Peggy Hays
McGUIRE, James   May 9, 1795
  Polly George
McHARGUE, William T.   June 29, 1843
  Julia A. F. Hendricks   James W. Godkin
McHENRY, James H.   May 30, 1843
  Sarah G. Poullain   Francis Bowman
McINTOSH, David   December 29, 1795
  Polly Dawson
McINTOSH, Jesse   June 19, 1802
  June Cartwright
McKENZIE, Josephus   March 15, 1866
  Nancy A. E. Mays   James Davison
McKINLEY, C.   January 12, 1832
  Antoinette Wingfield   Francis Cummins
McKNIGHT, John   July 28, 1842
  Susan Drake   William Manley
McLAIN, James   October 9, 1859
  Nancy Ward   J. M. Kelly

McLAIN, Samuel — April 15, 1841
  Adaline Landrum — Hardy Bridges
McLAUGHLIN, Owen A. — December 25, 1851
  Almarine C. Cheney — Enoch Calloway
McMAHAN, Noel — March 21, 1861
  Mary Jane Morgan — W. R. Wilson
McMAHAN, William I. — January 12, 1838
  Henrietta Higgins
McMICHAEL, Charles — October 17, 1807
  Polly Carmichael — James Holt
McMICHAEL, David — February 20, 1789
  Sarah Kimbro
McMICHAEL, Samuel — January 17, 1808
  Dicey Winslett — W. M. Johnson
McMICHAEL, Seaborn — February 17, 1824
  Elizabeth Riley
McMILLAN, Eli — June 25, 1822
  Candis Richards — William Wingfield
McMillan, Micajah — May 18, 1828
  Mary Harrison — A. Ray, M.G.
McMULLIN, David — December 19, 1803
  Hannah Pickard
McMURRAY, James — February 21, 1821
  Agnes Curtis — Francis Cummins
McWHORTER, Beeman C. — December 18, 1873
  Elizabeth Barnhart — W. A. Overton
McWHORTER, Frederick — December 28, 1841
  Elizabeth A. Johnson — N. H. Hill
McWHORTER, John — December 18, 1855
  N. H. Hall — T. B. Martin, M.G.
McWHORTER, Robert — November 2, 1843
  Nancy W. Jones — B. M. Sanders
McWHORTER, Robert — February 22, 1849
  N. Pope Thurmond — P. H. Mell
McWHORTER, Robert L. — April 20, 1875
  Mary E. Boyd — C. H. Strickland
McWHORTER, William H. — October 26, 1837
  Adaline Edmondson — Jack Lumpkin, M.G.
McWHORTER, William H. — November 14, 1865
  Mary E. Cheney — P. H. Mell, M.G.
McWHORTER, William P. — July 21, 1857
  Sarah J. Crawford — P. H. Mell, M.G.
MEADOWS, Benjamin — December 17, 1805
  Nancey Parker — B. Maddox
MEADDOWS, Benjamin — December 20, 1805
  Nancey Parker
MEADOWS, William — June 29, 1815
  Jean Meadows — Malichi Murden
MEALER, John W. — January 5, 1871
  Minnie Brooks — W. R. Wilson
MEANS, Francis M. — November 22, 1866
  E. Louisa Crutchfield — A. Hearns

MEDDOWS, Benjamin   October 12, 1805
  Nancy Parker
MEDDOWS, Alexander   February 11, 1875
  Mary A. Morgan   C. H. Strickland
MEDLIN, Andrew I.   April 13, 1845
  Mary Sherley   James T. Findley
MEEKS, Albert H.   September 12, 1872
  Naomi Brooks   James Griffen
MELBORN, Levi T.   April 15, 1824
  Roxana Bethune
MELTON, James K.   July 13, 1864
  Louisa H. Clements   L. B. Jackson
MELTON, Robert   October 10, 1804
  Patsey Boon
MELTON, William Allen   January 25, 1807
  Nancy Haynes   William Greer
MERRITT, Allen   March 5, 1873
  Mary Sherling   W. H. Wright
MERRITT, Benjamin   December 19, 1850
  Susan M. Heath   James Billingslea
MERRITT, James   March 18, 1875
  Nancy Williams   W. H. Wright
MEREDITH, James   August 13, 1843
  Harriet A. M. Fleetwood   John Robins
MERRITT, Franklin   August 31, 1865
  Cornelia C. Stewart   John C. Merritt
MERRITT, Henry   December 7, 1818
  Jackann Crawford
MERRITT, James   December 12, 1861
  Sarah Sidwell   James W. Godkin
MERRITT, John   April 30, 1844
  Lucy Clements   H. H. Laurence
MERRITT, John C.   July 15, 1849
  Louisa F. Crawford   James W. Godkin
MERRITT, Lovett   February 8, 1820
  Sarah Gatlin   John Harris
MERRITT, Lovett   September 25, 1837
  Mary O'Rear   Ephraim Bruce
MERRITT, Stephen   February 11, 1868
  Susan C. O'Neal   L. D. Caldwell
MERRITT, Thomas   February 28, 1815
  Patsey Roland   Robert Rea
MERRITT, Thomas   April 26, 1855
  Caroline A. Heath   L. C. Peek
MERRITT, William   August 22, 1854
  Nancy J. Burk   W. A. Florence, M.G.
MERRITT, William   October 29, 1865
  Sarah V. Ledbetter   William Bryan, M.G.
MERRIWETHER, Francis   November 3, 1818
  Sarah Watts   Lovick Pierce
MERRIWETHER, James   February 27, 1814
  Fanny Bradshaw

METCALF, Edward   May 22, 1851
  Ephronia M. Dawson   Francis Bowman
MICHAEL, Thomas J.   September 2, 1853
  Almeda T. Johnson   W. A. Partee
MIDDLEBROOKS, Zara B.   October 14, 1858
  Martha E. Maddox   J. M. Stilwell, M.G.
MIDDLETON, William   November 29, 1814
  Nancy Lumpkin   John Browning
MILLER, Charley   August 30, 1804
  Isabella Kennedy
MILLER, John   March 21, 1822
  Elizabeth Bird
MILLER, John A.   May 19, 1836
  Sarah Jane Smith
MILLER, Parker C.   September 13, 1843
  Martha Anne Caldwell   Wooten O'Neal
MILLER, Thomas S.   November 18, 1853
  Mary Jane Jackson   E. L. Whately, M.G.
MILLIGAN, James   August 19, 1788
  Elizabeth Cessna
MILLS, Henry   January 21, 1849
  Elizabeth Lindsey   Nevill Lumpkin
MILNER, Obadiah   January 4, 1806
  Precilia Meddows
MINER, Hermon   September 3, 1802
  Elizabeth Andrews
MIRNNER, William   May 21, 1816
  Cynthia Young   Walker Lewis
MITCHELL, Cicero A.   May 23, 1858
  Elmira C. Smith   O. L. Smith, M.G.
MITCHELL, Edward   February 1, 1821
  Essy Terzeach   Lovick Pierce
MITCHELL, Isaac   January 19, 1819
  Parizade Love   Lovick Pierce
MITCHELL, John   December 27, 1868
  Elizabeth Catching   James W. Godkin
MITCHELL, Joshua M.   October 17, 1867
  Valeria T. Randle   Francis S. Colley
MITCHELL, Reuben S.   July 9, 1843
  Elizabeth Forrester   E. S. Hunter
MITCHELL, Sterling   Augst 31, 1800
  Betsy Brewer
MIZE, Anderson   April 24, 1810
  Sally Wood
MIZE, Jo   September 7, 1804
  Jemima Wyatt
MONCRIEF, David   April 22, 1830
  Nancy Price   Jack Lumpkin
MONCRIEF, Isaac   December 30, 1819
  Nancy Kecker   A. Hutchenson
MONCRIEF, Marshall   December 18, 1845
  Elizabeth Bolles   Samuel Ely

MONCRIEF, Thomas I.   August 20, 1833
  Mary Ann Roberson   Thomas Stocks
MONCRIEF, William   September 6, 1849
  Nancy Booles   J. D. Williams
MONK, Tearson B.   December —, 1838
  Martha Watts   Vincent R. Thornton
MONTFORT, Alexander   November 25, 1852
  Elizabeth B. Smith   J. W. Yarbrough
MONTFORT, John   March 22, 1810
  Nancey Curry   C. Maddox
MONTFORT, John C.   November 26, 1850
  Elizabeth H. Quill   J. W. Godkin
MONTFORT, Oscar L.   December 16, 1858
  Margaret A. Hillsman   M. H .Hubbard
MONTFORT, William   January 3, 1822
  Matilda Jane Patrick   James Dunn
MONTGOMERY, James M.   January 14, 1836
  Margaret Culp   John G. Holtzclaw
MONTGOMERY, William   June 25, 1870
  Chloe Lewis
MOODY, Elias B.   September 14, 1845
  Susan Brook   Samuel Ely
MOODY, Elias B.   October 11, 1863
  Sarah E. Durham   W. R. Wilson
MOODY, George   February 21, 1833
  Eliza Velvin   Wm. H. Price
MOODY, George W.   December 28, 1835
  Emeline Moody   Wm. H. Price
MOODY, Greene   August 10, 1816
  Betsey Dove   Vincent Lanford
MOODY, Henry   April 19, 1855
  Frances Patrick   J. M. Davison
MOODY, James A.   March 13, 1836
  Elizabeth F. Brooks   John G. Holtzclaw
MOODY, James A.   May 10, 1860
  Maey Elizabeth Adkins   Wm. R. Wilson
MOODY, James A.   January 22, 1865
  Sarah Jane Mays   James Davison
MOODY, John   December 23, 1817
  Nancy Velvin   Hinton Crawford
MOODY, John C.   October 8, 1850
  Rebecca Robertson   James W. Godkin
MOODY, Lillte B.   September 28, 1865
  Mrs. Catherine S. Freeman   James Davison
MOODY, Waldman   July 24, 1864
  Georgia Ann Moore   Alfred L. Willis
MOON, Causby   December 22, 1868
  Louisa Melton   Joseph R. Parker
MOON, Franklin H.   January 5, 1869
  Sarah Crawford
MOON, George W.   March 25, 1866
  Phoebe J. Johnson   John O'Neal

MOON, George W.   November 20, 1866
  Electrian Wright   John C. Merritt
MOON, William L.   January 2, 1852
  Priscilla Bruce   D. Hightower
MOOR, David   October 20, 1807
  Sally Aubrey   William Greer
MOOR, Isaac   October 5, 1807
  Nancy Wyatt   J. Mapp
MOOR, Young   October 16, 1807
  Rebekah Aubrey   William Greer
MOORE, Anderson C.   May 4, 1868
  Georgia A. Howell   J. H. Kilpatrick
MOORE, Asbury Green   December 23, 1855
  Sarah Jane Caldwell   H. C. Peek
MOORE, Bertram   December 18, 1873
  Mattie Ely   J. H. Kilpatrick
MOORE, Curtis   September 14, 1789
  Agnes Smith
MOORE, David C.   December 24, 1857
  Sarah Ann Greer   James H. Wragg
MOORE, Freeling H.   January 7, 1869
  Sarah H. Crawford   W. R. Foote
MOORE, George   June 9, 1822
  Maria Wright   Stephen Hightower
MOORE, George   January 14, 1847
  Jincey Atkinson   James Rowland
MOORE, George   August 24, 1856
  Lucy Wilson   J. F. Wright
MOORE, George W.   November 16, 1872
  Margaret E. Hogg   John R. Young
MOORE, Gillis   December 22, 1798
  Betsey Cooper
MOORE, Henry H.   October 10, 1865
  Mrs. Martha W. Dooly   W. H. Blythe, M.G.
MOORE, Hiram   February 18, 1847
  Elizabeth I. Turner   Ephraim Bruce
MOORE, Isaac   July 2, 1855
  Mrs. Bethena Wilson   W. W. Moore
MOORE, Isaac D.   January 15, 1852
  Mary Jane Howell   D. Hightower
MOORE, Isaac J.   June 23, 1848
  Elizabeth Caldwell
MOORE, Jackson   July 7, 1821
  Nancy Stevens   Chesley Bristoe
MOORE, James   December 14, 1818
  Bethine Jordan
MOORE, James M.   February 2, 1837
  Eliza Ann Wilson   W. D. Coudrey
MOORE, Jeremiah   April 6, 1830
  Martha Gilbert   W. B. Barnett
MOORE, Jesse I.   January 28, 1844
  Frances A. Mapp   J. J. Howell

MOORE, John — March 19, 1800
  Elizabeth Hammond
MOORE, John — September 14, 1837
  Cordelia Ann Lumpkin — W. R. M. Moseley
MOORE, John B. — June 11, 1872
  Marian B. McHenry — C. W. Lane
MOORE, John C. — January 22, 1857
  Rebecca A. Wagnon — H. H. Parks, M.G.
MOORE, J. D. — November 4, 1869
  Mary Ely — J. H. Kilpatrick
MOORE, Joseph — January 18, 1810
  Matilda Goss — William McGiboney
MOORE, Osborn — December 18, 1873
  Latha Brake — J. H. Kilpatrick
MOORE, Oscar D. — December 22, 1874
  Mattie Newsom — J. H. Kilpatrick
MOORE, Ransom — December 29, 1819
  Mary Anne Hudgins — John Myrick
MOORE, Samuel — January 16, 1821
  Lucy Ward — Spencer Moore
MOORE, Spencer — September 24, 1801
  Luky Grimes
MOORE (or Brown) William — March 4, 1821
  Mary Wood — H. G. Slaughter
MOORE, William — December 5, 1822
  Jedidah Perkins — John Harris
MOORE, William — January 25, 1828
  Sydney Connell — John Harris
MOORE, William — December 12, 1831
  Jane Monfort
MOORE, William — April 25, 1844
  Frances Rea — Francis Bowman
MOORE, William — December 9, 1847
  Nancy Atkinson — J. J. Loudermilk
MOORE, William B. — May 20, 1858
  Mary Ann Credille — W. G. Johnson
MOORE, William H. — March 15, 1844
  Margary Veazey — E. P. Jarrell
MOORE, J. W. — April 26, 1871
  E. C. Park — Geo. W. Yarbrough
MORAN, Basil — March 2, 1789
  Nancy Harvey
MORELAND, James M. — December 29, 1853
  Elizabeth F. Bridges — L. E. Culver, M.G.
MORELAND, James M. — December 15, 1870
  Pheraby Wagnon — L. D. Caldwell
MORGAN, Adrain S. — December 20, 1865
  Annie M. Spencer — H. H. Tucker, M.G.
MORGAN, Adrain S. — December 25, 1867
  Amanda E. King — J. J. Brantley
MORGAN, Drury Chipsom — December 8, 1836
  Priscilla Southerland — Nathan Hobbs

MORGAN, Enoch C.   July 30, 1850
   Mary S. Johnson   P. H. Mell
MORGAN, Thomas H.   November 21, 1852
   Elizabeth D. Strozier   P. H. Mell
MORGAN, William   August 19, 1819
   Temperance Coleman   Lovick Pierce
MORGAN, William   April 29, 1830
   Caroline Wittick   James A. Andrews
MORGAN, William H.   May 13, 1830
   Mary Mounger   Lovick Pierce
MORREL, Simeon   December 10, 1818
   Mariah Harris   Robert Moore
MORRIS, Andrew Jackson   December 28, 1854
   Mary Jane Andrews   Hart C. Peek
MORRIS, George   June 3, 1824
   Frances Morris   Malichi Murden
MORRIS, Lemon   October 10, 1816
   Patsey Colclough   Thomas Legue
MORRISON, Isaac   March 23, 1837
   Rebecca Montfort   James W. Godkin
MORRISON, William J.   January 18, 1842
   Elizabeth J. Chew   James W. Godkin
MORROW, Hugh E.   June 26, 1839
   Ellen Mathew   Francis Bowman
MOSELEY, Benjamin   December 14, 1847
   Mary Ann Calloway   George F. Pierce
MOSELEY, John A.   January 8, 1839
   Eliza Ann Johnston   John W. Wilson
MOSELEY, Lewis   October 12, 1809
   Rebekah Jones   John Turner
MOSS, Carson F.   March 9, 1873
   Sarah F. Wheeler   W. A. Overton
MOSS, Henry   February 26, 1843
   Jane Nance   Samuel Ely
MOSS, Peter M.   December 12, 1867
   Emma Jernigan   J. H. Kilpatrick
MOTTE, Levi S.   May 15, 1866
   Sarah V. Chambers   Ezekiel S. Williams
MULKEY, James   June 25, 1807
   Betsey Dawson   Claborn Maddox
MULLINS, Charles   December 16, 1869
   Georgia Ann Andrews   W. A. Overton, M.G.
MULLINS, John   September 2, 1836
   Julia Ann Williams   B. M. Sanders
MULLINS, Julius S.   December 17, 1803
   Rosey Marcay
MULLINS, Thomas K.   December 9, 1830
   Pemelia H. Brockman   John Chew
MURDEN, Henning D.   April 12, 1837
   Cornelia F. Pinkston   J. G. Gilbert
MURDEN, Malicia   January 16, 1806
   Nancy Asbury

MURDEN, Redmond — March 16, 1864
  Sarah A. Mitchell — H. H. Tucker, M.G.
MURPHEY, Andrew — December 14, 1829
  Sydney White — John Chew
MURPHEY, John — December 19, 1811
  Polly Lake — Clayborn Maddox
MURRAH, James — March 5, 1821
  Ann Swindale — John Beattie
MURRAY, George — July 19, 1846
  Eliza Ann Glazier — T. M. Fambrough

N

NAZERY, Henry — October 3, 1801
  Polly Springer
NEAL, Alder — January 13, 1811
  Sally Cochran — Hinton Crawford
NEAL, George W. — July 12, 1850
  Eliza W. Edmondson — P. H. Mell
NEAL, Robert — December 26, 1872
  Alice Burnett — B. P. Taylor
NEELY, John F. — May 30, 1850
  Mary Ann Cone — John T. Cox
NELMS, Oliver — December 8, 1819
  Mary Shorter
NELMS, Samuel — December 28, 1815
  Sally Holland — George Owens
NELMS, Thomas — February 13, 1808
  Nancey Gillam — H. Gatlin
NELMS, Thomas — February 10, 1819
  Polly Worrell — Moore Robert
NELMS, Thomas — February 22, 1870
  Mary E. Haddaday
NELSON, Abram — December 23, 1799
  Elizabeth Ellis
NELSON, George W. — September 3, 1833
  Mary N. White
NELSON, John B. — October 21, 1818
  Sophia Roberts — Jesse Mercer
NELSON, John W. — December 29, 1874
  Mary Fenn — L. D. Caldwell
NELSON, Joseph F. — January 8, 1845
  Mary M. Parker — James Moore
NELSON, Perry — November 7, 1821
  Martha McGaughey
NESBIT, Dr. James — July 30, 1794
  Penelope Cooper
NEWELL, William — January 24, 1822
  Priscilla Jones — Walker Lewis
NEWSOM, David A. — February 9, 1869
  Mrs. Maggie W. Carlton — Philip Robinson
NEWSOM, Joseph N. — November 24, 1874
  Addie Lewis — John W. Swann

NEWSOM, Robert | September 29, 1808
　Nancey Asbery | Peter Joyner
NEWSOM, William J. | January 11, 1871
　Elizabeth W. Haley | P. H. Mell, M.G.
NEWTON, Elijah | May 14, 1822
　Betsey Collier | Lovick Pierce
NEWTON, William | January 3, 1804
　Betsey Dorough
NICHOLS, Thomas | December 29, 1858
　Emmaline Wiggins | R. B. Kelly
NICHOLSON, George W. | May 12, 1859
　Eliza C. Bridges | Jefferson F. Wright
NICKELSON, Archibald | September 27, 1846
　Sally Robinson | Abner R. Hill
NICKELSON, George | July 22, 1823
　Nancy Jackson | William Greer, M.G.
NICKELSON, Henry Clay | June 14, 1866
　Harriet M. Poullain | George F. Pierce
NICKELSON, Oscar E. | November 30, 1865
　Martha C. Maddox | V. A. Bell, M.G.
NICKELSON, Samuel S. | February 5, 1860
　Sarah A. Williams | John R. Young
NICKELSON, William | November 2, 1828
　Susan Williams | Jack Lumpkin
NICKELSON, William | August 24, 1862
　Elizabeth Atkinson | Wiley G. Johnson
NICKELSON, William B. | January 30, 1866
　Louisa C. Mullins | V. A. Bell, M.G.
NICKS, Henry | October 8, 1865
　Emily Bradley | Jefferson F. Wright
NORRIS, Jacob | November 23, 1819
　Liney Wood
NORRIS, James | July 23, 1800
　Sally Patrick
NORSWORTHY, Frederick | July 18, 1821
　Mary Alford
NORTHINGTON, James | September 26, 1814
　Sally Houghton | Evans Myrick
NORTON, Charles C. | June 3, 1844
　Anne M. Foster | William Arnold
NORWOOD, James M. | July 8, 1835
　Mary A. Maddox | James Moore
NORWOOD, William | January 26, 1836
　Mary F. Luckey | James Moore
NOWELL, Robert | December 3, 1839
　Martha Moncrief | B. M. Sanders
NUNN, C. W. | November 23, 1873
　Mattie Battle | W. A. Overton
NUNN, F. L. | April 22, 1874
　S. E. Moody | James A. Thornton
NUNN, John B. | February 28, 1875
　Mary A. Moody | James M. Griffen

O

O'CONNOR, John   June 28, 1822
   Nancy Braswell
OGLESBY, Thomas   October 7, 1818
   Mary Alford   L. Bethune
OGLETREE, Samuel T.   December 8, 1866
   Martha J. Williams
OGLETREE, Samuel T.   July 4, 1867
   Margaret A. Underwood   Hart C. Peek
OGLETREE, William D.   December 18, 1866
   Sarah C. Underwood   Hart C. Peek
O'KEEFE, Daniel   June 21, 1865
   Ann Walsh   P. J. Kirby, Cath. Priest
O'KEEFE, D. C.   May 7, 1851
   Sarah Branch   L. G. Hillyer
O'KELLEY, Patrick   January 6, 1843
   Nancy Reed   Lemuel Greene
OLCOTT, John   December 11, 1848
   Emmelin Moody   Thomas Stocks
OLIPHANT, Aaron P.   October 24, 1843
   Emily M. Wright   Francis S. Cooley
OLIVER, Alexander   November 15, 1846
   Mary Drenun   R. F. Griffen
OLIVER, Andrew   October 13, 1819
   Mary Dority
OLIVER, Charles C.   September 27, 1857
   Julia Frances Caldwell   Hart C. Peek
OLIVER, Columbus C.   November 28, 1868
   Maploa Flornoy Bowden
OLIVER, John   April 3, 1823
   Nancy Cartwright   Thomas Johnson
OLIVER, John G.   May 26, 1831
   Mary H. Cartwright   John N. Harris
OLIVER, Milus W.   December 3, 1874
   Maggie Heard   J. M. Loury
OLIVER, Thomas A.   November 29, 1855
   Julia F. Heard   Hinton Crawford
OLIVER, William   January 5, 1845
   Jane Cartwright   John L. Veazey
OLIVER, William I.   March 20, 1845
   Cena Bryan   Ephriam Bruce
O'NEAL, Alexander S.   November 12, 1872
   Malissa Ann Daniel   Hart C. Peek
O'NEAL, Alfred   October 17, 1868
   Martha King
O'NEAL, Augustus   December 12, 1843
   Georgia A. V. Stewart   H. F. Bunkley
O'NEAL, Daniel H.   December 16, 1874
   M. Fannie Johnson   Hart C. Peek
O'NEAL, Edward   October 2, 1799
   Elizabeth Roberts

O'NEAL, Hampton   February 19, 1834
  Charlotte T. Peek   James Moore
O'NEAL, Harrison   December 17, 1819
  Elizabeth Colclough   Malichi Murden
O'NEAL, Harrison   October 9, 1860
  Jane Williams   L. D. Caldwell
O'NEAL, James   July 8, 1849
  Julia Ann Rhodes   James T. Findley
O'NEAL, John   October 10, 1839
  Ecsah Caldwell   James Moon
O'NEAL, John   October 25, 1841
  Charlotte Hancock   James Moore
O'NEAL, Joshua   October 14, 1852
  Sarah Jane Davis
O'NEAL, William H.   December 23, 1873
  Fanny Irby   Hart C. Peek
O'NEAL, Williamson   December 9, 1823
  Rebeccah Holland   Malichi Murden
O'NEAL, Wooten   January 27, 1820
  Mary Stevens   Francis Cummins
OREAR, Benjamin   May 27, 1819
  Elizabeth Cook   William McGiboney
OREAR, Josiah   November 30, 1824
  Lucinda Lewis
OREAR, Osburn   December 27, 1829
  Lucissa Lewis   Dacheus Wright
OREAR, Robert   November 30, 1807
  Sally Knight   William McGiboney
ORR, William   February 10, 1820
  Jane Harris   Lovick Pierce
OSBORN, William T.   September 14, 1863
  Florida Wray   L. R. L. Jennings
OSTIN, John   December 16, 1819
  Rachel Anderson
OVERTON, Gilchrist   November 29, 1821
  Hannah R. Morris   Charles Baldwin
OVERTON, M. C.   December 19, 1871
  M. A. Caldwell
OVERTON, Simeon W.   January 20, 1874
  Emma Jones   A. A. Fluker
OWEN, Phillman   March 1, 1803
  Betsey Fluker
OWEN, John   December 5, 1822
  Nancy Woods   Henry Slaughter
OWEN, William   October 18, 1825
  Elizabeth Ann Crawford
OWEN, William   December 9, 1852
  Emily Durham   John R. Young
OWENS, Charles   May 26, 1861
  Mary Kirkendoll   E. S. Williams
OWENS, Charles W.   February 2, 1868
  Sarah M. Wiggins   W. M. Chapman, M.G.

OWENS, Daniel   February 10, 1847
  Louisa Hendricks   R. F. Griffen
OWENS, Daniel   April 26, 1857
  Caroline Marsh   William Hudson
OWENS, Jefferson   April 23, 1854
  Josephine Marsh   B. Rowland
OWENS, Morefield   August 30, 1821
  Martha Parker   A. H. Scott

P

PACE, Barnabus   March 12, 1807
  Patsey Harris   Thomas Crawford
PALMORE, Francis   September 21, 1840
  Ann Simmons
PALMORE, James   July 11, 1816
  Nancey Foster   William Armor
PALMORE, James   November 29, 1846
  Creasa Moore   Ephraim Bruce
PALMORE, James   August 17, 1860
  Lucy A. V. Devaney   Jefferson F. Wright
PALMER, James M.   October 23, 1847
  Sarah A. M. Jackson
PALMER, John C.   March 16, 1859
  Abbigail B. Littleton   James W. Godkin
PALMER, Landon   March 7, 1821
  Eliza Coleman   Lovick Pierce
PALMER, William W.   February 14, 1833
  Lorena Adkinson   J. P. Leveritt
PANTON, Abner   November 28, 1802
  Rebekah Barnheardt   Thomas Crawford
PARHAM, Darling P.   January 19, 1842
  Eliza Ann Tarpley   Vincent R. Thornton
PARK, Columbus M.   August 7, 1838
  Mary Ann W. Armor   Robert F. Griffin
PARK, Ezekial E. P.   April 11, 1833
  Frances A. Redd   A. M. Sanders
PARK, Hugh H.   January 21, 1874
  Anna S. Mays   W. A. Overton
PARK, James B.   Febrary 22, 1849
  Missouri Billingslea   Hinton Crawford
PARK, James L.   August 23, 1820
  Harriet F. Cunningham   Lovick Pierce
PARK, Richard   October 7, 1804
  Catherine Musgrove
PARK, Richard S.   July 15, 1841
  Nancy T. Walker   Reuben Arnold
PARK, Thomas   February 12, 1825
  Eliza Billingslea
PARK, William J.   October 6, 1857
  Mrs. Emily A. Carlton   B. H. Overby, M.G.
PARKER, Aaron   February 27, 1801
  Mary Williams

PARKER, Asa J. — December 20, 1849
  Susan M. A. Bates — W. W. Moore
PARKER, Austin — July 10, 1828
  Esther Williams — Reuben White
PARKER, David — June 30, 1803
  Lydia Radmore
PARKER, Edwin — January 11, 1846
  Rebecca Astin — James Moore
PARKER, Emanuel — January 30, 1807
  Polly Austin — B. Maddox
PARKER, James B. — April 1, 1867
  Virginia W. Sayers
PARKER, J. F. — January 18, 1849
  Sarah Jane Jackson — L. B. Jackson
PARKER, Lewis — January 6, 1825
  Martha H. Turner — Thos. W. Slaughter
PARKER, Robert F. — July 25, 1833
  Patima Simmons — J. P. Leveritt
PARKER, William — February 21, 1818
  Eunice Nelson
PARKS, William M. — June 23, 1864
  Elizabeth Bradshaw — John F. Zuber
PARMENTREE, Jason — September 21, 1799
  Catherine Heard
PARROTT, Asberry L. — December 9, 1875
  Lavinia R. Smith — W. H. Blythe
PARROTT, Asbury L. — October 12, 1869
  Fanny Turner — W. H. Blythe
PARROTT, Benjamin — July 28, 1828
  Patience Johnson — John Wood
PARROTT, Benjamin — February 14, 1838
  Nancy Williams — J. P. Leveritt
PARROTT, Curtis — December 30, 1833
  Sarah K. Rowland
PARROTT, Henry — February 13, 1812
  Patsey Dolvin — William Cone
PARROTT, James — October 16, 1804
  Amy King
PARROTT, James — February 2, 1840
  Matilda Harris — Reuben B. Armor
PARROTT, Obadiah — March 22, 1822
  Elizabeth Horn — Robert Booth
PARTEE, Walter A. — February 10, 1826
  Elizabeth Carr
PASCHEL, Samuel D. — December 7, 1854
  Georgia E. Hutcherson — —— Winchel
PATE, Edward — October 15, 1819
  Mary Fitzpatrick — Rich Gilbert
PATRICK, Benjamin B. — March —, 1833
  Adaline Maddox — John M. Cox
PATRICK, Charles L. — September 10, 1858
  Amanda J. Sidwell — William J. Parks

PATRICK, Constantine — January 9, 1797
  Polly Perkins
PATRICK, Josiah — December 30, 1801
  Bethsheba Phillips
PATRICK, Lucius — January 21, 1869
  Sarah C. Jarrell — Joe R. Parker
PATRICK, Robert — April 26, 1796
  Kitty Curry
PATRICK, Samuel, Jr. — April 26, 1875
  Mary E. Lewis — C. C. Davison
PARTRIDGE, Charles — October 27, 1874
  Mary Lankford — John T. Dolvin
PARTRIDGE, Thomas — December 22, 1868
  Elizabeth Loyd — E. B. Mosely
PATTERSON, John — November 25, 1817
  Susan Pryor — William Watson
PATTERSON, John G. — May 5, 1850
  Ann Smith — Joseph W. Drennan
PATTERSON, William H. — June 20, 1858
  Fannie C. Williams — J. H. Kilpatrick
PATTERSON, William P. — September 3, 1840
  Martha A. Moody — Robert Tolfree
PATTILLO, Charles — December 7, 1820
  Amelia Holt — Samuel Cowles
PATTILLO, Henry A. — June 20, 1866
  Henrietta H. Hall — V. A. Bell, M.G.
PATTILLO, James — January 11, 1810
  Elizabeth Jeter — Wm. McGiboney
PATTILLO, John — February 20, 1816
  Polly Winfield — Robert Rea
PATTILLO, Samuel — April 14, 1795
  Fanney Hall
PAULSON, Neel — April 16, 1819
  Rebeccah Cochran — John Myrick
PEAK, Leonard — July 8, 1832
  Jane Barnhardt — James M. Norwood
PECK, Hart C. — January 27, 1829
  Elizabeth C. Brooks
PEEK, Archibald P. — February 1, 1866
  Emily Robinson — Henry C. Weaver
PEEK, John C. — March 18, 1830
  Jane Adeline Michael — William Bryan
PEEK, John C. — August 15, 1838
  Frances Bryan — Reuben B. Arnold
PEEK, Leonard — December 7, 1841
  Sarah Patrick — James Davidson
PEEK, Leonard — May 14, 1846
  Sarah Patrick — James W. Godkin
PEEK, Littleberry — March 15, 1824
  Elizabeth Williams
PEEK, Micajah L. — December 24, 1833
  Judah Ann A. Johnson — William Bryan

PEEK, Robert   February 22, 1833
  Emily J. L. Trippe   William Bryant
PEEK, Simon T.   January 14, 1845
  Elizabeth Jones   M. F. Baker
PEEK, Singleton   December 28, 1843
  Louisa Moody   J. M. Davison
PEEK, William C.   December 29, 1874
  Martha C. Bell
PEEK, William J.   January 7, 1875
  Viney J. Porter   John R. Young
PEEK, William T.   October 30, 1874
  Amanda Colley   J. R. Parker
PEELER, Anderson J.   January 1, 1826
  Malinda Cook   E. Talley
PEELER, Anthony   December 2, 1827
  Mary Williams   William Austin
PEELER, Berry   December 30, 1829
  Emily McClellan   William Bryan
PEELER, Jacob   November 24, 1814
  Sally Martin   Thomas Riley
PEEVY, Allen   March 7, 1815
  Elizabeth Hightower   Thomas Bush
PENDERGRASS, Jesse   September 5, 1830
  Polly Devaney   Peter Johnson
PENN, Moss   June 25, 1804
  Penny Bird
PENN, William S.   December 16, 1834
  Eliza White   George Heard
PENNINGTON, James   October 2, 1845
  Martha Crawford   Thadeus Pennington
PEMBLETON, Joshua   September 20, 1805
  Jane Griffen
PEOPLES, Benjamin   November 4, 1824
  Mary Watts
PEOPLES, Dudley   October 6, 1819
  Matilda Park
PEOPLES, Hubbard   January 15, 1795
  Elizabeth Heard
PEPPIN, Noah   December 18, 1825
  Betsy Rowland
PEPPIN, Noah   November 12, 1868
  Emma Patrick
PERDUE, Daniel   November 7, 1815
  Rebekah Houghton   West Harris
PERDUE, Daniel   November 7, 1839
  Mary S. Finley   Hinton Crawford
PERDUE, George   August —, 1838
  Sarah Johnson
PERDUE, James H.   November 26, 1857
  Elizabeth Billingslea   G. Bright
PERDUE, John   September 24, 1839
  Dimny Hunt   P. C. Johnson

PERDUE, L. Crawford — January 13, 1870
  Ella Carey — J. M. Dickery
PERDUE, Thomas — December 10, 1807
  Peggy Gaston — C. Maddox
PERKINS, Absalom — October 29, 1870
  Frances A. Moore
PERKINS, Albert — October 21, 1847
  Mary C. Braddy
PERKINS, Ezekiel — February 1, 1810
  Sally English — William Greer
PERKINS, Hamilton — April 23, 1871
  Emma Lewis — J. M. Loury, M.G.
PERKINS, James H. — November 10, 1867
  Mary E. Gresham — J. M. Springer, M.G.
PERKINS, James I. — January 14, 1838
  Frances W. Terrell — Vincent R. Thornton
PERKINS, John — December 30, 1819
  Nancy Ransom — John Harris
PERKINS, Nicholas — December 9, 1834
  Cecile Jackson — Albert R. Jackson
PERKINS, Nicholas — December 7, 1850
  Mary Dixon
PERKINS, Robert — March 4, 1806
  Sarah B. Johnson
PERKINS, William — January 30, 1805
  Polly Harp
PERKINS, William — January 28, 1816
  Nancy Davis — L. Bethune
PERMAN, William — May 2, 1867
  Maria J. E. Merritt — A. H. Smith
PERRY, Dickerson — February 23, 1825
  Eliza McMillan
PERRY, Robert H. — March 25, 1875
  Lucy A. Stone — James W. Godkin
PETEET, William E. — November 18, 1869
  Mary Ann Brown — J. M. Dickey, M.G.
PETERS, John — February 1, 1807
  Sally Haynes — William Greer
PETERSON, Josiah S. — June 6, 1844
  Matilda Manley — J. N. Glenn
PETTY, William H. — December 15, 1870
  Mattie D. Fambrough — Malone M. Landrum
PEURIFOY, Jackson B. — December 18, 1851
  Virginia A. Hutchinson — William Bryan
PEURIFOY, McCarrol — October 31, 1865
  Phebe Anderson — John W. McCrary, M.G.
PHARR, Ephraim — April 12, 1819
  Mary Mathews
PHELPS, Augustus B. — April 27, 1861
  Sabrina Brown — R. A. Houston
PHELPS, Henry — June 16, 1842
  Rebecca H. Bowden — N. H. Hill

PHELPS, Jackson — April 1, 1840 — John G. Holtzclaw
  Rebecca Hobbs
PHILEMON, Edmundson — December 21, 1815 — Lemuel Greene
  Nancy McGee
PHILLIPS, Abner — January 3, 1853 — Ephraim Bruce
  Ann B. Burford
PHILLIPS, Daniel — April 26, 1835 — William Rowland
  Parthenia Vaughn
PHILLIPS, Elbert — September 25, 1810 — James Holt
  Charlotte Howell
PHILLIPS, Elijah — September 29, 1805
  Tabitha Walker
PHILLIPS, Hardy — October 23, 1814 — Archibald Watts
  Rebekah Veazey
PHILLIPS, Henry — February 2, 1831 — Thomas Grimes
  Eliza Fuller
PHILLIPS, Jackson — December 23, 1873 — W. A. Partee
  Daney Connell
PHILLIPS, Jesse — December 27, 1821 — W. W. Moore
  Betsey Martin
PHILLIPS, Jonathon — January 24, 1800
  Betsy Howell
PHILLIPS, Thomas E. — December 22, 1870 — Rev. J. S. Patten
  Cary Ann Connell
PHILLIPS, Zacharih — July 18, 1850 — E. S. Hunter
  Mary Ann Richards
PHILLUPS, Lancelot — June 22, 1852 — J. F. Billingslea
  Martha Anne R. Mapp
PIERCE, Bartley — February 3, 1802
  Betsey Gilmore
PIERCE, Edmund — September 16, 1818 — W. Cone
  Louiza Took
PIERCE, John — April 13, 1790
  Margaret Moon
PIERCE, Lazerous — February 4, 1803
  Mary Smith
PIERCE, Lovick — September 27, 1809 — Josias Randle
  Ann Martin Foster
PIERCE, Matthew — October 30, 1836 — James Moore
  Nancy Bates
PIERCE, Wiley M. — August —, 1863 — Eugenius L. King
  Sarah E. Wright
PIERCE, Wyly — September 28, 1806 — Henry English
  Rebekah Harrell
PILGRIM, Green — August 26, 1855 — David R. Elder
  Nancy Ann Bryan
PIMM, Joseph — February 19, 1863 — R. A. Houston, M.G.
  Martha A. Paynter
PINTHART, John — December 17, 1807 — George Tuggle
  Judith Jett
PIPER, William — December 18, 1805
  Jane McMichael

PIPER, Zadick February 8, 1805
  Amy Bearden
PITMAN, Joel J. January 30, 1853
  Phenaley Emaline Peek Hart C. Peek
POESY, Bennett March 21, 1796
  Nancy Griffin
POLLARD, Brittian C. November 24, 1834
  Sarah E. Benham Vincent R. Thornton
POLLARD, Frederick September 23, 1819
  Mary Wright John Harris
POLLARD, James November 22, 1824
  Louisa King
POLLARD, Josiah November 20, 1866
  Susan L. Goodman
POLLARD, Stephen July 23, 1818
  Anna Willson John Harris
PONSONBRY, George July 6, 1803
  Catherine Howe
POOL, Gilmon July 3, 1807
  Janey Patrick Clabourn Maddox
POOLE, John March 15, 1840
  Martha Stovall Thomas Stocks
POPE, John Hardeman October 15, 1850
  Demarias Carter Hubbard N. M. Crawford
POPE, Littleberry December 15, 1865
  Martha A. Cockram
POPE, Willson December 8, 1818
  Nancy Rowland James Riley
PORTER, David O. November 27, 1855
  Elizabeth Anne Mays William English
PORTER, John November 28, 1799
  Mary Chesser
PORTER, Robert August 21, 1856
  Mrs. Willie Thompson J. G. Holtzclaw
POTTER, Charles February 13, 1868
  Sarah F. Worthy E. H. Burgess
POTTER, George Washington January 11, 1855
  Mary Thurmond W. A. Partee
POTTS, William October 25, 1788
  Isabel Simons
POULLAIN, Feliz November 11, 1841
  Evaline H. Foster George Pierce
POULLAIN, Thomas N. December 4, 1873
  Mildred P. Sanford C. H. Strickland
POWERS, Allinus February 16, 1872
  Eugenia A. Stewart
POWERS, Isaac November 22, 1839
  Mary Louisa Stovall John Harris
POWERS, John November 8, 1829
  Elizabeth Palmore Butt L. Cato
POWERS, William August 9, 1804
  Nancy Houghton

PRATT, James   August 3, 1857
  Susan Wellmaker   Larkin R. Sisson
PRATT, Thomas S.   October 11, 1853
  Lillian H. Logan   Robert Logan
PRESTON, James A.   March 1, 1860
  Cornelia C. Davis   T. J. Bowen
PRICE, Adam A.   December 28, 1854
  Emily Frances Jones   Vincent R. Thornton
PRICE, Enoch N.   December 1, 1859
  Nancy Colley   A. A. Jernigan
PRICE, Ephrum   August 28, 1828
  Elizabeth Sayers   Robert Booth
PRICE, Hansford   December 21, 1828
  Mary Cook   Ephraim Bruce
PRICE, James T.   July 30, 1854
  Mary A. Jones   I. A. Williams
PRICE, Theophilus A.   January 16, 1868
  Mary A. Clifton   W. H. Blythe
PRICE, William E.   January 23, 1842
  Alvina Anne Burkes   George Lumpkin
PRIDGES, Laurence (Alonzo) G.   February 1, 1855
  Susan Rhodes   W. W. Partee
PRIEST, Miles M.   December 9, 1875
  Emma Bennett   R. A. Credelle
PRIMROSE, James   November 19, 1822
  Sarah Moore   William Winfield
PRINCE, George   December 27, 1807
  Patsey Lawrence   W. M. Johnson
PRINCE, John   November 1, 1805
  Nancy Clark
PRIOR, Harden M.   November 3, 1836
  Nancy Montfort   Thomas Stocks
PRITCHELL, James   September 14, 1831
  Winney Cone   Benj. F. Martin
PRUDDEN, Sydney C.   March 30, 1843
  Isabella Simonton   Francis Bowman
PRYER, Jackson   July 7, 1844
  Sarah Waggoner   I. N. Wilson
PRYOR, Allen   September 18, 1799
  Elizabeth Cole
PRYOR, Marlow   September 12, 1816
  Mary Armor   Lovick Pierce
PUCKELL, John   October 3, 1811
  Tabitha Richards   Wm. McGiboney
PUGH, Bervy   January 7, 1874
  Martha J. Vine   W. A. Partee
PUGH, James   February 12, 1874
  Ann Vine   W. A. Partee
PULLEN, Sanford   January 10, 1828
  Susannah Pullen   John Harris
PURDEE, George   June 17, 1840
  Sarah Johnson

PURDEE, John — September 24, 1839
  Dimmy Hunt — P. C. Johnson, J.P.
PURDELL, John Thomas — July 12, 1869
  Sarah Frances Nunn — William K. Wilson
PURDUE, John T. — November 26, 1843
  Eliza F. Smith — James W. Godkin
PURKS, William — June 25, 1857
  Sarah E. M. King — Wm. M. Crumly, M.G.
PYRON, Charles — March 20, 1827
  Nancy Pyron — Joshua Cannon

Q

QUINN, Charles — February 6, 1801
  Dilly Houghton
QUINN, John C. — November 11, 1854
  Frances E. Branch

R

RABURN, Mathew — November 11, 1802
  Hannah Walls
RADEN, John — October 6, 1814
  Nancy Curry — John Browning
RADEN, J. N. — January 28, 1855
  Anita A. M. Dixon — B. E. Spencer
RADIN, George — January 22, 1829
  Elizabeth Ray — Elijah Holtzclaw
RAGAN, Ibzan — February 15, 1841
  Caroline Perkins — Vincent R. Thornton
RAGAN, John — December 21, 1789
  Susanna Battle
RAGAN, Moses — May 25, 1847
  Martha Newsom — Vincent R. Thornton
RAGARD, John — June 9, 1814
  Maria Harper — O. Porter
RAINEY, Etheldred — March 10, 1840
  Elizabeth Amanda Johnson — B. M. Sanders
RAINEY, John H. — August 31, 1871
  Mattie Lunsford — John R. Young
RAINEY, William J. — November 19, 1868
  Ella V. Sanford — J. M. Dickey, M.G.
RAINWATER, Charles A. — April 6, 1875
  Cornelia J. Veazey — J. H. Kilpatrick
RAINWATER, Joseph H. — December 28, 1875
  Letitia Williams — N. M. Jones, M.G.
RAINWATER, Lacy D. — September 5, 1846
  Dorothy Bell — R. F. Griffen
RAINWATER, W. T. — June 16, 1856
  Asthenath Wright — Greene Thompson
RALLS, Hector — December 22, 1814
  Nancy Atkinson — John Browning
RALLS, James H. — May 14, 1846
  Sarah Newsom — E. S. Hunter

RANDALL, Thomas W.   October 3, 1831
   Mirium Hunter   Thomas Stocks
RANDLE, Augustus Henry   July 27, 1836
   Emily Reid Asbury   Vincent R. Thornton
RANDLE, James G.   January 26, 1808
   Sally Coleman   Peter Early
RANDLE, J. W.   November 20, 1870
   Avarilla Boatsman   W. R. Wilson
RANDLE, Thomas   February 2, 1830
   Elizabeth E. Sanford
RANDLE, William C.   November 5, 1835
   Mary S. Hart   G. A. Chappell
RANKIN, Adam W.   June 11, 1828
   Sarah Burke   William Cone
RANKIN, David   January 27, 1823
   Mary Moore
RANKIN, James R.   May 13, 1837
   Eliza A. Irby   Peter C. Johnson
RANSOM, Joseph   June 26, 1818
   Patsey Carrel   Wm. McGiboney
RANSOM, Robert   July 26, 1807
   Polly Ransom   Francis Ross
RANSOM, Thomas H.   April 23, 1871
   Mrs. Nancy Price   J. M. Loury
RAY, Andrew   January 12, 1820
   Nancy Barker
RAY, Benjamin   December 29, 1822
   Elizabeth Bennett   John Bowles
RAY, Benjamin   April 6, 1848
   Sarah E. Lanham   T. M. Fambrough
RAY, David   September 18, 1827
   Elizabeth Jackson   Joshua Cannon
RAY, Emanuel   January 29, 1822
   Martha James   J. A. Leftwich
RAY, Isaac   February 19, 1825
   Elizabeth Sayers
RAY, John H.   August 23, 1852
   Sarah Ann Barksdale   B. Rowland
RAY, John T.   November 26, 1868
   Nannie S. Watts
RAY, Nimrod   March 22, 1825
   Polly Mays
RAY, Shadrach E.   September 11, 1860
   Delia A. Smith   William Bryan
RAY, William   November 13, 1807
   Mary Orr   William Greer
RAY, William   July 5, 1830
   Susannah Burk
RAY, William   November 17, 1836
   Mary Kennedy   Nathan Hobbs
REA, Benjamin F.   July 13, 1847
   Laura Gresham   Francis Bowman

REA, Robert	August 26, 1818
Jane Smith	
REA, Robert	December 27, 1821
Nancy Akins	O. Porter
READ, James	November 26, 1804
Rhoda Brown	
REDD, Albert G.	April 25, 1849
Henrietta E. Daniel	Francis Bowman
REDD, James	May 27, 1830
Mary Lewis	Lovick Pierce
REDDIN, James	October 9, 1816
Elizabeth Bledsoe	John Browning
REDDIN, James	April 30, 1818
Polly Nickelson	John Myrick
REDDING, Thomas	June 25, 1825
Mary Brockman	
REDMOND, John	August 6, 1871
Frances Aaron	W. C. Birchmore
REED, Freeman	December 10, 1835
Nancy Ray	Wm. H. Price
REED, James	February 6, 1842
Ann Bickers	Thomas Stocks
REED, Robert N.	June 15, 1865
Julia K. Brown	P. H. Mell, M.G.
REED, William	February 6, 1828
Nancy Jarrell	Hermon Mercer
REED, Zachariah	March 3, 1789
Ginney Adams	
REESE, Charles	April 15, 1830
Lucy Merriwether	M. Reed
REESE, Drury	June 11, 1849
Phidella Phillips	
REEVES, J. I.	July 24, 1840
Elizabeth M. Hodge	
REID, Felix C.	October 15, 1863
Sallie C. Lightfoot	J. M. Kilpatrick
REID, Reuben	December 15, 1788
Polly Alford	
REID, William T.	April 28, 1859
Mary A. E. Kendall	C. W. Key
REID, Zachariah	January 14, 1790
Polly Lawrence	
REYNOLDS, James	December 27, 1840
Lucretia Perkins	David Daniel
REYNOLDS, James	March 25, 1856
Eliza Wright	J. P. Duncan
REYNOLDS, James H.	November 12, 1867
Emily J. Stewart	W. R. Wilson
REYNOLDS, John	January 3, 1858
Cynthia S. Reynolds	T. Callahan
REYNOLDS, John	September 5, 1875
Martha J. Freeman	John S. Callaway

REYNOLDS, John C.   December 31, 1868
  Emma Moody   Wm. A. Overton
REYNOLDS, Levy   October 15, 1811
  Metsey Moore   Arthur Foster
REYNOLDS, Mordecai J.   May 29, 1858
  Ann A. Tuggle
REYNOLDS, Mordecai J.   September 5, 1865
  Electra A. Durham   William R. Wilson
REYNOLDS, William E.   July 20, 1875
  Lizzie A. Newton   Henry Newton
REID, Brice   February 15, 1821
  Sarah Tanner   John Harris
RHIMES, William   September 18, 1821
  May Wilkerson   Francis West
RHODES, A. S. W.   December 8, 1841
  Sarah Smith   Ephraim Bruce
RHODES, Henry   September 16, 1823
  Rebecah Day
RHODES, Henry   December 17, 1850
  Eliza Williams
RHODES, Johnson   April 2, 1855
  Martha Potter   I. R. Hall
RHODES, Johnson R.   January 11, 1868
  Caroline Horton   R. B. Kelley
RHODES, Martin V.   April 25, 1841
  Elizabeth Finley   I. M. Wilson
RHODES, Thomas   October 29, 1817
  Frances Gresham   Jesse Mercer
RHODES, Wiley   December 17, 1840
  Mararet Mitchell   Vincent R. Thornton
RHODES, Wiley A. T.   October 5, 1840
  Elizabeth Ann Patterson   S. G. Jenkins
RHODES, William   December 10, 1820
  Milly Evans   Mallichi Murden
RHODES, William C.   November 15, 1868
  Mary F. Gordon   James Davison
RICHARDS, Azaria   October 3, 1820
  Lelila Woods
RICHARDS, Calvus   August 12, 1873
  Myrtus Thornton   W. A. Overton
RICHARDS, Pickerel   November 30, 1799
  Hannah Beardin
RICHARDS, Terah   December 17, 1818
  Lucy Bates   John Harris
RICHARDS, William A.   September 9, 1851
  Savannah W. Ledbetter   John C. Merritt
RICHARDS, Willis   December 29, 1846
  Elizabeth Irby   I. A. Williams
RICHARDSON, James   July 1, 1807
  Betsey Kineman   John Mapp
RICHARDSON, Robert   January 2, 1831
  Nancy Carter   Butt L. Cato

RICHTER, Charles W., Jr.   September 12, 1866
  Mary L. Hunter   Philip B. Robinson
RIGHTS, John   November 6, 1804
  Rebeccah Panton
RILEY, Henry N.   May 14, 1851
  Lavina Bell
RILEY, James G.   June 8, 1843
  Mary F. Brunt   R. G. Griffin
RILEY, James G.   March 19, 1848
  Sarah Ann Sims Woodard   Hinton Crawford
RILEY, Joseph   April 2, 1811
  Betsey Smith   Robert Rea
RILEY, Thomas   January 10, 1808
  Sally Hill   George Smith
RILEY, Thomas P.   October 18, 1870
  Linnie Armor   J. M. Dickey
RILEY, William M.   January 8, 1835
  Louisa Ann Mallory   James Anderson
RISSEL, William   June 29, 1799
  —— McCulloch
ROAD, Benjamin   March 27, 1803
  Sally Whitlock
ROARKS, Joel   November 28, 1845
  Emily Wright   Ephraim Bruce
ROBARTS, David   December 20, 1818
  Eliza Green Robarts   A. Gresham
ROBERTS, Andrew   June 21, 1856
  Susan Bennett
ROBERTS, Frederick   November 12, 1826
  Martha Lewis   Abraham Baugh
ROBERTS, Jo   September 5, 1804
  Clarey Goode
ROBERTS, John   June 24, 1803
  Polly Milton
ROBERTS, Richard   September 13, 1804
  Sally Baker
ROBERTS, R. F. G.   May 10, 1846
  Nancy Meredith   J. B. Chappel
ROBERTS, William   December 30, 1801
  Frankey Samson
ROBERTS, William B.   December 22, 1842
  Emily Greer   Hinton Crawford
ROBERTSON, Jesse   March 6, 1820
  Mary Irby
ROBERTSON, John   April 13, 1832
  Jennett Evans   John Park
ROBERTSON, Willis   December 13, 1804
  Polly Coleman   Thomas Crawford
ROBERTSON, William   February 4, 1818
  Anny Stringfellow   O. Porter
ROBERTSON, Z.   January 2, 1800
  Susannah Bridges

ROBINS, Albert M.   April 5, 1859
  Dianah D. Walker   L. B. Jackson
ROBINS, James R.   April 29, 1873
  S. M. Wilkins   E. Heiat, M.G.
ROBINS, John   July 22, 1827
  Elizabeth Stoutamire   William Aston
ROBINS, Thomas S.   October 17, 1850
  Sarah A. Avery   James M. Kelly
ROBINS, William   October 23, 1827
  Sarah Williams   Nat. Harris
ROBINSON, Benjamin   November 14, 1815
  Narcisa Harris   Thomas Lyne
ROBINSON, Benjamin   August 11, 1868
  Martha Cochran   A. J. S. Jackson
ROBINSON, Benjamin   August 15, 1871
  S. M. Bruce   W. H Wright
ROBINSON, James   August 3, 1826
  Eliza Kicker   Reuben White
ROBINSON, John Pope   April 8, 1828
  Sarah Williams   E. Tally
ROBINSON, John Pope   January 9, 1873
  Julia Pearman   John P. Wagnon
ROBINSON, Joseph   August 25, 1836
  Martha Ellis   William L. Pullen
ROBINSON, Joseph W.   October 12, 1841
  Caroline B. Smith   F. R. Golding
ROBINSON, Lewellin   June 24, 1819
  Amelia Coleman   Lovick Pierce
ROBINSON, Phillip B.   October 26, 1858
  Mrs. Nancy T. Sweet   William J. Parks
ROBINSON, Milford   December 29, 1830
  Francina Parker   Mathew Winfield
ROBINSON, Thomas W.   June 25, 1861
  Mary E. Park   Albert Gray
ROBINSON, William H.   October 17, 1866
  Malinda Patrick   Lorenzo D. Carlton
ROBINSON, William H.   April 16, 1872
  Henrietta Bruce   John Dolvin
RODGERS, Andrew J.   December 24, 1872
  Mary J. Owens   John D. Copeland
ROGERS, Joel B.   February 22, 1872
  Lizzy Jones   John D. Copeland
ROGERS, John   January 23, 1802
  Mary Kizerk
ROSE, William   June 13, 1804
  Frankey Burch
ROSS, Samuel   February 23, 1815
  Polly McCombs   John Armor
ROUM, Charles   February 22, 1847
  Adelaid King   J. F. Billingslea
ROUNSEVALL, Robert   December 20, 1821
  Grace Finley   Francis Cummins

ROUZEL, Hiram — March 21, 1840
  Emaliza Williams — John G. Holtzclaw
ROWLAND, Charles R. — August 26, 1875
  Mattie Ledbetter — W. H. Blythe
ROWLAND, Barksdale — October 1, 1837
  Elizabeth Parrott — Lemuel T. Crossley
ROWLAND, David R. — December 22, 1868
  Cornelia Smith — W. H. Blythe, M.G.
ROWLAND, James — May 7, 1824
  Emily Jackson
ROWLAND, James — April 22, 1842
  Julia F. Hutcherson — James Godkin
ROWLAND, John — January 8, 1854
  Harriett Stines — B. Rowland
ROWLAND, John G. — December 1, 1857
  Sarah Virginia Cutwright — Wm. J. Park, M.G.
ROWLAND, John J. — November 15, 1849
  C. L. Hutcherson
ROWLAND, Jordan — May 17, 1797
  Sally Swan
ROWLAND, Jordan — July 12, 1829
  Lucinda Wright — William Bryan
ROWLAND, Wiley — October 12, 1826
  Elizabeth Akers — Jacob Riley
ROWLAND, William — January 26, 1819
  Mary Jackson — John Harris
ROWLAND, William, Sen. — February 23, 1862
  Winnie R. Newton — W. J. Cotter, M.G.
ROWLAND, William A. — December 13, 1859
  Sallie M. Hudson — O. L. Smith
ROWLAND, William D. — November 2, 1855
  Sarah F. R. Bryan — William Bryan
ROYSTON, John — January 6, 1803
  Polly Cesna
ROZIER, William — January 23, 1852
  Rhoda C. Drennon — J. T. Finley
RUARKS, Joel J. — July 11, 1858
  Mrs. Mary F. Hooks — L. B. Jackson
RUMNEY, James E. — January 2, 1868
  Mary E. Hendrey — L. D. Carlton
RUMIEL, Greenberry — March 2, 1805
  Polly Jones
RUNDLES, James — September 20, 1819
  Amy Willson
RUSSELL, Ignatious — July 20, 1801
  Eleanor Kimbrough
RUSSELL, Samuel H. — January 12, 1826
  Elizabeth Parrott — Benj. Gildersleeve
RUTLAND, Wiley — January 2, 1819
  Pamelia Chewning
RYAN, Haynes S. — September 8, 1836
  Mary M. Roberts — James Moore

RYE, Joseph July 10, 1790
　Betsey Wilson
RYLES, James G. January 13, 1852
　Mary E. Jones B. M. Sanders

S

SAMS, James October 2, 1828
　Adeline Wright
SAMSON, Robert June 29, 1805
　Polly Mosely
SAMSON, William June 27, 1806
　Delphy Clay
SANDERS, Alser February 27, 1805
　Elizabeth Newberry
SANDERS, George May 29, 1824
　Sarah Clarke
SANDERS, George January 28, 1825
　Polly Jones
SANDERS, James June 13, 1805
　Polly Hall
SANDERS, James Ragan January 4, 1842
　Cornelia M. Jones B. M. Sanders
SANDERS, John Q. July 4, 1833
　Cordelia E. Hard (Hart) Thomas Stocks
SANDERS, Thomas L. February 19, 1852
　Parmelia White F. W. Prior
SANDERS, William December 15, 1835
　Elizabeth Jenkins Thomas Stocks
SANDERS, Zadock December 12, 1819
　Holly Sayers Reuben White
SANDERSON, George W. March 30, 1866
　Eugenia H. Sayers H. C. Peek, M.G.
SANFORD, Ben August 11, 1805
　Jimmy Armor
SANFORD, Henry April 2, 1840
　Susan Ann Smith Thomas Stocks
SANFORD, Shelton P. July 30, 1840
　Maria F. Dickerman Otis Smith
SANFORD, William March 11, 1805
　Polly Harris
SANFORD, William July 3, 1814
　Sally B. Darnel Nicholas Lewis
SANKEY, Dr. John T. ———, 1801
　Anna Daniel
SANKEY, Richard O. May 4, 1854
　Mary M. Watts S. G. Hillyer
SANKEY, Dr. Richard T. October 20, 1831
　Frances Love J. N. Glenn, M.G.
SANKEY, William D. March 2, 1824
　Margaret Daniel
SAPP, Richard H. August 24, 1852
　Sarah M. Kellam N. M. Crawford, M.G.

SARGEANT, John C.   February 15, 1852
  Nancy Anne Bruce   B. Rowland
SAXON, Lewis W.   October 8, 1867
  Eliza Parnell   E. A. Burgess
SAYERS, David   September 15, 1804
  Elizabeth Robinson
SAYERS, James M.   November 24, 1825
  Delana Richards
SAYERS, James M.   January 8, 1835
  Nancy A. Lucky   James Moore
SAYERS, John S.   March 3, 1834
  Frances Price   G. W. West
SAYERS, Joshua L.   November 18, 1834
  Permelia Ansley   James F. Hillyer
SCAMPER, Daniel   April 1, 1803
  Polly Finley
SCOGGINS, John   April 15, 1829
  Mary Ann Nelms   Robert Burdell
SCOGGINS, John T.   December 14, 1826
  Mary Forrester
SCOTT, James N.   December 12, 1856
  Mary J. Bowles
SCOTT, John T.   September 2, 1834
  Ann B. Cartwright   Thomas W. Grimes
SCOTT, Pulaskie S.   May 1, 1838
  Charity N. Grimes   Francis Bowman
SCUDDER, Samuel C.   November 13, 1848
  Eunice Safford   H. Safford
SEALS, Henry   November 3, 1827
  Angelina Carrel
SEALS, John H.   October 1, 1857
  Mary E. Sanders   William Williams
SELF, James E.   September 8, 1850
  Artemisa Jordan   Daniel Hightower
SELF, William   March 11, 1828
  Matilda Knowles   William Austin
SESSIONS, Jeremiah M.   November 5, 1856
  Sarah E. Porter   W. H. C. Cone
SEYMORE, Evabon   April 10, 1822
  Lucy E. M. Wingfield   Francis Cummins
SEYMOUR, Henry C.   April 20, 1841
  Anne Cornelia Wingfield
SHACKELFORD, Charles   October 5, 1836
  Rebecca Elizabeth Hunter   Jonathan Davis
SHACKELFORD, Josephus   April 18, 1855
  Cordelia Stowe   L. R. L. James
SHACKELFORD, Lloyd   January 20, 1869
  Ida J. Mitchell   J. J. Brantley
SHANNON, William   October 1, 1820
  Margaret Nickelson   Lovick Pierce
SHARKLEY, Silas   December 23, 1818
  Dorcas Tait

SHARP, Benjamin   January 25, 1843
  Martha Jackson   B. M. Sanders
SHARP, John   June 12, 1801
  Sally Peeples
SHARP, Martial   November 30, 1819
  Matilda McGuire
SHARP, Richard   May 11, 1815
  Polly Guinn   Wm. McGiboney
SHARP, Robert   February 15, 1818
  Lucindia Newell   Thomas Johnson
SHAW, Creytin   August 7, 1870
  Caroline Barnes   W. C. Birchmore
SHAW, James E.   December 13, 1868
  Josephine M. Davis   Wm A. Overton
SHAW, John   November 18, 1818
  Della Findley   L. Bethune
SHAW, Samuel   December 28, 1869
  Emma Roe   James W. Godkin
SHEATS, Benajah   July 23, 1838
  Mary Ann Richardson   Thomas Grimes
SHED, Prelow   March 20, 1861
  Nancy Nichols
SHED, William   July 4, 1860
  Amanda M. Parks   R. B. Kelly
SHELL, Reuben R.   January 2, 1843
  Jane Lucas
SHELL, T. I.   December 9, 1846
  Clarissa Bruce   L. A. Williams
SHELTON, George W.   October 5, 1858
  Mary Ann Morris   J. H. Wragg
SHELTON, John L.   December 8, 1864
  Rebecca A. Sidwell   James W. Godkin
SHERIDAN, Dennis   May 24, 1815
  Polly Riley   Robert Rea
SHERIDAN, R. W.   March 7, 1852
  Lucienda Shell   B. Rowland
SHERLEY, Richmond   June 10, 1820
  Delila Blythe   Wm. McGiboney
SHERRELL, Littleberry   March 9, 1825
  Elizabeth Bedell
SHERWOOD, Adial   May 18, 1821
  Ann Early
SHEY, Samuel   September 3, 1846
  Mary B. Crawford   Wm. I. Parks, M.G.
SHIELDS, William   August 25, 1801
  Catherine Cone
SHIPP, John H.   December 27, 1866
  Elizabeth O'Neal   John C. Merritt
SHIPP, Lemuel   July 18, 1844
  Elizabeth Peek   James Moore
SHIPP, Stephen   May 15, 1834
  Luciena Irby   James Moore

SHIRLING, James N.   September 12, 1841
   Martha Anne Peek   Ephraim Bruce
SHIRLING, Rabun W.   December 29, 1846
   Mary Ann Gaston   R. F. Griffen
SHIRLING, Richard   August 3, 1855
   Rebecca W. Lewis   William Bryan
SHIRLING, Richard   July 6, 1858
   Nancy Lewis   William Bryan
SHIVERS, Thomas J.   February 25, 1836
   Sarah Ann Martin   George F. Pierce
SHOCKLEY, Benjamin   December 28, 1819
   Patsy Gatlin
SHROPSHIRE, James H.   December 17, 1805
   Sally Henly
SHROPSHIRE, Joshua   December 1, 1822
   Elizabeth Booles   William Greer
SHROPSHIRE, Wesley   January 5, 1826
   Nancy Swanson
SHY, William H.   November 23, 1868
   Eliza May Bowden
SIDWELL, John   June 10, 1866
   Sallie E. Bruce   Lucious C. Broome
SIGNAW, Thomas   May 30, 1805
   Betsey Daniell
SILVEY, Hinton C.   November 8, 1864
   Sarah Jane Holder
SIMMONS, Charles   November 20, 1793
   Polly Parker
SIMMONS, Charles J.   December 25, 1836
   Nancy Little   Mathew Oliver
SIMMONS, Frank M.   December 30, 1860
   Mary Styans   J. M. Kelly
SIMMONS, Franklin   July 23, 1856
   Susan Channell
SIMMONS, Henry S.   June 15, 1833
   Aseneth Parker   J. P. Leveritt
SIMMONS, Jack   August 7, 1821
   Polly Leonard   H. G. Slaughter
SIMMONS, Simeon   December 30, 1828
   Nancy Parrott
SIMMONS, Stephens   July 31, 1823
   Matilda Leonard   Thos. W. Slaughter
SIMMS, Frederick   April 3, 1804
   Sally Baine
SIMONTON, Ezekiel   January 17, 1816
   Sophia Greer   William Cone
SIMONTON, Joel   September 7, 1814
   Sarah Powers   Archibald Watts
SIMONTON, John A.   October 18, 1843
   Catherine A. Jossey   W. D. Martin, M.G.
SIMONTON, Thomas   March 14, 1787
   Rebecca Potts

SIMPSON, William H.   December 29, 1865
  Sarah J. Hancock   Lorenzo D. Carlton
SIMS, A. F.   April 1, 1855
  Lavinia Williams   J. F. Thrasher, Jr.
SIMS, John M.   November 29, 1824
  Beheathalon Grigsby
SIMS, William   June 26, 1822
  Falbra Richards
SINCLAIR, William F. M.   February 27, 1868
  Camilla J. Rowles
SINGLETON, Joseph   January 4, 1825
  Mary Ann Terrell
SKIDMORE, Crosley S.   May 21, 1843
  Eliza W. Smith   Vincent R. Thornton
SLADEN, Arthur   January 29, 1825
  Frances Evans
SLAUGHTER, George   October 8, 1818
  Susannah Copeland
SLAUGHTER, Henry G.   December 14, 1815
  Elizabeth Kimbrough   Gilly Moore
SLAUGHTER, John   November 8, 1803
  Elizabeth Sayers
SLAUGHTER, John   September 27, 1827
  Temperance Harris   Francis Cummins
SLAUGHTER, Raney S.   November 22, 1838
  Nancy L. Credille   Nathan Oliver
SLAUGHTER, Reuben   August 19, 1789
  Polly Lawson
SLAUGHTER, Thomas   December 7, 1815
  Nancy Lewis   Walker Lewis
SLAUGHTER, William   December 16, 1796
  Nancy Kimbrough
SMALLWOOD, James   December 8, 1850
  Mary O'Neal
SMITH, Alexander H.   December 12, 1833
  Elizabeth L. Blythe   William Bryan
SMITH, Alexander H.   January 18, 1871
  Sallie F. Swann   Thos. F. Pierce
SMITH, Azariah   January 5, 1871
  Celestia Brooks   L. D. Caldwell
SMITH, Burgess   June 3, 1875
  Eleva Carlton   Clement A. Evans
SMITH, Daniel N.   April 25, 1848
  Sophronia Ann Channel   W. F. Gaston
SMITH, Ebenezzer   March 12, 1818
  Cynthia Lewis   John Harris
SMITH, George N.   September 16, 1873
  Sarah C. Bryan   James L. Pierce
SMITH, George W.   January 19, 1864
  Leonora McCommons   John R. Young, M.G.
SMITH, Hilliard A.   December 18, 1866
  Mary E. F. Tarpley   Jefferson F. Wright

SMITH, Isaac   August 28, 1806
  Eliza Moore   A. Hays
SMITH, Isaac   January 28, 1819
  Mary Martin   Reuben White
SMITH, Isaac   July 28, 1852
  Elizabeth Kelly   A. L. Willis
SMITH, Isaac F.   January 31, 1867
  Susan A. Phelps   Thomas J. Peek
SMITH, Isaac H.   September 11, 1866
  Eliza Ruark   William Bryan
SMITH, Isaac H.   February 11, 1873
  Amanda M. Smith   N. M. Jones
SMITH, James   October 4, 1824
  Rebecca Winfield
SMITH, James   December 19, 1833
  Jane E. Houghton   C. T. Beeman
SMITH, James, Jr.   July 31, 1842
  Patience Atkinson   Hartwell H. Lawrence
SMITH, James   June 1, 1845
  Mary Anderson   R. F. Griffen
SMITH, James   November 30, 1868
  M. Fredonia Smith
SMITH, James C.   December 8, 1868
  Fredonia Credille   W. H. Blythe
SMITH, James D.   July 31, 1866
  Mary Jane Oliver   L. O. Carlton
SMITH, James H.   January 22, 1874
  Anna L. J. Hendry   W. A. Overton
SMITH, James M.   December 16, 1875
  Mattie N. Moreland   L. D. Caldwell
SMITH, James R.   November 26, 1850
  Edna Cheak   James M. Kelly
SMITH, James W.   October 14, 1852
  Caroline M. Swindell   J. W. Yarbrough
SMITH, Jedeah   September 5, 1822
  Flora Williams   John Harris
SMITH, Jeremiah   October 4, 1818
  Mary Peters   John Willson
SMITH, Joel   May 6, 1847
  Frances McLellan   William Bryan
SMITH, John   February 15, 1810
  Milly Hightower   W. McGiboney
SMITH, John   April 1, 1812
  Harriet Park
SMITH, John   March 14, 1839
  Elizabeth Catherine Oliver   Ephraim Bruce
SMITH, John   December 14, 1848
  Martha A. Miller   Francis Bowman
SMITH, John F.   June 1, 1858
  Mary A. Hargrove   L. R. L. Jennings
SMITH, Nathan   March 30, 1815
  Fanny Smith   Robert Rea

SMITH, Nathaniel	November 24, 1808
Elizabeth Hutson	Henry English
SMITH, Reddick	December 20, 1811
Polly Hall	A. Veazey
SMITH, Reddick	January 11, 1816
Mary Clarke	Robert Rea
SMITH, Reuben C.	November 21, 1836
Sarah Kimbrough	
SMITH, Richard A.	October 9, 1860
Susan R. Smith	A. Gray, M.G.
SMITH, Thomas	November 21, 1817
Anna Peters	John Williams
SMITH, Thomas	April 22, 1847
Patience Smith	James W. Godkin
SMITH, Thomas H.	November 19, 1840
Emily A. Perdue	James Jones
SMITH, William	February 6, 1802
Betsey Holland	
SMITH, William C.	January 25, 1859
Lavinia A. Swinney	W. J. Parks, M.G.
SMITH, William G.	March 6, 1845
Patience Smith	William Bryan
SMITH, William T.	June 26, 1866
Susan M. E. Armor	Albert Gray, M.G.
SMITH, Young	December 28, 1814
Rebekah Channel	James Baldwin
SMITH, Youngset	April 18, 1816
Elizabeth Smith	Thomas Snow
SNEED, William	November 24, 1836
Caroline Scoggins	Nathan Hobbs
SNOW, John P.	January 24, 1819
Susannah Smith	Osborne Rogers
SNOW, Samuel G.	December 18, 1807
Polly Copeland	J. Holt
SORRELL, George	November 16, 1799
Sally Cameron	
SORROW, Joseph C.	February 2, 1869
Sarah E. Allen	John C. Merritt
SORROW, Nicholas	September 2, 1866
Sidney E. A. Nickelson	Jefferson F. Wright
SOUTHALL, Hollman	January 21, 1819
Nancy Greer	
SOUTHERLAND, John	April 17, 1808
Sally Hobbs	Henry English
SPARKS, James	May 8, 1815
Susan Meadows	Malichi Murden
SPARKS, Thomas H.	February 20, 1845
Ann Linton	
SPENCER, John	November 17, 1804
Fanny Whatley	
SPENCER, Levi	November 25, 1822
Rebecca DeLoach	

SPINKS, Henry N.   April 24, 1861
   Anna E. Miller   R. A. Houston
SPIVEY, Francis M.   October 6, 1859
   Irena Saxon   J. M. Kelly
SPIVEY, William   October 10, 1831
   Amey Batchelor   George Hall
SPIVEY, William H.   February 25, 1874
   Effie J. Armor   Albert Gray, M.G.
SPRADLING, James   January 7, 1805
   Sally McMurray
SPRADLING, William   February 15, 1804
   Hannah McMurray
SPURLOCK, John   November 26, 1815
   Judith Blackmon   Alex. Johnson
STACK, Henry H.   December 24, 1865
   Eliza Reynolds   Thos. F. Pierce
STALLINGS, John E.   March 11, 1819
   Mary Bass   O. Porter
STALLINGS, Moses   January 8, 1827
   Mary Mabry
STALLINGS, Wilson   July 14, 1822
   Susanna Smith   H. P. Mabry
STANDIFER, Jesse   November 19, 1799
   Elizabeth Houghton
STANFORD, George   November 25, 1874
   Indiana Treadway   Hart C. Peek
STANLEY, Isaac   January 1, 1802
   Nancy Hough
STANLEY, Thomas   March 26, 1857
   Margaret A. E. Oliver   Hart C. Peek
STANLEY, William T.   August 3, 1856
   Martha A. Irby   T. J. Beck
STANLY, James   June 27, 1806
   Amy Ellis
STANTAMIN, Newell   March 15, 1821
   Elizabeth Tally   John Beattie
STAPP, Stephen   September 15, 1825
   Sarah Curry   Robert Booth
STARR, Elijah   April 15, 1805
   Hannah Townsend
STATHAM, Memory   July 28, 1826
   Malissa Campbell
STEELE, Alexander   June 8, 1804
   Polly Harper
STELL, Archibald   June 7, 1855
   Sarah Sanders   B. Rowland
STEPHENS, Henry   May 20, 1839
   Matilda Stephens   W. L. Strain
STEPHENS, Jesse   November 22, 1842
   Mary Jane Irby   James Moore
STEPHENS, John   November 23, 1841
   Charlotte Bragg   James Moore

STEPHENS, Silas August 18, 1842
  Illisa Rankin F. R. Golding, M.G.
STEPHENS, Walter May 27, 1840
  Sarah Ann O'Neal James Moore
STEPHENS, William August 2, 1825
  Henrietta Ogletree Horatio Nunnelly
STEPHENSON, Thomas August 18, 1818
  Sarah Rounsavale John Harris
STERLING, Jenkins I. June 4, 1833
  Sevener Ann Borders Reuben Thornton
STEVENS, Edmund February 4, 1810
  Mary Goss W. McGiboney
STEVENS, John December 26, 1803
  Patsey Parker
STEVENS, John November 30, 1854
  Mary Christopher Daniel Hightower
STEVENS, Rollin W. December 18, 1860
  Mary A. Greene Albert Gray, M.G.
STEVENSON, Stephen W. November 14, 1835
  Mary J. Jenkins
STEWART, Frederick December 30, 1847
  Margaret Nelson James Moore
STEWART, George March 10, 1859
  E. Augusta Weaver W. J. Parks, M.G.
STEWART, William D. August 14, 1845
  Martha Ann Stovall Hinton Crawford
STILLMAN, Samuel December 22, 1829
  Nancy R. Harris Thomas Sanford
STIMSON, William October 25, 1824
  Elizabeth Anderson
STISHER, Solomon June 18, 1822
  Mary Bays Chesley Brislow
STOCKS, John May 14, 1800
  Nancy Fitzpatrick
STOCKS, Thomas November 26, 1848
  Frances A. Davis P. H. Mell
STOKES, John G. December 14, 1856
  Anna M. Matthews John P. Duncan, M.G.
STONE, John T. November 7, 1850
  Mary Anne Daniel James W. Godkin
STONE, Hardy June 19, 1815
  Jenny Bankenship W. McGiboney
STONE, John W. October 26, 1865
  Effie L. Carson R. A. Houston
STOVALL, John December 22, 1830
  Martha M. Pryor John Park, J.P.
STOVALL, Littleberry June 14, 1819
  Mary Buchannon L. Bethune
STOVALL, Powhattan November 15, 1824
  Temperance Bishop
STOVALL, Powhattan November 14, 1827
  Sarah Ann Crawford

STOVALL, William H.　　　　　　　October 29, 1874
　Sallie K. Bunkley　　　　　　　　J. H. Kilpatrick
STRAIN, W. W.　　　　　　　　　　October 28, 1799
　Sally Spruce
STRANGE, James W.　　　　　　　　August 25, 1864
　Margaret McLellan　　　　　　　　R. A. Houston, M.G.
STRICKLAND, James K.　　　　　　　April 9, 1864
　Susan E. Rhymes
STRICKLAND, C. C. O.　　　　　　　February 4, 1872
　M. G. A. Chandler　　　　　　　　W. T. Foster
STROUD, John　　　　　　　　　　October 13, 1787
　Sarah Phillips
STROZIER, Reuben I.　　　　　　　December 13, 1846
　Mary W. Wright　　　　　　　　　W. J. Parks
STUBBLEFIELD, Gustavus　　　　　　April 3, 1828
　Eliza Perry　　　　　　　　　　　William Winfield
STURDIVANT, George W.　　　　　　February 16, 1854
　Frances Z. Y. Nelson　　　　　　　Daniel Hightower
STURGIS, Charles M.　　　　　　　April 14, 1868
　Martha C. Thornton　　　　　　　William A. Overton
SWAIN, John　　　　　　　　　　　October 14, 1831
　Mary Whitlock
SWANN, George　　　　　　　　　　December 21, 1819
　Elizabeth Baker
SWANN, John　　　　　　　　　　　December 22, 1819
　Elizabeth Musgrove
SWANN, John W.　　　　　　　　　April 20, 1848
　Lucy P. Jernigan　　　　　　　　W. H. Evans
SWANN, Joseph　　　　　　　　　　May 17, 1804
　Anne Surnden
SWANSON, Graves　　　　　　　　　December 8, 1808
　Sally C. Brown　　　　　　　　　George Tuggle
SWANSON, Graves　　　　　　　　　March 18, 1819
　Nancy Wilkinson　　　　　　　　　John Browning
SWEET, James F.　　　　　　　　　January 18, 1854
　Nancy J. Park　　　　　　　　　　N. M. Crawford, M.G.
SWINDALL, Daniel　　　　　　　　　March 6, 1828
　Eunice Ward　　　　　　　　　　William Bryan
SWINDALL, Thomas　　　　　　　　June 17, 1837
　Mary Curtwright
SWINDLE, Thomas　　　　　　　　　August 7, 1832
　Levina Curtwright　　　　　　　　Samuel Curtwright
SWINNEY, Henry　　　　　　　　　December 21, 1819
　Martha Lasseter　　　　　　　　　John Park
SWINNEY, Jothram　　　　　　　　November 5, 1827
　Nancy McIntosh　　　　　　　　　Thomas Grimes
SWINNEY, Marcus　　　　　　　　　February 17, 1824
　Dianah Jackson
SWINNEY, William　　　　　　　　　February 20, 1819
　Peggy Moore

T

TALBOT, James Sarah Ann Phillips	November 26, 1829 J. W. Glenn, M.G.
TALLEY, William L. S. Nancy R. Smith	September 6, 1838 James W. Godkin
TALLY, Elkanah Sarah Anderson	February 1, 1821 John Simmons
TALLY, Nathan Catherine Sagar	January 22, 1819 D. L. McBride
TALLY, Nathan Martha Travis	February 6, 1851 Hinton Crawford
TALLY, Thomas Lucy Tippett	November 12, 1822 George Watkins
TANNER, Floyd Judith Tanner	November 1, 1810 Robert Rea
TANNER, Jesse Martha Ware	February 27, 1820 A. Hutchinson
TAPPAN, A. B. Anne A. Wright	February 21, 1854 Daniel Hightower
TAPPAN, Alexander Adelaine Wright	December 8, 1850 J. C. Simmons
TAPPAN, Randolph Eliza Ely	March 22, 1861 A. Gray, M.G.
TAPPAN, Samuel W. Cornelia Merritt	January 16, 1873 J. L. Pierce
TARPLEY, Archibald Ann Lee	October 24, 1811 Thomas Stocks
TARPLEY, Archibald Nancy M. Tunnell	July 18, 1866 John W. Talley
TARPLEY, Augustus Genette Broughton	October 19, 1843 B. M. Sanders
TARPLEY, John Jane Bowden	February 21, 1839 Hinton Crawford
TARPLEY, John L. Mary F. Bryan	September 30, 1861
TARWATER, James S. Rebecca Phelps	November 20, 1847 B. M. Sanders
TATTUM, Joel Polly Price	November 9, 1808 Stephen Gatlin
TAYLOR, Abraham Elizabeth Peeler	May 17, 1818 James Hall
TAYLOR, Archibald C. Eliza Head	October 26, 1831 Matthew Winfield
TAYLOR, Archibald Martha Dean	August 20, 1844 Matthew Winfield
TAYLOR, Brantley Ellen Smith	September 29, 1870 W. C. Birchmore
TAYLOR, Henry Martha Ann Houghton	August 1, 1822 Lovick Pierce
TAYLOR, James Charity Howard	December 8, 1831 Thomas J. Park

TAYLOR, John   March 6, 1853
  Martha Kirkley   J. R. Hall
TAYLOR, John   February 11, 1866
  Susan Herron   Wm. M. Chapman
TAYLOR, Rudolph   December 22, 1874
  Nancy Andrews   J. H. Kilpatrick, M.G.
TAYLOR, Samuel S.   December 20, 1855
  Esther E. Williams   T. R. Morgan, M.G.
TAYLOR, Seaborn H.   May 8, 1865
  Fatima Smith
TAYLOR, Semion   January 5, 1832
  Elizabeth Ann Carr   A. Perkins
TAYLOR, Thomas   September 29, 1819
  Sarah Maddox   Thomas Johnson
TEMPLER, Stuart   November 30, 1799
  Frances Fitzpatrick
TERRY, William   July 4, 1804
  Prudy Wester
THAXTON, Daniel   June 27, 1875
  Mary English   James M. Griffen
THAXTON, James   September 21, 1825
  Polly Lindsey   John Hatchett
THAXTON, James N.   January 2, 1862
  Sarah N. Nash
THAXTON, Jeremiah   December 29, 1836
  Mary Booles   John G. Holtzclaw
THAXTON, Nathaniel   September 28, 1815
  Susan Lindsey   Lemuel Greene
THAXTON, Simon   January 15, 1823
  Nancy Lindsey   Robert Newsome
THOMAS, James H.   November 19, 1850
  Avarilla Harper   Thomas Scott
THOMAS, John   November 1, 1823
  Caroline M. Gregory
THOMAS, John   December 4, 1827
  Sarah Ann Hunter   Rev. Anderson Ray
THOMAS, John I.   August 25, 1853
  Claudia F. McKinley   Nathan Hoyt
THOMAS, Seth   December 19, 1826
  Ruthy Ashley Furlow   David Terrell
THOMAS, William   December 21, 1789
  Polly Richardson
THOMAS, William   July 28, 1831
  Susan E. Burke   Thomas W. Grimes
THOMAS, William   July 27, 1858
  Lucy Ann Harper   J. H. Wragg
THOMPSON, George   November 5, 1837
  Rebecca Greene   John G. Holtzclaw
THOMPSON, Henry B.   November 9, 1865
  Mrs. Mary J. Seals
THOMPSON, Hiram   November 10, 1835
  Emily Evans   Mathew Winfield

THOMPSON, James   August 17, 1814
  Eliza Jane Harn   Nicholas Lewis
THOMPSON, James   February 4, 1818
  Christian Collocan   O. Porter
THOMPSON, James   October 22, 1820
  Elizabeth Penny   A. Hutchinson
THOMPSON, Jeremiah   September 9, 1828
  Elizabeth Edmundson   James Park
THOMPSON, John   December 20, 1821
  Nancy Conyers   Jack Lumpkin
THOMPSON, Joseph   December 20, 1827
  Nancy Greer   Isaac Brockman
THOMPSON, Joseph M.   July 15, 1841
  Nancy B. Lucas   H. Bridges
THOMPSON, Matthew   October 8, 1803
  Lydia Goldsby
THOMPSON, Moody   January 31, 1824
  Elizabeth Thompson
THOMPSON, Moses   November 4, 1828
  Matilda Ray   John Armstrong
THOMPSON, Richard M.   May 6, 1834
  Martha Hubbard   Thos. B. Thompson
THOMPSON, Samuel   February 22, 1805
  Polly Sumsden
THOMPSON, Thomas   December 14, 1819
  Mary Murrah   A. Hutchinson
THOMPSON, Thomas   January 28, 1844
  Susanna Woodard   I. M. Wilson
THOMPSON, Thomas B.   January 4, 1841
  Margaret Finley
THOMPSON, Thomas H.   December 24, 1846
  Elizabeth Lucas   A. G. Hutchinson
THOMPSON, William   November 30, 1799
  Mary Patrick
THOMPSON, William A.   May 11, 1852
  Mary Genett Safford   Francis Bowman
THOMPSON, William F.   October 2, 1839
  Sarah Elizabeth Jones   Francis S. Colley
THORNBURY, William   July 27, 1827
  Sarah Bryan
THORNTON, Henry C.   May 20, 1861
  Laura Beasley
THORNTON, Jesse   April 27, 1847
  Mary Holtzclaw   Vincent R. Thornton
THORNTON, Jesse M.   August 6, 1861
  Mrs. Catherine D. Dickinson
THORNTON, Joe F.   January 19, 1871
  Annie Foster Pierce   George W. Yarbrough
THORNTON, Otis S.   September 5, 1865
  Elizabeth Heard   John R. Young, M.G.
THORNTON, Richard   March 25, 1828
  Elizabeth B. Eley

THORNTON, Samuel
  Margaret Reid
THORNTON, Vincent
  Phereba Lynes
THORNTON, William R.
  Zymonia A. Randle
THRASHER, Alexander B.
  Mary Ann Smith
THRASHER, Early W.
  Martha S. Oliver
THRASHER, John F.
  Mary A. Rowland
TIGNER, Hope H.
  Liza Ann Glenn
TIGNER, Philip
  Nancy Hall
TILLER, Martin
  Temperance Newsom
TINDAL, W.
  Martha Harris
TIPPETT, Frederick
  Nancy Hubbard
TIPPETT, John
  Matilda Cartwright
TIPPETT, William
  Fathax Wilkinson
TIPPIN, Noah
  Lucy Lindsey
TODD, John H.
  Eliza F. King
TORBERT, Benjamin F.
  Mary E. Bacon
TORBERT, John Q.
  Mary A. Jones
TORBERT, Samuel A.
  Jane E. Walker
TORRENCE, Ebenezer
  Louisa Beard
TORRENCE, John
  Mary Bledsoe
TOUCHSTONE, William
  Georgia Stevens
TOWNS, Benjamin
  Mahala Hunter
TOWNS, Drury
  Ann Sankey
TOWNS, Drury
  Sarah Watson
TOWNS, John W.
  Elizabeth Lyne
TOWNSEND, Duncan C.
  Lenora Clayton

March 6, 1823
Herman Mercer
July 23, 1827
Jonathon Davis
December 27, 1859

August 17, 1851
William Bryan
September 24, 1854
Hart C. Peek
April 4, 1850
Hinton Crawford
January 13, 1819
Lovick Pierce
February 1, 1794

January 20, 1853
Vincent R. Thornton
December 21, 1789

November 27, 1821
A. N. Scott
June 2, 1836
James W. Godkin
November 22, 1825
John Harris
February 3, 1833
Thomas W. Grimes
February 17, 1827

December 5, 1871
W. D. Atkinson, M.G.
May 31, 1864
P. M. W. Arnold, M.G.
April 14, 1870
Philip Robinson
January 19, 1830
Lovick Pierce
July 8, 1819
Lovick Pierce
May 11, 1871
W. C. Birchmore
April 6, 1823
Herman Mercer
October 17, 1814

February 9, 1828
Augustine Greene
December 30, 1824

May 23, 1872
R. W. B. Elliot

TOWNSING, Anderson C.	January 24, 1809
Betsey Ann Barnet	
TOWNSON, William	May 21, 1807
Betsey Shropshire	George Tuggle
TREADWAY, Elijah	December 3, 1820
Rachael Sweeney	John Parks
TRIBBLE, John	March 28, 1845
Nancy A. Anderson	
TRIP, James M.	December 17, 1835
Rhoda H. Rowland	A. Hutcheson
TRUIT, Jobe	January 26, 1804
Ellivia Besbit	
TUCKER, Jeremiah	January 10, 1818
Alice Hunt	
TUCKER, Jeremiah	December 2, 1821
Tabatha Houghton	Robert Newsom
TUCKER, John	December 31, 1818
Mary Daniel	Thomas Stocks
TUCKER, Treuheart	April 10, 1808
Judith Hall	George Tuggle
TUGGLE, Augustus See	December 3, 1840
Sarah Ann Haynes	Neville Lumpkin
TUGGLE, Augustus W.	January 21, 1868
Martha Brimberry	William A. Overton
TUGGLE, E. B.	November 29, 1869
M. E. Bledsoe	W. A. Overton, M.G.
TUGGLE, G. H.	July 7, 1872
Dora Overton	Henry Newton, M.G.
TUGGLE, Hillard	December 7, 1815
Nancy Henley	
TUGGLE, Leonard	December 7, 1815
Nancy Henley	Thomas Lyne
TUGGLE, Littleberry	December 19, 1837
Mary Ann McWhorter	Jack Lumpkin, M.G.
TUNNEL, Jesse W.	September 6, 1857
Martha A. Heard	T. J. Beck, M.G.
TUNNISON, William C.	October 23, 1874
Sallie E. Comer	Albert Gray
TURNER, A.	March 15, 1806
Jenny Ransome	
TURNER, Boswell	June 8, 1801
Virtuous Love	
TURNER, David	March 16, 1796
Francina Veazey	
TURNER, David	January 12, 1830
Nancy Credille	William Bryan
TURNER, Eli	February 13, 1816
Rebekah Baker	William Cone
TURNER, Henry C.	September 8, 1859
Louisa J. O'Rear	A. A. Jernigan
TURNER, James	September 8, 1811
Elizabeth Cox	A. Gresham

TURNER, James W.   March 19, 1839
  Mary Jane Grimes   M. P. Peurifoy
TURNER, Jarrell L.   July 5, 1855
  Rebecca Slaughter   William Bryan
TURNER, John   December 1, 1824
  Lorinor Dawson
TURNER, Reuben T.   May 29, 1835
  Phebe Ann Bishop   James W. Godkin
TURNER, S. S.   October 4, 1855
  Penelope F. Gatlin   J. M. Kelly
TURNER, Thomas   December 5, 1833
  Lurana Credille   C. D. Teurnfog
TUTT, George C.   September 15, 1873
  Annie McDaniel   James L. Pierce
TYLER, Alexander   February 4, 1822
  Martha Catchings   William Winfield
TYLER, Robert   November 1, 1865
  Mary E. Crutchfield   S. J. Pinkerton
TYLER, Willis   September 3, 1819
  Sallie Jackson

U

UMPHREY, Erastus   December 21, 1834
  Matilda Olephant   Joseph Roberts
UNDERWOOD, Benjamin F.   January 14, 1845
  Elizabeth Veazey   Wooten O'Neal
UNDERWOOD, Daniel   July 19, 1832
  Nancy Fillinggame   Vincent R. Thornton
UNDERWOOD, George C.   August 17, 1851
  Mary Veazey   I. A. Williams
UNDERWOOD, Jesse H.   December 9, 1875
  Melvina Jackson   N. M. Jones
UNDERWOOD, Miles P.   March 5, 1834
  Sarah McLelland   Vincent R. Thornton

V

VAN TRIEAU, Constantine   May 20, 1852
  Louisa Jane Peek   Hart C. Peek
VAN VALKINBURG, Alonza Wandison   October 27, 1829
  Catherine Park   H. Reid
VARNER, Joseph W.   October 28, 1867
  Martha E. Durham   P. H. Mell, M.G.
VASON, John   May 21, 1803
  Rebeccah Newton
VAUGHN, Isaac   July 13, 1865
  Adaline M. Harris   Jefferson F. Wright
VAUGHN, Wyatt   January 30, 1845
  Eliza Parker   E. C. I. B. Thomas
VEAL, James H.   January 27, 1842
  Matilda Underwood   John L. Veazey
VEAZEY, Albert A.   March 30, 1841
  Frances Gresham   Francis Bowman

VEAZEY, Allanson E.   March 8, 1827
  Mariah McGiboney   Absalom Baugh
VEAZEY, Eli A.   October 14, 1851
  Mary A. Jackson   I. A. Williams
VEAZEY, Eli A.   July 28, 1868
  Josephine A. Jackson   Hart C. Peek
VEAZEY, Ezekiel   August 21, 1814
  Jean Parker   Wm. McGiboney
VEAZEY, James   December 12, 1811
  Polly Morris   Jesse Mercer
VEAZEY, Jesse   March 28, 1816
  Ruth Veazey   William Cone
VEAZEY, Jesse   February 13, 1823
  Sarah Aikens   John Harris
VEAZEY, John   November 8, 1825
  Permelia Veazey   John Harris
VEAZEY, Timothy   October 25, 1821
  Martha Phillips   Thomas Johnson
VEAZEY, William C.   December 5, 1840
  Mary Ann Lucas   John Veazey
VEAZEY, William D.   March 7, 1861
  Emaline Oliver   Hart C. Peek
VEAZEY, William D.   May 30, 1871
  Mary E. Jackson   W. A. Overton
VEAZEY, William I.   September 11, 1853
  Tranquilla C. Parrott   W. H. Blythe
VELVIN, Thomas   December 8, 1810
  Nancy Coleman   Robert Dale
VENABLE, Robert A.   January 7, 1873
  Mildred A. Stovall   D. W. Elder, M.G.
VINCENT, Charles A.   April 17, 1851
  Susan A. Williams   Richard Lane, M.G.
VINCENT, Sanford, Jr.   November 14, 1822
  Ann Broughton   A. H. Scott
VINCENT, William   September 18, 1823
  Nancy Simonton   Wm. McGiboney
VOUGHT, J. L.   April 26, 1848
  Adaline Walker   James Rowland

W

WADDELL, Marshall   January 18, 1825
  Jane Payne
WADDLE, Isaac W.   September 14, 1831
  Sarah R. Daniell   Nathan Hoyt, M.G.
WADE, James   June 26, 1840
  Mary Elizabeth Thompson   B. M. Sanders
WADE, John   December 23, 1787
  Aggie Peek
WADE, John   May 31, 1822
  Anny Cook   William Moore
WADE, Joshua   February 2, 1820
  Nancy Tucker   William Cone

WAGGONER, Thomas
  Mary Ann Lawrence
WAGGONER, William
  Elizabeth Finley
WAGNON, Daniel M.
  Martha M. Swindelle
WAGNON, Eugenius N.
  Mary E. Gantt
WAGNON, George H.
  Susan F. Ruarks
WAGNON, John P.
  Mary J. Moore
WAGNON, Joshua H.
  Emily Southerland
WAGNON, Pittman M.
  Frances A. Leveritt
WAGNON, Thomas
  Harriet Houghton
WAGNON, William S.
  Martha M. McLellan
WALDEN, Smith
  Elizabeth Whatley
WALDEN, Towner
  Susannah Greer
WALKER, Andrew
  Polly Graham
WALKER, Edwin T.
  Josephine Alexander
WALKER, Edwin T.
  Mary Lenora Fleetwood
WALKER, Henry
  Vicey Phillips
WALKER, Henry
  Mary Ann Hutcherson
WALKER, James T.
  Ruthy A. Phillips
WALKER, John
  Elizabeth Talley
WALKER, John
  Betsey Murphey
WALKER, John
  Elizabeth Brown
WALKER, John E.
  Mary E. Gaston
WALKER, Johnson
  Sarah Swindall
WALKER, Mena M.
  Martha Anne Hardeman
WALKER, Robert
  Frances A. E. Walker
WALKER, Samuel R.
  Falby Moore

December 13, 1846
T. M. Fambrough
November 12, 1818
L. Bethune
December 18, 1834
A. Hutcheson
January 23, 1866
John W. Talley
March 21, 1861
Hinton Crawford
December 1, 1848
Vincent R. Thornton
August 21, 1845
Thomas H. Dawson
February 1, 1866
Lorenzo D. Carlton
October 15, 1818
Lovick Pierce
July 5, 1860
Hart C. Peek
January 28, 1806

November 26, 1804

October 28, 1801

December 10, 1868
Thomas F. Pierce
September 8, 1874
J. L. Pierce, M.G.
May 19, 1800

April 24, 1828
A. Ray, M.G.
October 31, 1849
R. F. Griffen
May 10, 1805

May 4, 1807
James Holt
March 13, 1823
Lovick Pierce
October 12, 1847
J. L. Rowland
November 30, 1815
William Cone
October 12, 1855
B. R. Elder
February 26, 1846
R. C. Smith
December 5, 1840
E. P. Jarrell

WALKER, William   April 24, 1788
  Elizabeth Wynn
WALKER, William   January 26, 1803
  Nancy Connell
WALKER, William H.   January 9, 1872
  Mary L. Fillingim   Hart C. Peek
WALKER, William R.   January 8, 1833
  Martha T. Colquitt   J. P. Leveritt
WALKER, Z. T.   December 18, 1873
  Fanny Ely   J. H. Kilpatrick
WALKER, William T.   December 23, 1856
  Anna E. Tuggle   T. D. Martin, M.G.
WALL, Frank   May 22, 1787
  Catherine W. Culloch
WALL, Richard W.   December 23, 1830
  Elizabeth Gilbert   Augustine Greene
WALLACE, Aaron B.   December 18, 1860
  Elizabeth Wallace   Elisha Elliot
WALLACE, Augustus   November 3, 1831
  Rebecca Shell   J. P. Leveritt
WALLACE, Bartley   September 29, 1836
  Susan Ann Parker   James Moore
WALLACE, B. G.   January 16, 1875
  Alice Cofer   Henry Newton
WALLACE, Woodford   October 11, 1849
  Martha Ann Crosley   Ephraim Bruce
WALLER, Benjamin B.   January 20, 1870
  Louisa Turner   W. H. Blythe, M.G.
WALLER, James   April 8, 1849
  Susan J. Epps   R. F. Griffen
WALLER, Thomas   March 20, 1850
  Rachael Blackman   Joseph W. Drennan
WALLER, William   April 9, 1867
  Sidney W. Tunnell   J. R. Young, M.G.
WALLS, Jubal   September 16, 1828
  Nancy Forrester   Robert Newsom
WARD, Austin   November 21, 1852
  Sarah Staples   J. T. Finley
WARD, Eneas   January 29, 1828
  Altetha Winfield   William Bryan
WARD, Enos Wesley   September 25, 1825
  Elizabeth Smith
WARD, Enos W.   July 14, 1831
  Mary Rowlin   William Rowland
WARD, Enos W.   August 13, 1836
  Louisa Rowland   A. Hutcheson
WARD, George   March 10, 1857
  Frances C. Perdue   J. S. K. Axson
WARD, James S.   February 17, 1824
  Milly Harp   Butts L. Cato
WARD, John   February 14, 1828
  Carey Fambrough   Joshua Cannon

WARD, Joseph S.   September 18, 1839
   Sarah Ann Bryant
WARD, Richard   March 10, 1825
   Urethea White
WARD, Stephen   April 6, 1802
   Jane Wood
WARD, Stephen   February 13, 1822
   Jane Davis   Lovick Pierce
WARD, Wiley   December 13, 1824
   Atherla L. R. Snow
WARE, Edward H.   November 27, 1873
   Mrs. Harriet M. Nichelson   Eustace W. Speer
WARE, Henry C.   December 19, 1839
   Harriet Rainey   Francis Bowman
WARE, Hudson   October 27, 1821
   Elizabeth Farrell
WARE, James   November 24, 1787
   Elizabeth Walker
WARE, John   August 13, 1819
   Patsy Peeler   Thomas Riley
WARE, Robert   May 23, 1821
   Martha Norris   Thomas Riley
WARE, Thomas   June 2, 1818
   Phoebe Peeler   George Dillard
WARE, William   November 29, 1825
   Susan Perkins
WARNER, Robert   March 5, 1804
   Betsey Sims
WARNER, William   January 31, 1825
   Ann Watson
WARREN, George W.   October 27, 1838
   Emily Swindalle   Robert T. Griffin
WARREN, James R.   May 18, 1834
   Burnetta Caldwell   James Moore
WARREN, Slady   August 17, 1820
   Elizabeth Johnson   John I. Beatee
WASHAM, John   October 30, 1806
   Sally Studman   Isaac McClendon
WATERS, Arthur   December 16, 1799
   Sally Sherrill
WATERS, Isaac   March 17, 1809
   Elizabeth Fitzpatrick   William Johnson
WATERS, Matthew   January 27, 1824
   —— Stringfellow
WATERS, James W.   January 8, 1787
   C. C. Gustavious
WATKINS, George   December 26, 1801
   Polly Early
WATKINS, John   September 18, 1816
   Elizabeth Atkinson   Robert Rea
WATKINS, Josiah   July 31, 1805
   Dicey Sropsheer

WATKINS, William   October 31, 1811
  Polly Kennedy   Wm. McGiboney
WATSON, Andrew Jackson   November 26, 1840
  Louisa Jane English
WATSON, Briant   December 27, 1827
  Priscilla Perkins   John Harris
WATSON, Douglas C.   November 1, 1832
  Elba N. Stovall   Thomas W. Grimes
WATSON, Elias   December 11, 1829
  Arean M. Lellan   John Harris
WATSON, Jesse   March 21, 1847
  Amanda Jones   Vincent R. Thornton
WATSON, John   August 12, 1829
  Minerva Mabry   George Hall
WATSON, John A.   May 10, 1833
  Eliza Copeland   L. P. Leveritt
WATSON, Marcus L.   July 20, 1854
  Emily Houghton   S. G. Hillyer
WATSON, Nicholas A.   April 1, 1852
  Mary Harris   Hart C. Peek
WATSON, Solomon   December 18, 1823
  Nancy Akins
WATSON, William   March 5, 1806
  Abagail Brewer
WATSON, William   December 18, 1824
  Sarah Williams
WATSON, William B.   December 5, 1871
  Lavinia Catchings   Q. L. Lupe, M.G.
WATTS, Hampton   January 14, 1825
  Amanda Davenport
WATTS, Hardy K.   December 10, 1834
  Martha Bunch   Bennet A. Ely
WATTS, Harrison   November 2, 1824
  Mary Daniel
WATTS, Harrison H.   January 12, 1834
  Jane Forrester   Bennett Hillsman
WATTS, Holton   July 22, 1805
  Selattia Smith
WATTS, Jacoby   February 24, 1804
  Elizabeth Harrison
WATTS, John R.   September 23, 1833
  Elizabeth T. Asbury   Bennett Hillsman
WATTS, Joseph   July 30, 1818
  Eliza Jenkins   John Willson
WATTS, Lillte B.   February 21, 1801
  Nancy Whatley
WATTS, Presley   July 20, 1808
  Abbey Andrews   John Cox
WATTS, Richard   October 27, 1839
  Martha Watts   C. D. Kennebrew
WATTS, Richard N.   May 30, 1837
  Mary S. Watts   Vincent R. Thornton

WATTS, William — September 21, 1845
  Nancy Williams — E. S. Hunter
WATTS, William H. — February 17, 1804
  Patsey Roberts
WATTS, William H. — December 10, 1828
  Mary Robinson
WEATHERLY, John S. — March 18, 1861
  Rhoda Cheney — P. H. Mell
WEATHERLY, William — November 28, 1818
  Frances Smith
WEATHERS, Jesse — July 18, 1815
  Unity Johnson — Robert Rea
WEATHERS, John — November 17, 1808
  Polly Kelley — James Holt
WEAVER, Francis — April 15, 1847
  Priscilla Ely — John Harris
WEAVER, James M. — December 28, 1847
  Jane Amanda Harris — S. G. Hillyer
WEAVER, John — February 6, 1812
  Elizabeth Harralson — A. Veazey
WEAVER, William M. — March 14, 1860
  Margaret Nickelson — George F. Pierce
WEAVER, William — April 8, 1824
  Caroline M. Mango — Lovick Pierce
WEBB, John — August 10, 1859
  Jane Fambrough — James H. Wragg
WEBB, John G. — February 28, 1827
  Lucy Clarke
WEBB, Robert — February 10, 1812
  Polly Sorrell — Thomas Rhodes
WEEKS, Samuel — September 5, 1788
  Anne Jackson
WELBORN, William — October 12, 1842
  Martha Elizabeth Sanders
WELBORN, Jonathon — May 18, 1806
  Rebekah Williams — John Robinson
WELBOURN, Jeremiah — December 13, 1824
  Polly Morris — George Johnson
WELBURN, James — April 12, 1832
  Mary Elizabeth Harris — R. Q. Dickerson
WELLS, George — February 27, 1823
  Polly Moore — Lovick Pierce
WELLS, John — May 15, 1826
  Emily J. Booles
WEST, Edward — August 18, 1801
  Elizabeth Copelan
WEST, Elijah — February 4, 1808
  Matilda Sorrell — William Browning
WEST, George — November 4, 1830
  Matilda Prior — Jonathon Davis
WEST, J. T. — December 24, 1872
  C. T. Horton — J. T. Wood

WEST, Reuben S.   October 27, 1842
  Margaret Hogg   N. M. Lumpkin
WEST, Thomas J.   November 25, 1841
  Matilda Asbury   W. H. Stocks
WEST, Warren   February 4, 1803
  Betsey Whaley
WEST, William   August 22, 1827
  Sarah Butts
WEST, William E.   November 7, 1875
  Lizzie Moncrief   John R. Young
WEST, William M.   December 12, 1844
  Harriett Brooks   Samuel Ely
WESTBROOKS, Allin   October 20, 1818
  Frances Huff
WESTBROOKS, Thomas   December 7, 1819
  Aley Ball
WESTBROOKS, William   February 5, 1816
  Susanna Lee   Richard Baugh
WESTER, Edward   November 17, 1804
  Elizabeth Yancey
WESTER, John   January 20, 1803
  Anne Wester
WHALEY, Burwell   March 14, 1803
  Polly Whitlock
WHALEY, Edward   Augst 20, 1803
  Elizabeth Caldwell
WHALEY, James   October 11, 1803
  Nancy Lake
WHALEY, Thomas   October 21, 1828
  Mary Smith   Jos. Roberts, M.G.
WHATLEY, Floyd   December 16, 1823
  Alsay Hunt   Robert Newsome
WHATLEY, John   June 24, 1803
  Polly Blanks
WHATLEY, John   January 28, 1806
  Patsey Bowles
WHATLEY, Michael   August 26, 1799
  Elizabeth Peoples
WHATLEY, Robert   July 10, 1808
  Polly Swann   George Tuggle
WHATLEY, Thomas W.   November 8, 1853
  Julia Davis   E. L. Whatley, M.G.
WHATLEY, Wyatt   January 11, 1800
  Elizabeth Wright
WHEALY, John   March 17, 1789
  Mary Porter
WHEAT, Jonathan   November 29, 1838
  Mary Ann Horn   Thomas Stocks
WHEAT, Jonathon   January 21, 1847
  Elizabeth Merritt   R. F. Griffen
WHEELAS, Hardy   June 12, 1806
  Hannah Rimes   J. Mapp

WHEELAS, Joab — August 20, 1807
  Jane Spradling — James Holt
WHEELER, Avery — October 10, 1804
  Rebeccah Cunningham
WHEELER, Elijah — August 25, 1800
  Elizabeth Jackson
WHEELER, Lawrence F. — December 16, 1841
  Mary Anne Watkins — N. H. Hill
WHEELOUS, William — January 16, 1859
  Arry Fambrough — W. A. Partee
WHETSONE, John A. — January 8, 1827
  Ann C. Banks
WHITAKER, William — March 20, 1873
  Mrs. L. D. Florence — W. A. Florence
WHITE, Andrew — December 10, 1803
  Mary Smith
WHITE, Coleman — August 29, 1821
  Ann Allen — A. Hutchinson
WHITE, David M. — December 6, 1842
  Nancy Woodard — John L. Veazey
WHITE, D. A. — December 24, 1848
  Rebecca Reynolds — W. H. C. Cone
WHITE, Edmund — April 19, 1827
  Sarah Rea — John Armstrong
WHITE, James T. — July 23, 1823
  Sarah Tolly — John N. Harvey
WHITE, James — January 26, 1837
  Caroline Gatlin — James W. Godkin
WHITE, John — November 24, 1803
  Lucy Jones
WHITE, Reuben — January 5, 1802
  Nancy Hines
WHITE, Samuel — June 20, 1822
  Sarah Nelson — Thomas Johnson
WHITE, Wiley M. — November 28, 1833
  Mary S. Moore — George Heard
WHITE, William — April 24, 1806
  Anna Maddox — Ewing Morrow
WHITE, William H. — December 9, 1823
  Jane S. McIntyre — Francis Cummins
WHITE, William H. — June 27, 1826
  Permelia Baldwin
WHITE, William — October 2, 1863
  Georgia Anna Daniel — James W. Godkin
WHITEHEAD, John W. — December 22, 1874
  Inez English — W. A. Cheney
WHITELY, Richard Henry — November 29, 1849
  Margaret Eliza Divine — William Bryan
WHITESIDE, Andrew J. — May 12, 1848
  Mary Ann Greer
WHITFIELD, Ivy I. — November 3, 1850
  Susan P. Ramsey — J. T. Findley

WHITFIELD, James A.   December 13, 1866
   Mary E. Shipp   Hart C. Peek
WHITLAW, James H.   December 25, 1859
   Anna A. Broach   James Davison
WHITLOCK, William A.   April 3, ——
   Louisa Emily Johnson   Vincent R. Thornton
WIGGINS, Benjamin   February 28, 1845
   Sara Ann Rhodes
WIGGINS, John   June 29, 1815
   Nancy Hall   John Browning
WIGGINS, Whittenton   November 29, 1830
   Nancy Atkins
WIGGINS, William   February 20, 1789
   Sarah Lawrence
WILFORD, Walter   March 22, 1802
   Nancy Hester
WILKERSON, Dempsey   January 21, 1807
   Lydia Bishop   Thomas Crawford
WILKINS, John   January 16, 1816
   Cynthia Lanier   John Armor
WILKINS, John   May 4, 1820
   Lucy Thompson   George Watkins
WILKINSON, Abner   December ——, 1803
   Ami Mathews
WILKINSON, Henry   September 17, 1822
   Maria Towers   Francis Cummins
WILKS, John A.   December 19, 1852
   Rebecca Jackson   J. T. Findley
WILLIAMS, Albert   February 13, 1866
   Julia Ann Linch   Jefferson F. Wright
WILLIAMS, Anderson   December 17, 1835
   Martha Lancastor   James W. Godkin
WILLIAMS, Benjamin   February 18, 1868
   Anna B. Billingslea   James L. Pierce
WILLIAMS, Crawford   December 18, 1839
   Mahala Frances Wade   James M. Davidson
WILLIAMS, David   September 17, 1850
   Elizabeth Scott
WILLIAMS, Ed. G.   January 19, 1871
   Kate M. Pierce   George W. Pierce
WILLIAMS, Elisha   October 21, 1827
   Mary Phillips   Abraham Yeates
WILLIAMS, Ezekiel   December 17, 1818
   Cynthia Swann
WILLIAMS, Ezekiel S.   January 10, 1867
   Emma L. Parrott   William Bryan
WILLIAMS, Francis Key   April 13, 1856
   S. A. McLellan   Hart C. Peek, M.G.
WILLIAMS, Frederick H.   January 8, 1815
   Nancy Daniels   Jesse Mercer
WILLIAMS, Henry P.   October 18, 1865
   Mildred J. P. Burk   N. M. Crawford, M.G.

WILLIAMS, Henry P.   December 18, 1873
   Eliza J. Alfriend   W. H. Blythe
WILLIAMS, Isaac   February 7, 1836
   Emily Atkinson   A. Hutcheson
WILLIAMS, Isaac   April 28, 1842
   Almira A. Bowden   James Jones, M.G.
WILLIAMS, Isaac   December 21, 1869
   Ella Dora Bruce   W. H. Blythe, M.G.
WILLIAMS, Isaac   January 30, 1869
   Sarah Andrews
WILLIAMS, James   October 24, 1847
   Susan A. Copelan   John C. Lucas
WILLIAMS, James B.   April 6, 1841
   Nancy V. Terrell   Vincent R. Thornton
WILLIAMS, James D.   September 10, 1871
   Matilda Goodroe   Rev. J. S. Patten
WILLIAMS, Jesse   June 4, 1826
   Elizabeth McMichael
WILLIAMS, Jo   November 26, 1804
   Polly Boon
WILLIAMS, John   November 10, 1788
   Anne Wade
WILLIAMS, John   November 21, 1803
   Delpha Watkins
WILLIAMS, Jonathan   May 18, 1808
   Rebeccah Williams   John Roberson, J.P.
WILLIAMS, Joseph   June 10, 1804
   Mary Boon   Thomas Crawford
WILLIAMS, Littleberry   May 1, 1827
   Amanda Cato
WILLIAMS, Orrin   August 19, 1808
   Rebekah Stephens   Stephen Gatlin
WILLIAMS, Patrick   November 15, 1832
   Ariam Ingram   Thomas I. Park
WILLIAMS, Peter   February 3, 1818
   Lucindia Park   Lovick Pierce
WILLIAMS, Pleasant   June 5, 1856
   Harriet Perkins   B. R. Elder
WILLIAMS, Poleman   May 7, 1846
   Nancy May   E. S. Hunter
WILLIAMS, Richard S.   March 5, 1860
   Emma J. West   Thomas B. Cooper
WILLIAMS, Robert   January 9, 1800
   Rebekah Whatley
WILLIAMS, Robert B.   September 23, 1869
   Georgia Ann Fisher   James W. Godkin
WILLIAMS, James   May 1, 1827
   Nancy Dingler   E. Tally
WILLIAMS, Thomas   June 12, 1822
   Edney Scroggins   Robert Newsome
WILLIAMS, William   April 9, 1829
   Elizabeth Atkinson   William Bryan

WILLIAMS, William   August 8, 1847
  Louisa R. Parrott   Ephraim Bruce
WILLIAMS, William A., Jr.   January 22, 1854
  Martha A. Robinson   J. R. Hall
WILLIAMS, William B.   February 25, 1868
  Susan Ann M. Bruce   Joseph R. Parker
WILLIAMS, William N.   January 11, 1843
  Nancy Baldwin   Thomas Stocks
WILLIAMS, William T. J.   December 30, 1860
  Rhodice Ann Crossley   J. M. Kelly
WILLIAMS, Willis   February 17, 1848
  Jane F. Booles   B. M. Sanders
WILLIAMS, Wilson   July 8, 1820
  Sarah Kimbrough
WILLEY, James H.   April 29, 1841
  Julia Foster   George Pierce
WILLIS, Alfred L.   June 2, 1856
  Florida C. Duncan   J. P. Duncan
WILLIS, Eugene L.   January 29, 1865
  Serepta A. Hackney   John R. Young, M.G.
WILLIS, James   February 13, 1834
  Margaret Ann Chew   Thomas Stocks
WILLIS, London   May 27, 1815
  Priscilla Thompson   Sol Lockett
WILLIS, Louden   September 30, 1819
  Sarah D. Ferrel   Jesse Mercer
WILLIS, Richard   January 25, 1848
  Sarah Foster   Thomas Stocks
WILLIS, Robert   June 13, 1820
  Lucy Baugh   Lovick Pierce
WILLIS, Washington   November 14, 1825
  Susan Martin
WILLOUGHBY, William R.   October 21, 1856
  Sarah N. Ray   John W. M. Barton
WILLSON, James   June 2, 1789
  Phebe White
WILLSON, Joshua   April 8, 1807
  Cumfort Knowles   W. M. Johnson
WILLSON, Larkin   December 22, 1803
  Polly Cabiness
WILSON, A. A.   Janary 6, 1876
  Ann Hailes   John T. Dolvin
WILSON, George S.   January 8, 1874
  Mary F. Lankford   John F. Dolvin
WILSON, James   January 4, 1826
  Nancy Heard
WILSON, James   November 26, 1835
  Mary Ann McAuly
WILSON, James L.   May 22, 1870
  Emma Lankford   W. A. Colclough
WILSON, Jesse P.   October 30, 1860
  Cornelia C. Wright   Homer Hendee, M.G.

WILSON, John L.   August 21, 1839
  Mary Jane Harris
WILSON, John M.   September 10, 1874
  Mrs. Talitha J. Jackson   J. L. Pierce, M.G.
WILSON, John R.   January 12, 1858
  Martha A. Gentry   W. W. Moore
WILSON, John T.   March 7, 1852
  Naomi Gilmer   B. Rowland
WILSON, Joseph P.   June 3, 1862
  Caroline L. Whetstone   P. H. Mell, M.G.
WILSON, Lewis   February 9, 1841
  Eliza T. Kittrell   Thomas Stocks
WILSON, P. F.   December 29, 1844
  Julia Ann Fambro   John Zuber
WILSON, Samuel G.   January 6, 1875
  Sarah N. Poullain   G. F. Pierce, M.G.
WILSON, Thomas B.   September 8, 1872
  Ellen A. Durham   W. A. Overton
WILSON, William   January 6, 1789
  Elizabeth Jones
WILSON, William   March 1, 1825
  Arenath Pullen
WILSON, William   March 3, 1859
  Mrs. Caroline Durke   George C. Clarke
WILSON, William A.   January 2, 1867
  Mary T. Lankford   Luciuc C. Broome
WILSON, William W.   August 6, 1834
  Lucy Perkins   James Moore
WILSON, Willis   June 20, 1875
  Carrie F. Morris   James A. Thornton
WINFIELD, James   July 20, 1826
  Frances Duncan
WINFIELD, James   May 18, 1828
  Mary Gooch   Robert Burdell
WINFIELD, James   February 7, 1856
  Claudia Jackson   N. M. Crawford
WINFIELD, John   December 21, 1817
  Barsheba Wade   Lauchlien Bethune
WINFIELD, Matthew   November 26, 1828
  Rebecca Wade   Robert Burdell
WINGFIELD, Alfred   October 1, 1845
  Frances Cunningham   Francis Bowman
WINGFIELD, Junius A.   November 9, 1836
  Mary T. Mosely   Thomas M. Grimes
WINFREY, H. L.   September 13, 1868
  Lydia L. Greer   P. H. Mell, M.G.
WINN, J. H.   November 22, 1870
  Nettie V. Smith   John M. Loury
WINN, Thomas   December 23, 1819
  Nancy Greer   James Brockman
WINN, Thomas E.   December 13, 1865
  Sophia I. Park   Thos. F. Pierce

WINNINGHAM, Jarrett Lukey Woods	July 18, 1801
WINSLETT, I. I. Mary A. E. Bickers	August 31, 1851 A. T. N. Vandivere
WINSLETT, Jonathon Gelly D. Bagley	June 11, 1818 R. White
WINSLETT, L. B. Mary N. Copelan	December 14, 1871 James W. Godkin
WINSLETT, Richard Perthene Bagley	March 5, 1815 Thomas Bush
WINSLETT, William Elizabeth Harp	September 14, 1799
WINSLETT, William Peggy Woods	June 13, 1801
WINSLETT, William Eliza B. Copeland	May 3, 1831 Thomas W. Grimes
WINTER, Albert H. Dora Tunnell	February 26, 1874 Albert Gray
WINTER, D. Henry Nancy Carlton	December 15, 1850 James M. Davison
WINTER, D. Henry Lucy Ann Grier	October 16, 1859 James Davison
WIRSLEY, John Sarah Hammons	June 13, 1807 J. Bethune
WOMACK, Mancey Sarah Rogers	September 11, 1790
WOOD, Aristarchus Fanney Newton	January 14, 1799
WOOD, Elial Martha Bunn	June 21, 1827 E. Talley
WOOD, Etheldred Dicey Bagby	June 10, 1790
WOOD, James Isabellah Patrick	February 8, 1802
WOOD, John Sally Reid	April 2, 1807 Adam Hays
WOOD, John Elizabeth Saxon	May 30, 1854 A. L. Willis
WOOD, John C. Nancy F. Greene	June 3, 1856 J. S. R. Axon
WOOD, John Henry Harriet C. B. Crawford	May 4, 1854 J. W. Yarbrough
WOOD, Richard Tabitha Glass	April 21, 1790
WOOD, Taylor Mary Burger	December 5, 1872 W. A. Partee
WOOD, Thomas Polly Hill	March 28, 1810 W. Johnson
WOOD, William T. Ugenia J. Talley	October 18, 1838 Robert F. Griffen
WOODALL, Jamie Beckey Watson	May 15, 1801

WOODALL, June Martin	June 18, 1803
Polly Lacey	
WOODALL, Michael	August 11, 1790
Betsey Bird	
WOODARD, Jonathan	January 16, 1825
Elizabeth Brunt	
WOODJIN, William G.	July 21, 1860
Helen James	
WOODHAM, Everett	January 25, 1821
Harriett Phillips	Lovick Pierce
WOODHAM, James	April 21, 1814
Peggy Peek	John Turner
WOODHAM, John E.	March 31, 1859
Miriam J. Callahan	William Bryan
WOODS, Cyrus	June 24, 1823
Frances Pinkard	Aug. B. Longstreet
WOODS, Matthew	January 19, 1826
Myrum Woods	William L. Asten, J.P.
WOOTEN, James	April 6, 1789
Elizabeth Lawrence	
WOOTEN, John	June 22, 1801
Polly Beavers	
WORTHY, Zachariah P.	May 9, 1839
Emily Caldwell	James M. Davison
WRAY, Pleasant J.	November 10, 1864
Mrs. Rebecca Bagby	W. A. Partee
WRAY, Sylvanus	December 20, 1864
Mrs. Rebeccah Ogletree	W. A. Partee
WRAY, William T.	December 20, 1864
Mrs. Martha G. Edmondson	W. A. Partee
WRIGHT, Christopher C.	May 13, 1838
Rebecca B. Moore	James N. Porter
WRIGHT, Jacob T.	May 7, 1838
Eliza W. Few	James Madison Porter
WRIGHT, James A.	October 23, 1873
Scott Branch	W. H. LaPrade
WRIGHT, James Osborn	June 24, 1866
Alice E. Reynolds	Thos. F. Pierce
WRIGHT, Jefferson	April 29, 1849
Louisa Kimbrough	J. C. Simmons
WRIGHT, John	December 18, 1804
Nancy Jones	
WRIGHT, John	January 11, 1825
Celia Rowland	E. Tally
WRIGHT, John	November 23, 1868
Frances Bowden	
WRIGHT, John E.	April 9, 1839
Sarah H. Bickers	Thomas Stocks
WRIGHT, John W.	May 31, 1855
Sarah Lewis	J. S. Williams
WRIGHT, Joseph	December 11, 1817
Mary Ann Stark	John Browning

WRIGHT, J. F.   October 29, 1846
  L. A. Burk   William I. Parks
WRIGHT, Lorenzo D.   January 11, 1866
  Mary Lewis   Jefferson F. Wright
WRIGHT, Nathaniel   January 12, 1852
  Eliza M. Robson   A. L. Willis, J.P.
WRIGHT, Redock T.   November 16, 1832
  Merium Malory   Thomas W. Grimes
WRIGHT, Reuben   July 3, 1827
  Jane Hays   Robert W. Bardell
WRIGHT, Reuben   December 4, 1828
  Mary Conner   Anderson Ray, M.G.
WRIGHT, Robert   May 31, 1808
  Margaret Bledsoe   William Browning
WRIGHT, Samuel   December 1, 1835
  Frances Julian Perkins   Wesley P. Arnold
WRIGHT, Thomas   February 14, 1823
  Nancy Tucker
WRIGHT, Wiley   April 28, 1821
  Sarah Lewis   Robert Flourney
WRIGHT, William   January 11, 1816
  Rhoda Cummings   C. Maddox
WRIGHT, William   October 12, 1831
  Maria Brunt   L. P. Leveritt
WRIGHT, William   June 7, 1844
  Hannah Orr   James Moore
WRIGHT, William   August 13, 1844
  Susan Mapp   J. J. Howell
WRIGHT, William   April 17, 1846
  Eleanor Johnson   James W. Godkin
WRIGHT, William H.   December 22, 1858
  Sarah Isadora Colclough   L. B. Jackson
WRIGHT, Willis   December 9, 1833
  Sarah T. Ketterall   A. Hutcheson
WRIGHT, Zachaeus   November 19, 1820
  Asentha Lewis   John Harris
WYNN, John   January 27, 1842
  Martha H. Smith   James W. Godkin
WYNN, R. I.   January 28, 1841
  Sarah M. Rawls   James W. Godkin
WYMAN, Samuel H.   May 29, 1856
  Mary E. Sidwell

MARRIAGE RECORDS
Oglethorpe County, Georgia

A

AARON, Daniel and Polly Wilson	November 25, 1807
ABLE, John F. and Nancy Reed	October 9, 1827
ADAMS, James and Dorcas Pratt	October 9, 1810
ADAMS, William and Sally Hatley	November 24, 1806
ADAMS, William and Nancy Huddleston	September 14, 1818
ADKINS, William and Martha Drake	January 5, 1837
ADKINSON, — and Elizabeth A. Landrum	October 8, 1845
AKINS, Joseph and May D. Walker	November 9, 1824
ALDRIDGE, Abner and Rebekah House	March 20, 1798
ALEXANDER, Edmund and Polly Grass	June 23, 1801
ALEXANDER, Peyton and Ann T. Blanton	January 29, 1834
ALEXANDER, R. U. and Frances Lumpkin	January 21, 1851
ALEXANDER, William and Polly Blanton	February 3, 1825
ALLDRIDGE, Reuben and Elizabeth House	September 19, 1819
ALLEN, A. A. and Mariah E. Cook	February 21, 1843
ALLEN, Charles and Jenny Bradshaw	December 27, 1798
ALLEN, Chas. H. and Sarah Ann Gilham	July 13, 1852
ALLEN, Clement Y. and Martha West	January 4, 1822
ALLEN, David and Sally Walker	April 12, 1806
ALLEN, George A. F. and Nancy Porter	July 6, 1825
ALLEN, Henry and Elizabeth Colbert	November 13, 1816
ALLEN, Henry J. and Frances E. Farmer	August 30, 1851
ALLEN, Henry W. and Martha A. E. Rainey	January 1, 1838
ALLEN, John and Sally Maxwell	November 6, 1805
ALLEN, John and Nancy Wood	May 5, 1816
ALLEN, Richard and Emily Kidd	May 11, 1837
ALLEN, Stephen and Sally Brown	December 25, 1821
ALLEN, William and Betsy Carder	September 20, 1806
ALLEN, William and Eleanor Bailey	January 5, 1813
ALLEN, William and Jane Kines	March 14, 1835
ALLEN, William G. and Lucy Jane Mattox	July 7, 1845
ALLEN, Wm. G. and Margaret A. E. Smith	July 28, 1848
ALLEN, Young S. and Frances M. Allen	December 28, 1823
ALLGOOD, Henry S. and Sarah Ann Elizabeth Davis	March 22, 1843
ALMON, William and Catharine Landrum	February 7, 1839
ALMOND, Wm. D. and Martha A. J. Curtis	May 4, 1843
AMBROSE, Marcus and Martha Sterling	June 23, 1818
ANDERSON, Alexander and Winiford Thornton	December 1, 1798
ANDERSON, James and Polly Combus	March 22, 1802
ANDERSON, James and Salley Trible	September 16, 1807
ANDERSON, Mathew and Frankey Ellis	September 30, 1800
ANDERSON, Sidney and Betsey Carruth	February 2, 1809
ANDERSON, William and Mary Nowell	January 9, 1808
ANDERSON, William and Judith Colquitt	January 24, 1815
ANDREWS, John M. and Julia Ann Smith	November 27, 1832
ANDREWS, William and Elizabeth Smith	December 6, 1816

ANDREWS, William and Patsey Guthrey	March 6, 1822
ANDREWS, Wyatt and Johanna A. Smith	December 7, 1816
ANGLE, John and Sally Johnson	January 8, 1808
ANGLE (or Augle) Thomas and Susannah Morris	August 16, 1802
ANGLEN, John and Sally Bradshaw	December 2, 1813
ANGLIN, Henry and Lucy Bradshaw	June 18, 1820
ANGLIN, Silas M. and Elizabeth A. Chaplin	December 23, 1841
ANTHONY, Mark C. and Elizabeth Olive	May 4, 1833
ANTHONY, Micajah and Isabella Vernon	March 23, 1835
ANTHONY, Middleton and Rebecca Black	November 22, 1819
ANTHONY, Thomas B. and Ann R. Carter	April 16, 1833
ANTHONY, Wade and Rebecca York	March 4, 1834
ANTHONY, William B. and Susan A. Arnold	January 18, 1842
APLIN, Lewis and Susannah B. Farmer	October 10, 1815
APPLING, Burwell and Betsy Walker	January 2, 1823
APPLING, James and Martha Hoell (Howell)	December 29, 1847
APPLING, Joel and Penna Bolton	October 17, 1811
ARMSTED, John and Amy Owen	March 29, 1818
ARMSTRONG, Alexander and Malissa Martin	October 5, 1835
ARMSTRONG, George and Lucinda Edmondson	March 12, 1824
ARMSTRONG, John and Sara Swanson	January 17, 1822
ARNOLD, Allen and Grady Owen	December 21, 1801
ARNOLD, Berry and Sally Slaton	December 22, 1819
ARNOLD, Chesley and Susannah Andrews	May 2, 1808
ARNOLD, David and Martha Ann Gibson	February 14, 1850
ARNOLD, George W. and Salina K. Sims	August 24, 1838
ARNOLD, Hopson and Avy Nicks	January 14, 1800
ARNOLD, Hugh P. and Elizabeth Johnson	September 7, 1840
ARNOLD, John and Elizabeth Raney	October 27, 1813
ARNOLD, John and Rebeckah Powell	December 16, 1799
ARNOLD, John and Susannah Young	December 25, 1808
ARNOLD, John J. and Frances Jackson	November 20, 1832
ARNOLD, John L. and Patsy Beaty	February 7, 1807
ARNOLD, John T. and Mrs. Mary E. Drake	March 19, 1852
ARNOLD, Joseph D. and Centhy Davis	July 6, 1820
ARNOLD, Moses and Catherine Jones	December 19, 1823
ARNOLD, Moses and Catherine M. Ashton	September 17, 1833
ARNOLD, Moses and Martha Ann Jackson	July 17, 1844
ARNOLD, Park E. and Susan Glenn	May 1, 1828
ARNOLD, Samuel and Nancy Rainey	July 24, 1808
ARNOLD, Samuel O. and Elender M. Johnson	March 11, 1833
ARNOLD, Stephen and Susannah Arnold	February 14, 1795
ARNOLD, Washington and Martha H. Johnson	September 23, 1845
ARNOLD, William and Elizabeth Echols	January 12, 1807
ARNOLD, William and Anna Patterson	March 31, 1812
ARNOLD, William W. and Chloe Ann Arnold	January 1, 1826
ARTHUR, John and Matilda Gibson	September 8, 1817
ARTHUR, John B. and Susan Jane Jackson	August 19, 1850
ARTHUR, Talbot and Sarah Fambrough	November 25, 1841
ARTHUR, William and Margaret Eason	June 5, 1837
ARTHUR, William and Patsy Bryant	July 27, 1840
ASBURY, David R. and Sarah B. Kimbell	March 22, 1848

ASBURY, Richard and Susan Ann Young — December 4, 1834
ASHTON, John and Nancy Nichols — April 10, 1837
ASPAY, Thomas and Elizabeth Bailey — August 14, 1802
ATKINSON, John and Mary H. Landrum — July 21, 1845
ATKINSON, Samuel and Jane Andrews — November 2, 1815
ATKINSON, William and Mary Pinson — January 21, 1819
AUSTIN, William W. and Elizabeth Bradbury — December 30, 1820
AUTREY, Alexander and Milly Digans — March 28, 1805
AVENT, Benjamin and Olive Patton — October 17, 1822
AVENT, William and Hannah Goolsby — February 15, 1823
AVERHEART, Jacob W. and Martha W. Weaver — May 28, 1828
ACOCK, Burwell and Mable A. Young — January 11, 1834
AYCOCK, Isaac P. and Lucy Marable — November 3, 1832
AYCOCK, Reddick and Fanny Anderson — December 28, 1809
AYCOCK, Richard M. and Nancy Amis — January 24, 1828
AYCOCK, Zachariah and Tabitha Edwards — July 10, 1817
AYCOCK, Seaborn R. and Mary Jane Christopher — January 6, 1845

B

BABER, Elisha and Betty Bradshaw — October 8, 1807
BABER, George and Ann Haynes — September 15, 1825
BABER, Robert and Assinah Haynes — November 12, 1823
BACKHAMON, John and Russell Edmondson — July 23, 1811
BACKWELL, Major and Oney Varner — November 4, 1818
BACON, John W. and Mary E. Jordan — April 20, 1846
BACON, Thomas W. and Liza Warnack — January 11, 1810
BAILEY, Elijah and Caroline Tiller — December 26, 1820
BAILEY, Jacob and Prudence Garrett — January 21, 1819
BAILEY, James and Nancy Dicks — March 2, 1813
BAILEY, James J. and Mary Smith — November 2, 1822
BAILEY, John and Polly Smith — October 5, 1801
BAILEY, Richard and Nancy Hay — December 5, 1797
BAILEY, Russell and Peggy Bailey — January 1, 1803
BAILEY, William and Jane Bailey — January 20, 1819
BAILS, Christopher and Betsey Morgan — April 7, 1794
BALDWIN, Samuel and Clara Pope — July 20, 1819
BALDWIN, Thomas B. and Cynthia E. Chaffin — September 22, 1849
BALDWIN, William W. and Ann R. Billups — April 30, 1818
BANIAN, Thomas and Milley Traylor — July 25, 1799
BANKS, Eaton and Sally Hodnett — December 3, 1806
BANKS, Eli and Celina Jenkins — January 10, 1842
BANKS, James and Mason Calvary — November 6, 1797
BANKS, Lacey and Mrs. Ann Pemberton — March 7, 1848
BANKS, Richard and Betsy Lacy — June 22, 1802
BANKS, Richard and Peggy Rice — April 25, 1796
BANKS, Robert and Susana Dunson — August 26, 1801
BANKS, Thompson and Susan Hale — January 29, 1832
BANKSTON, Abner J. and Rebecca Short — December 21, 1832
BANKSTON, Willabe and Martha Smith — August 12, 1828
BARBER, Jesse and Prudy Hargrove — December 17, 1808
BARBER, Mathew and James Johnson — February 24, 1803

BARBIN, James and Sally Kidd	September 18, 1806
BARKER, Harris and Frances Hammonds	December 30, 1836
BARKER, John and Jane Hatchett	May 24, 1824
BARKER, John and Mary Ann Mastris	January 30, 1844
BARNES, Daniel and Gruney Bagard	September 26, 1807
BARNES, Samuel and Isbell Edwards	December 18, 1805
BARNETT, Abel and Rachel Medows	January 11, 1832
BARNETT, Benjamin A. and Irena Yancey	December 6, 1842
BARNETT, Benjamin and Lucy Barnett	December 17, 1834
BARNETT, Charles and Eliza W. Gresham	December 23, 1824
BARNETT, David A. J. and Hanah Meadows	March 31, 1834
BARNETT, Francis M. and Sarah G. Ponder	February 24, 1825
BARNETT, George and Susannah Martin	October 21, 1799
BARNETT, James and Sarah Webb	October 16, 1822
BARNETT, John D. and Emily A. Bridges	December 5, 1837
BARNETT, John F. and Sarah E. Hardeman	January 12, 1849
BARNETT, Nathan and Eary Griffin	February 1, 1797
BARNETT, Nathan and Eliza Goolsby	December 8, 1825
BARNETT, Pleasant L. and Polly Johnson	July 4, 1820
BARNETT, William and Elisabeth Barnett	March 3, 1823
BARNETT, William H. and Elisabeth M. Brockman	January 2, 1817
BARNETT, William H. and Elizabeth Goss	August 29, 1822
BARNETT, William J. and Winifred Aycock	May 18, 1823
BARRON, Barnabas and Libbyann Wheelers	December 27, 1836
BARROW, David C. and Sarah E. Pope	October 22, 1838
BARTLET, Burwell B. and Edith Cobb	July 24, 1833
BATEY, Hugh and Sally Anderson	July 10, 1807
BATTLE, William and Kezziah Wright	December 12, 1818
BATTLES, Samuel and Nancy Right	November 18, 1805
BAUGHN, John and Nancy Hubbard	December 26, 1813
BAUGHN, John T. and Frances E. Borum	December 12, 1844
BAXTER, Allen T. and Elizabeth A. Tuck	December 20, 1847
BEADLE, William and Sally Lester	March 19, 1804
BEASLEY, John and Lucy Gresham	March 28, 1801
BEASLEY, John and Elisabeth Moody	May 14, 1811
BEASLEY, John P. and Nancy Beasley	February 13, 1821
BEASLEY, William and Adeline Lumpkin	December 15, 1832
BEAVERS, William and Silvey Johnson	November 8, 1808
BEATY, James and Patsey Jones	February 17, 1812
BELIAH, Samuel and Polly Phillips	January 2, 1798
BELL, Dr. Addison A. and Frances McWhorter	June 3, 1851
BELL, Andrew and Winney Knox	October 12, 1805
BELL, Enoch and Elizabeth Johnson	August 19, 1847
BELL, Francis and Marion J. Jackson	October 10, 1850
BELL, Frederick and Lucinda Pace	November 7, 1848
BELL, Green and Susan G. Tiller	November 13, 1837
BELL, James and Rebecca E. Gresham	August 3, 1824
BELL, James J. and Ann McCowan	December 10, 1846
BELL, Jesse and Nancy Tarpley	December 23, 1812
BELL, John and Polly Brown	March 5, 1818
BELL, John and Nancy Dowdy	November 24, 1825
BELL, John and Elisabeth Peyton	February 24, 1826

BELL, John and Mary Ward   September 20, 1831
BELL, John L. and Georgia Ann Clark   December 15, 1834
BELL, Joseph and Priscilla E. Drake   November 22, 1821
BELL, Joseph and Louisa S. Hopper   April 9, 1846
BELL, Marcus D. F. and Rebecca M. Collier   October 25, 1821
BELL, Richard and Martha Ann Bledsoe   September 3, 1849
BELL, Samuel and Gilley Pye   December 29, 1798
BELL, Sylvanus, Jr. and Frances M. Lumpkin   September 16, 1828
BELL, Thomas A. and Martha Raines   May 6, 1844
BELL, William J. and Jane Caroline Beasley   October 6, 1835
BELL, William J. and Eliza Bugg   March 1, 1837
BELLAH, James and Polly Pharr   October 20, 1807
BELLOUGH, Beubin and Bee Whatley   September 27, 1802
BELSHER, William and Jemima Smith   October 30, 1809
BENFORD, John and Elisabeth Pope   December 11, 1806
BENNETT, Benjamin and Susanah Waters   December 19, 1811
BENNETT, Reubin and Sally Edwards   November 17, 1804
BENTLEY, Isaac and Lizzy Williams   April 6, 1798
BENTLEY, Isaiah and Nancy Dale   January 7, 1813
BENTLEY, James and Zilly Thornton   March 8, 1827
BENTLEY, John T. and Polley Maxey   October 22, 1807
BERRING, John and Holly Ragan   May 30, 1795
BERRY, Bradley and Sarah Davis   December 26, 1819
BERRY, Bradley and Lucy Smith   October 31, 1833
BERRY, Edmond and Betsey Hailes   December 27, 1815
BERRY, John D. and Nancy Herring   February 13, 1816
BERRY, Lawrence and Betty Wilson   August 9, 1800
BERRY, Talliferro and Sally Wilson   May 8, 1810
BERRY, William M. and Jane Brock   April 23, 1836
BERRY, William W. and Harriet L. Ogden   October 23, 1844
BIBB, Benj. S. and Lucy Ann Sophia Gilmer   January 19, 1819
BILLUPS, Thomas C. and Sarah Ann Moon   February 25, 1823
BIRD, John and Delilah Brewer   June 10, 1795
BIRD, Wiley M. and Elizabeth Smith   March 12, 1822
BIRDSONG, Benjamin and Martha P. Owen   December 12, 1820
BIRDSONG, Edward and Nancy Susan Hawkins   May 15, 1834
BIRDSONG, Geo. W. and Serena Birdsong   March 9, 1829
BIRDSONG, John and Polly Strong   June 14, 1808
BIRDSONG, Paris and Margaret S. Scroggin   May 21, 1835
BIRDSONG, Robert B. and Sarah W. Dozier   December 8, 1837
BLACK, George W. and Jane Vann Vaughn   March 23, 1835
BLACK, James S. and Nancy J. Martin   October 30, 1832
BLACK, John and Elinor Scott   August 23, 1794
BLACK, John and Catherine Ramsey   September 19, 1801
BLACK, Samuel Joseph and Katharine Jane Grover   August 24, 1846
BLACK, Thomas and Polly Callahan   February 23, 1795
BLACKBURN, John and Frances Morris   October 10, 1816
BLAKE, Sisson and Silvey Bohannon   April 13, 1796
BLANTON, Benjamin and Sally Freeman   December 12, 1801
BLANTON, Benjamin and Lucinda M. Hill   July 17, 1843
BLEDSOE, John and Polly Birdsong   June 13, 1804
BLEDSOE, Miller and Mary W. Asbury   December 20, 1841

BLEDSOE, Morton and Polly Brockman	March 19, 1809
BLEDSOE, Moses and Polly Turner	September 7, 1805
BELDSOE, Moses and Lucy Ann Bowling	September 1, 1834
BLEDSOE, Peachy and Nancy L. Atkinson	January 5, 1818
BLEDSOE, Travey G. and Ann D. Broughton	December 11, 1821
BLEDSOE, Whitfield and Eunice Bledsoe	February 10, 1824
BODINE, John and Nancy Gunnels	December 25, 1810
BOGGS, James R. and Lucy R. Brock	March 27, 1835
BOGGS, Jeremiah and Luckey Dorsey	January 20, 1798
BOHANNON, Edmond and Sealy Peacock	December 26, 1797
BOHANNON, Kinehan and Dolly Peacock	January 20, 1807
BOLES, Benjamin and Mrs. Hannah Reid	December 28, 1851
BOLES, Henry and Effa Hogue	December 16, 1807
BOLLING, Thornberry and Lucy Ramey	January 26, 1798
BOLTON, George W. and Cornelia Ann Jennings	July 17, 1838
BOLTON, Dr. James N. and Mary Frances Johnson	February 24, 1852
BOLTON, Leonard and Mary C. Jennings	December 16, 1816
BOLTON, Maneau and Mary Goolsby	August 15, 1815
BOMAN, Isham and Polly Davison	May 7, 1804
BOMAN, William and Rebeckah Wall	May 26, 1804
BOND, Joel and Pena Read	April 1, 1818
BOND, Joel and Susanah Kitchens	June 6, 1819
BOND, John and Jane Eberhart	November 28, 1822
BOND, John C. and Margaret Reynolds	December 25, 1823
BONE, William and Malissa Carter	September 19, 1850
BOOTH, Reubin and Polly Moss	July 11, 1803
BOOTH, William and Polly Davis	November 22, 1820
BOOTH, William and Martha Powell	September 3, 1832
BOOTH, Wootson C. and Louisa Ann Pace	December 30, 1845
BOREN, James and Eliza B. Stovall	October 4, 1813
BORN, Daniel and Jenny Buzbain	September 30, 1807
BOWDEN, Charles and Mary Ann Waters	December 3, 1812
BOWDEN, James and Betsy McCord	April 22, 1805
BOWDEN, Jesse and Sally Yarbrough	October 30, 1808
BOWDEN, John and Anna Blackburn	September 7, 1802
BOWDEN, William and Amy Finch	June 4, 1813
BOWDRE, Albert J. R. and Lucy C. Merriwether	September 21, 1847
BOWLING, Alexander B. and Elizabeth Kines	May 9, 1839
BOWLING, Thornberry and Mary Wright	June 19, 1828
BOWLING, Samuel and Susannah Brewer	September 15, 1797
BRADBERRY, James and Judith Carter	January 3, 1803
BRADBERRY, Wm. C. and Elisabeth Wright	September 3, 1827
BRADBURY, Edward and Anna Eliott	July 5, 1803
BRADFORD, James and Margaret Hale	September 25, 1832
BRADFORD, Bartholomew and Lucy Bailey	July 26, 1807
BRADFORD, Jefferson M. and Catherine Watkins	February 22, 1841
BRADFORD, Reese and Mary Jones	September 17, 1839
BRADFORD, Richard B. and Betsy Edwards	January 26, 1802
BRADFORD, Samuel and Elisabeth Tompkins	March 17, 1814
BRADLEY, Francis and Pheniby Goolsby	November 20, 1823
BRADLEY, James and Martha G. Jordan	July 15, 1801
BRADLEY, John and Peggy J. Meriwether	June 23, 1798

BRADLEY, John A. and Elizabeth Noel — May 14, 1819
BRADLEY, John A., Sr., and Martha Stephens — January 17, 1828
BRADSHAW, Charles and Caroline Bailey — October 6, 1852
BRADSHAW, George and Vina Radford — May 11, 1798
BRADSHAW, Joshua and Nancy Bradshaw — June 5, 1834
BRADSHAW, Peter and Fanney Smith — February 28, 1799
BRADSHAW, Peter and Lucy Allen — August 25, 1808
BRADSHAW, William and Elizabeth Hinson — August 20, 1841
BRADSHAW, William and Martha Bradshaw — November 9, 1852
BRAGGARD, Richard P. and Martha Galbreath — February 5, 1824
BRAND, Cashwell and Syntha Williams — January 22, 1818
BRAND, Gail and Tabitha King — February 27, 1812
BRAND, Malliard and Charity Jinks — March 17, 1814
BRAY, John and Polly Hammond — March 3, 1825
BRAY, Martin and Sarah Berry — October 1, 1846
BREWER, Franklin and Mary Ann Brooks — January 17, 1842
BREWER, Hendley and Lury Loyd — March 23, 1799
BREWER, Jacob and Jemima Morgan — January 1, 1805
BREWER, William and Sally Dogget — April 17, 1800
BREWER, William and Genny Farmer — November 27, 1804
BRIANT, Braxton and Sarah C. Bacon — October 24, 1843
BRIANT, Edward and Mary Stewart — February 26, 1824
BRIANT, William and Sally Mills — July 23, 1812
BRIDGES, Aaron and Amey McDaniel — July 30, 1818
BRIDGES, Berry and Mary Freeman — July 12, 1797
BRIDGES, Burwell and Nancy Gunnels — January 26, 1809
BRIDGES, Daniel and Bekey Huddleston — April 13, 1803
BRIDGES, Hollis C. and Patsy W. Colbert — October 24, 1816
BRIDGES, James and Kizziah Jennings — February 23, 1826
BRIDGES, James and Emily Bell — April 17, 1849
BRIDGES, Jeremiah and Sarah Hail — October 25, 1796
BRIDGES, Jeremiah and Rebecca Hails — March 30, 1800
BRIDGES, Jonathan and Sally Bridges — December 10, 1807
BRIDGES, Joseph and Obedience Bridges — September 24, 1809
BRIDGES, Merrill and Pasence (Patience) Grunnolds — April 5, 1800
BRIDGES, Moses and Sally Hill — November 16, 1826
BRIDGES, Nathaniel C. and Martha Arnold — August 6, 1850
BRIGHTWELL, Andrew T. and Lucinda Robinson — January 3, 1837
BRIGHTWELL, John M. and Elizabeth Patrick — November 1, 1843
BRIGHTWELL, Samuel and Frances Beary — August 29, 1809
BRISCOE, Abednego W. and Sarah Ann Gresham — June 11, 1839
BRITAIN, Berry and Winny Biggs — July 21, 1806
BRITAIN, Jack L. and Mary J. Bush — February 19, 1852
BRITAIN, James H. and Nancy Gillum — December 14, 1836
BRITAIN, John B. and Lucinda Walker — February 6, 1828
BRITAIN, Thomas J. and Permelia Lumpkin — October 25, 1838
BRITTAIN, Burwell and Polly Hinton — October 22, 1807
BRITTAIN, George and Nancy Brewer — July 23, 1800
BRITTAIN, Thomas and Susannah Bolling — January 3, 1797
BRITTON, Henry and Nancy Lunsford — November 28, 1811
BROACH, George and Lucy Glenn — August 10, 1801
BROACH, George A. and Mary B. Butler — October 11, 1843

BROCKMAN, James and Margaret Bledsoe — March 16, 1824
BROOKS, Addison and Lucinda Bray — September 2, 1852
BROOKS, Albert and Nancy Butler — January 29, 1848
BROOKS, Edward G. and Mary Ann Farro — December 4, 1832
BROOKS, Gilbert and Rachel Beavers — April 17, 1797
BROOKS, Hillery and Nancy Andrews — January 16, 1826
BROOKS, Jesse and Ann Callahan — April 15, 1824
BROOKS, John and Elisabeth Davis — October 13, 1818
BROOKS, Jonathan and Sarah English — January 18, 1826
BROOKS, Robert and Sarah Moore — June 9, 1825
BROOKS, Silas and Tabitha Mickelberry — January 12, 1826
BROOKS, Thomas and Betsy Hardman — January 12, 1801
BROOKS, Thomas P. and Mary Amis — January 26, 1826
BROOKS, William M. and Amanda Jane Stewart — February 4, 1848
BROOKS, William P. and Amanda F. Bridges — October 19, 1852
BROOKS, William R. and Lucinda B. Rainey — February 5, 1833
BROOKS, Wilson W. and Katherine L. Yancey — December 17, 1829
BROUGHTON, William and Nancy Akins — February 4, 1807
BROWN, Alexander and Syntha Brown — March 2, 1817
BROWN, Allen W. and Martha Gresham — January 19, 1820
BROWN, Benjamin and Milley House — April 13, 1807
BROWN, Charles W. and Matilda Williamson — May 17, 1836
BROWN, David and Mary Stewart — August 7, 1814
BROWN, Ezekiel and Mary Low — April 12, 1810
BROWN, Ezekiel and Sarah Sims — August 20, 1839
BROWN, Gideon and Sarah Glenn — November 13, 1802
BROWN, Isaac and Anna Thompson — December 24, 1818
BROWN, John G. and Sally Caruthers — November 6, 1811
BROWN, John and Ann Moore — November 17, 1845
BROWN, Joseph and Charity Cullum — April 10, 1806
BROWN, Joseph and Delania Suddeth — December 16, 1813
BROWN, Nathaniel and Eliza Smith — December 31, 1815
BROWN, Samuel B. and Parthenia Stewart — December 28, 1823
BROWN, Thomas and Fanny Finch — September 30, 1801
BROWN, Thomas and Mahala Finch — December 3, 1814
BROWN, Thomas W. and Elisabeth Holmes — June 14, 1829
BROWN, William G. and Jane Thompson — June 18, 1818
BROWN, William and Polley Suddeth — August 19, 1826
BROWN, William W. and Louisa G. Sims — June 10, 1836
BRYANT, Braxton E. and Emaline Roberts — December 15, 1847
BRYANT, James and Sarah Ann Ward — February 26, 1849
BRYANT, John and Eliza Kimbell — December 3, 1836
BRYANT, William and Ann Kimbell — January 27, 1837
BRYANT, William and Elizabeth Langford — December 13, 1841
BUCHANNAN, James and Sally Gunnels — September 18, 1826
BUFORD, Alfred and Sarah E. Jackson — April 9, 1839
BULLOCK, Hardy and Polly Dorherty — June 16, 1808
BULLOCK, Nathan N. and Selasty Colbert — November 3, 1821
BULLOCK, Thomas B. and Nancy Jackson — December 19, 1837
BULLOCK, Wyatt and Betsey Allen — June 6, 1803
BUNDREN, Josiah and Miss Johnson — January 1, 1798
BUNYARD, John and Sally Harwell — January 22, 1807

BUPREE, William and Betsey Embry	June 1, 1808
BUREGARD, James and Delilah McLeroy	December 19, 1803
BURFORD, Mitchell and Salley Bragg	March 18, 1809
BURGESS, Francis M. and Lucy A. E. L. Veal	June 19, 1847
BURKE, Elisha and Pacience Dunston	June 30, 1801
BURKE, Francis and Viney Goolsby	January 21, 1824
BURKE, William and Mary Dunston	March 29, 1800
BUROUGHS, William F. and Mary Cheatham	October 16, 1838
BURT, Anderson and Sally Finch	March 20, 1809
BURT, Ernesly P. and Jane Tiller	June 15, 1843
BURT, James N. and Elizabeth Fambrough	September 5, 1807
BURTON, John and Amanda Booth	December 29, 1852
BURTON, Joseph and Elizabeth Edwards	September 9, 1848
BURTON, Robert and Lydia Clayton	March 13, 1798
BURTON, William and Nancy Hugh	August 25, 1804
BUSBIN, Benjamin and Temperance Bridges	October 2, 1816
BUSBIN, David and Lucy Bishop	January 31, 1815
BUSBIN, Isaac and Harriet Ann Johnson	August 20, 1833
BUSBIN, Jacob and Dorothy R. Gunnels	September 29, 1824
BUSBIN, John and Jerusha Corbin	December 22, 1814
BUSBIN, John and Mrs. Martha Andrews	April 14, 1852
BUSBIN, Josiah F. and Eliza Ann Short	December 3, 1844
BUSHBIN, Jonathan and Dicey Lively	September 3, 1832
BUSH, William Wade and Eliza Wise	November 11, 1846
BUTLER, David and Matilda Kent	September 24, 1838
BUTLER, Frederick and Amy Martin	October 24, 1827
BUTLER, Joseph and Sarah Jane Landrum	October 28, 1846
BUTLER, Seaborn and Elva A. Green	December 20, 1837
BUTLER, Western and Juliann Hancock	December 22, 1847
BUZBIN, J. M. and Nancy Cheatham	September 23, 1839
BYRD, Samuel and Elisabeth Finch	September 2, 1808
BYRNE, Richard and Joanah Gresham	April 21, 1808

C

CABANISS, George and Betsy Goolsby	May 15, 1806
CALAWAY, Young and Sarah D. Hardman	September 14, 1835
CALENHEAD, John and Patsey Whitehead	December 29, 1798
CALLAHAN, John B. and Harriett Bowen	May 11, 1835
CALLAHAN, William and Sally Thompson	September 24, 1805
CALLAHAN, William, Sr. and Lucy Burton	August 5, 1844
CALLAWAY, Abner R. and Sarah Jane Howard	October 15, 1852
CALLAWAY, David and Judith Tillery	December 24, 1800
CALLAWAY, Eli and Martha Lumpkin	October 9, 1818
CALLAWAY, George W. and Elizabeth Wilson	November 15, 1832
CALLAWAY, John and Mary Milner	June 4, 1796
CALLAWAY, Seaborn G. and Mildred O. Gordon	January 1, 1839
CALLAWAY, Thomas P. and Lucy F. Oliver	August 26, 1848
CALLAWAY, Wm. R. and Mrs. Jane Hudson	October 16, 1849
CALLOWAY, Jesse and Anna Wier	December 9, 1807
CAMPBELL, Andrew and Nancy Patrick	October 26, 1818
CAMPBELL, Bailey A. and Mary A. Betts	January 6, 1835

CAMPBELL, Charles and Milley Bailey — January 20, 1800
CAMPBELL, James F. and Margaret Jane McLaughlin — October 16, 1849
CAMPBELL, William and Elizabeth Jewell — January 14, 1825
CANTABURG, Jeremiah and Celery Martin — August 2, 1796
CARDIN, James and Elizabeth Tillery — December 13, 1807
CARDWELL, John and Pheby Gosden — December 24, 1816
CARITHERS, Samuel L. and Elizabeth Johnson — July 30, 1822
CARLEY, John G. and Nancy Arnold — October 16, 1841
CARLTON, Richard and Mary Bowling — September 26, 1833
CARLTON, Richard and Eugenia A. Ragan — November 3, 1840
CARMICAL, Richard and Elizabeth Moore — December 26, 1810
CARR, Jonah and Mazy Eason — January 6, 1805
CARR, Robert E. and Elizabeth Mattox — January 6, 1813
CARRINGTON, John and Sarah Lester — May 15, 1818
CARRINGTON, Osborn and Polley Thompson — August 10, 1810
CARROLL, Benjamin and Elizabeth Robertson — February 28, 1796
CARRUTH, James and Eliza Carruth McEnder — October 12, 1798
CARRUTH, Robert and Mary Hitchcock — April 6, 1815
CARRUTHERS, Robert and Polley Anderson — January 31, 1803
CARRUTHERS, William and Semby Sims — September 8, 1813
CARSON, John S. and Martha Littlefield — July 4, 1838
CARTER, Armstead and Jane McWhorter — March 17, 1814
CARTER, Edward and Polly Kidd — December 14, 1805
CARTER, Edward and Sally Carter — June 29, 1811
CARTER, Eli and Catharine Harwell — November 24, 1838
CARTER, Eli and Mary A. Graham — September 21, 1840
CARTER, George W. and Lucy A. Carter — December 14, 1844
CARTER, Henry W. and Matilda A. McCarty — November 8, 1827
CARTER, Henry W. and Ardecy Lacy — December 21, 1835
CARTER, J. and Mary Charlotte Walker — December 5, 1842
CARTER, James R. and Elizabeth A. Espy — November 22, 1819
CARTER, Jesse and Mary Eliza Carter — December 11, 1841
CARTER, Joseph and Nancy E. Tucker — December 12, 1848
CARTER, L. and Minney Tribble — January 17, 1804
CARTER, Lesley G. and Elizabeth N. England — September 22, 1825
CARTER, Magnus and Dothia Farmer — February 2, 1826
CARTER, Obediah and Carando Wilson — May 30, 1810
CARTER, Paul and Winney Bridges — November 16, 1815
CARTER, Thomas and Hicksey Carter — March 9, 1813
CARTER, William and Holly Carter — November 28, 1812
CARTER, William and Ann Barber — September 21, 1824
CEAY, William B. and Elizabeth M. Hill — December 3, 1839
CESSNA, Samuel and Frances Huddleston — September 20, 1820
CHAMBERS, Asa and Mary E. Howard — February 23, 1822
CHANDLER, James O. and Emily A. Sims — December 1, 1838
CHANDLER, James O. and Susan Avery Anthony — December 6, 1845
CHANDLER, Pleasant B. and Mary O'Kelley — August 10, 1835
CHANDLER, William A. and Susan E. Sims — June 15, 1843
CHANDLER, William D. and Polly C. Lacy — August 15, 1842
CHANY, John and Caley E. Owen — April 1, 1803
CHAPLIN, Jackson and Susan Allen — September 6, 1839
CHAPLIN, William and Peggy Bradshaw — July 24, 1808

CHAPLIN, William and Lucy Kelly — February 23, 1833
CHAPMAN, Benjamin and Lidia Brown — December 6, 1812
CHAPMAN, Thomas and Sally Brown — June 7, 1809
CHAPPELL, Rev. John B. and Mrs. Margaret Griffin — September 12, 1845
CHEATHAM, Isham and Rebecca England — April 9, 1851
CHILDRESS, John and Sally Golesby — March 19, 1796
CHILUZ (Chilluss) David and Lilla Hardman — September 28, 1835
CHRISTIAN, Gabriel and Hannah B. Gilmore — July 9, 1810
CHRISTIAN, Ira and Anna Wood — February 28, 1845
CHRISTIAN, Thos. D. and Martha Ann Harman — November 11, 1833
CHRISTOPHER, David and Judah Clark — December 7, 1798
CHRISTOPHER, John and Elizabeth Varner — March 3, 1812
CHRISTOPHER, Richard and Martha Akins — January 7, 1826
CLAGHORN, James and Nancy Jones — June 10, 1795
CLARK, Josiah and Nancy Garrett — July 17, 1825
CLARK, William and Susannah Graves — July 11, 1803
CLAY, Samuel and Tabitha Clay — August 20, 1798
CLEMENS, Jesse and Betsy Webb — January 3, 1809
CLEMENT, Benjamin and Malinda Gilbert — February 16, 1795
CLEMENT, Isham and Hannah Morrow — December 20, 1797
CLEMENT, John S. and Sarah Kidd — August 27, 1822
CLEMENT, John S. and Margaret Wise — August 25, 1852
CLEMENTS, Jesse and Betsy Webb — January 5, 1809
CLIFT, William and Happy Olive — October 19, 1799
CLOUD, Ezekiel and Elizabeth Harrison — January 26, 1804
COATS, William H. and Sarah Jackson — October 24, 1842
COBB, Thomas R. R. and Marion G. Lumpkin — January 8, 1844
COBB, Thomas W. and Polly W. Moore — May 14, 1807
COBBY, John and Cathy Kent — December 11, 1804
COCHRAN, John and Julie Sims — December 1, 1824
COCHRAN, Lewis F. and Barbara M. Glenn — July 27, 1840
COCHRAN, Samuel and Rhoda Scroggin — October 2, 1797
COCHRAN, Seaborn and Clary Harris — December 20, 1827
COCHRAN, William and Betsey Owen — December 22, 1798
COIL, James and Mary Barnett — July 6, 1825
COILE, Warren and Matilda Webb — May 15, 1827
COLBERT, William P. and Louisa M. Sims — May 4, 1850
COLDWELL, Curtis C. and Sarah McCowan — May 4, 1826
COLE, Robert and Elizabeth Phambro — October 3, 1796
COLE, William and Anna Walden — August 21, 1799
COLEMAN, John W. and Rebecca C. Armstrong — October 28, 1852
COLLEY, David and Winifred Hardin — April 8, 1822
COLLEY, Francis M. and Lucinda Arnold — December 25, 1840
COLLEY, Joel and Polly Lindsey — January 18, 1804
COLLEY, Jonathan and Nancy Tuck — February 1, 1819
COLLEY, Thomas and Polly Wilson — April 4, 1801
COLLIER, Berry and Polly Howard — December 4, 1805
COLLIER, Charles V. and Rebecca M. Owen — June 4, 1829
COLLIER, Cuthbert and Nancy Dikes — December 13, 1803
COLLIER, Cuthbert and Rebecca Franklin — January 10, 1816
COLLIER, Edward V. and Davidley O'Gilvie — August 25, 1835
COLLIER, Wm. Joe and Jemima Powell — December 6, 1803

COLLIER, John and Patsy Gresham — February 5, 1795
COLLIER, John V. and Olive J. Mathews — November 12, 1833
COLLIER, John V. and Mrs. Elizabeth Bush — August 25, 1846
COLLIER, Nathaniel H. and Mary W. Brooks — October 16, 1825
COLLIER, Vines and Molly Rafferty — December 24, 1805
COLLIER, William and Sally Powell — October 12, 1801
COLLIER, William and Mahala Brooks — January 6, 1820
COLLIER, William P. and Maryann G. L. Nutt — November 18, 1835
COLLINS, Beverly T. and Sarah A. Kent — September 14, 1841
COLLINS, James and Mary Spurlock — January 2, 1809
COLLINS, James P. and Susan B. Patman — August 20, 1836
COLLINS, John and Polly O'Kelley — September 11, 1807
COLLINS, Randolph and Martha Brown — December 25, 1839
COLLINS, William and Nancy Guttery — September 26, 1813
COLLINS, William and Calenda Howell — January 1, 1839
COLLINS, William E. and Mary Jordan — November 5, 1827
COLLINS, Wm. G. and Maryann M. Davis — January 8, 1850
COLQUITT, F. M. and Mary E. Hargrove — September 9, 1852
COLQUITT, Henry P. and Mildred Pinson — April 28, 1824
COLQUITT, James and Ann Wise — May 12, 1825
COLQUITT, John and Sally Smith — October 27, 1813
COLQUITT, Jonathan and Sarah S. Banks — December 2, 1823
COLQUITT, Joseph E. and Ava A. Lee — March 17, 1834
COLQUITT, Nath. G. and Elizabeth Jane Arnold — December 14, 1836
COLQUITT, Thomas and Betsey Franklin — May 5, 1808
COLQUITT, Wm. H. and Zelpha Kidd — March 2, 1820
COLSON, Thomas and Nancy Hollaway — February 4, 1812
COLWELL, Glenn and Sally Moore — July 8, 1820
COLWELL, William and Anna Stubblefield — November 17, 1818
COMER, James and Faney Finch — April 1, 1794
COMPTON, John and Peggy Smith — December 31, 1807
COMPTON, Pleasant and Elizabeth Harris — March 14, 1796
CONDON, John and Elizabeth Hartley — December 21, 1813
CONE, James and Aggatha Bostwick — August 25, 1796
CONE, Richard and Frances Thornton — June 25, 1832
CONE, Robert and Frances Thaxton — March 21, 1833
CONE, William and Rebecca S. Briscoe — December 21, 1835
CONNELLY, John W. and Mary Brewer — March 24, 1845
CONNEY, Robert and Delilah Patton — March 15, 1794
CONNORS, Charles H. and Lucy J. Jordan — May 11, 1849
CONRAD, Benjamin G. and Nancy Maxey — April 8, 1824
COOK, Frederick W. and Louise A. McKinley — April 3, 1827
COOPER, Drewry and Polly Fields — November 2, 1809
COOPER, Harrison and Dicey Self — June 6, 1803
COOPER, James and Nancy Chaplin — February 29, 1816
COOPER, Kinnon and Salley E. Carter — December 11, 1822
COOPER, Thomas and Margaret Harrys — March 14, 1809
COOPER, Vines S. and Rebecca M. Carter — September 24, 1844
*COPLAND, Colson and Polly Silvey — November 11, 1807

*Certificate of marriage certifies they were married May 7, 1807. Clerk of Court has foot-note: "I recorded two certificates as above."

COPLAND, Obadiah and Susannah Dorsey — January 19, 1801
COPLAND, William and Beckey Dunn — May 12, 1800
COPLIN, John and Nancy Dorsey — January 19, 1795
CORINTHE, Alex and Polly Ragan — January 16, 1805
COUPPET, Vining and Sally Hitchcock — July 30, 1804
COX, John and Elizabeth Hide — October 2, 1809
COX, John M. and Mary Hawkins — November 7, 1821
COX, Swepson H. and Sarah E. Upson — July 2, 1838
COX, Wm. H. and Amelia S. Brailsford — April 4, 1842
COX, William J. and Matilda Bridges — December 5, 1837
CRAIN, George and Amelia Tompkins — June 28, 1799
CRAIN, Spencer and Polly Tompkins — June 16, 1803
CRAMER, Samuel and Jenny Brown — December 27, 1806
CRAMER, Samuel A. and Eliza N. Whitlock — December 17, 1850
CRAMER, Simeon and Jane Campbell — February 6, 1837
CRAMER, Wm. H. and Lucy Ann Stewart — December 30, 1852
CRANE, William and Nelly Thompkins — January 12, 1801
CRAWFORD, Charles G. and Mary J. Baughn — January 8, 1852
CRAWFORD, Hinton and Martha Barnett — January 19, 1820
CRAWFORD, Joseph and Susan Dupree — January 20, 1820
CRAWFORD, William H. and Caroline E. Thomas — March 25, 1839
CROCK, John and Mary Fequett (Fickett) — January 11, 1815
CROOK, Osborn and Elizabeth G. Leigh — October 16, 1826
CROOK, Valentine and Nancy Fuguitt — December 16, 1819
CROOK, Valentine and Mary Jarvis (?) — June 3, 1845
CROOK, William R. and Nicy Buzbin — February 5, 1838
CROSBY, John and Martha Kinnebrew — February 11, 1823
CROSS, Harris and Fanny Turner — June 18, 1810
CROSS, Richard and Edney Turner — October 10, 1813
CROWDER, George and Lucinda Lansford — November 14, 1822
CROWDER, George W. and Emily Jones — March 10, 1839
CROWLEY, Abraham and Susanna Brittain — January 13, 1800
CROWLEY, Abraham and Wingfield Pinson — August 11, 1824
CROWLEY, Benjamin and Catherine Wiley — December 15, 1795
CROWLEY, Bengy and Elizabeth Jewel — January 7, 1841
CROWLEY, James and Dorcas Smith — February 23, 1799
CROWLEY, Price and Susana Landsford — August 19, 1805
CROWLEY, Spencer and Mary Smith — January 8, 1826
CRULE, John and Polly Belsher — November 5, 1810
CRUSE, Martin and Ginny Jordan — November 22, 1800
CRUTCHFIELD, John H. and Permelia F. Young — December 3, 1833
CRUTCHFIELD, Washington and Olive Jordan — October 1, 1810
CUDSON, William G. and Jane Smith — May 4, 1833
CULBERTSON, Madison and Susan Hopper — January 18, 1832
CULBERTSON, Newton and Phitterne Wray — January 1, 1838
CULBERTSON, W. P. and Aletha Jennings — June 2, 1800
CULBREATH, Francis M. and Elizabeth Smith — January 29, 1838
CULBREATH, James P. and Mary Adaline Everett — January 11, 1849
CULBREATH, Wm. Wert and Sarah Ann Brown — October 2, 1845
CUMMINGS, Elijah and Margaret Moore — June 14, 1832
CUMMINGS, John and Genny Martin — October 13, 1809
CUMMINGS, Thomas and Sally Wilkes — March 5, 1812

CUNNINGHAM, Benj. F. and Elizabeth S. Sanders   October 21, 1848
CUNNINGHAM, Benj. F. and Martha E. Winfrey   February 5, 1850
CUNNINGHAM, George and Agnes Patrick   March 6, 1798
CUNNINGHAM, James and Martha Watson   October 4, 1831
CUNNINGHAM, Robert and Betsey Ann Parks   October 6, 1795
CUNNINGHAM, William and (blank)   June 8, 1812
CUNNINGHAM, Wm. A. and Henrietta D. Poss   November 29, 1842
CURTIS, Emit and Elisabeth C. Stephens   August 29, 1822

D

DABNEY, William O. and Delilah Dillard   October 21, 1823
DADE, Reubin and Bebay Sorrow   December 9, 1800
DALTON, Jesse and Betsey Ann Finch   April 8, 1829
DAMBY, John C. and Martha C. Meriwether   January 6, 1823
DANCE, Matthew and Mary A. Adams   December 17, 1827
DANCE, William and Martha Jane Richards   December 16, 1847
DANIEL, Berry and Susana Berry   June 18, 1810
DANIEL, David C. and Mary Gresham   June 29, 1842
DANIEL, Edmond and Julia A. Wellborn   January 5, 1825
DANIEL, James and Frances Andrews   October 25, 1813
DANIEL, John W. and Mary Beman   September 18, 1850
DARBY, Richard and Sidney Bledsoe   April 20, 1822
DAUSBY, Albert H. and Elizabeth Johnson   November 7, 1832
DAVID, Isaac and Susanah Vaughn   October 14, 1798
DAVIE, Edward and Olive Smith   May 23, 1794
DAVIS, Aaron and Prisilla McElroy   September 10, 1796
DAVIS, Benjamin and Grunney McKee   October 10, 1801
DAVIS, Benjamin and Nancy Johnson   April 4, 1826
DAVIS, Berry and Martha Taylor   March 27, 1816
DAVIS, David and Polly Colwell   September 25, 1802
DAVIS, Dudley and Matilda Embry   December 19, 1809
DAVIS, Isham and Sally Edwards   November 27, 1796
DAVIS, Isham M. and Maryann Dorough   November 1, 1850
DAVIS, John and Permelia Richardson   March 19, 1829
DAVIS, John and Nancy Copeland   May 27, 1833
DAVIS, John and Jane Bradshaw   June 29, 1833
DAVIS, John C. and Rebecca Wooten   January 2, 1829
DAVIS, John L. and Polly Kelly   September 18, 1828
DAVIS, Jonathan and Pening Gunnels   March 1, 1821
DAVIS, Malachi R. and Susan Elizabeth Power   October 2, 1846
DAVIS, Manly and Caroline Ogden   July 26, 1832
DAVIS, Moses and Caty Finch   November 13, 1807
DAVIS, Pryor L. and Elizabeth Sims   April 5, 1834
DAVIS, Seyborn and Mary B. Collins   September 10, 1818
DAVIS, Sherwood and Lovraney Watkins   February 15, 1797
DAVIS, William and Catey Dorsey   September 11, 1809
DAVIS, William and Patsey Johnson   August 17, 1811
DAVIS, William and Angeline Lumpkin   December 26, 1827
DAVIS, Wm. J. and Mary Watkins   January 6, 1851
DAVENPORT, Jewett and Susanah Hewell   February 24, 1814
DAVENPORT, John and Elisabeth Bridges   January 9, 1811

DAVENPORT, Martin and Lucy Woodruff — October 4, 1841
DAVENPORT, Ransom and Nancy Bradshaw — January 8, 1798
DAVENPORT, Smith and Frances Davenport — January 17, 1807
DAVENPORT, William and Elizabeth Adams — December 3, 1818
DAVENPORT, Dr. Wm. W. and Maryann Glenn — January 6, 1852
DAWSON, William and Judith Hopper — March 7, 1801
DAY, Edward and Susan A. Edwards — December 15, 1849
DAY, William and Susan H. Britain — June 24, 1841
DEADWYLER, Asa and Mary Ann D. Johnson — December 21, 1842
DEADWILDER, Henry R. and Lucinda Bugs — December 17, 1832
DEAL, John W. and Sousan King (or Kines) — September 18, 1840
DEAVORS, Isaac B. and Elizabeth Farmer — January 10, 1822
DEGRAFTENREAD, William and Elizabeth Maxey — October 2, 1815
DENNARD, Wiley C. and Margaret E. M. Smith — December 12, 1849
DENT, Richard and Nancy Thomas — May 15, 1799
DICKENS, John W. and Mary Owen — December 15, 1821
DICKINS, James and Nancy H. Smith — March 27, 1810
DICKSON, Hugh and Sally Sanders — July 18, 1810
DICKSON, William and Elizabeth Sanders — March 4, 1806
DILLARD, Humphrey and Nancy Williams — December 14, 1813
DILLARD, Isaac and Sarah J. Stephens — February 24, 1834
DILLARD, Reubin and Delilah Ponder — September 18, 1817
DILLARD, Richard and Jane Ellington — April 21, 1833
DILLARD, Richard Antionette A. Chaffin — August 21, 1843
DIX, James L. and Nancy Swanson — December 19, 1826
DODD, George I. and Jane Born — January 28, 1821
DOGGETT, Thomas and Susannah Smith — August 16, 1802
DOGGETT, Thomas and Jane Bell — July 28, 1825
DONAHOE, John and Susan Patman — September 4, 1832
DONOHOE, Patrick and Polly Johnson — October 6, 1817
DOROUGH, Nathan S. and Harriett Landrum — August 11, 1841
DORSEY, Thomas B. and Sally Lemon — February 2, 1803
DOUSENBERRY, William and Sarah Degrafenreid — February 3, 1817
DOWDY, Francis Will and Mary T. Carithers — December 6, 1845
DOWDY, John M. and Lucinda Wise — January 15, 1824
DOWDY, John and Margaret Macklen — September 6, 1826
DOWDY, Richard and Nancy Jones — February 12, 1815
DOWDY, Richard and Ann Johnson — May 25, 1840
DOWDY, Willis W. M. and Eliza W. Jones — January 18, 1826
DOZIER, Albert G. and Margaret J. Powers — August 16, 1837
DOZIER, Augustus and Martha E. Howard — November 22, 1832
DRAKE, Archebold and Esther Martin — June 18, 1803
DRAKE, Averet and Mary Brown — December 26, 1844
DRAKE, Etheldred and Elizabeth Finch — February 3, 1820
DRAKE, William and Selina Hawks — December 26, 1843
DRAPER, William G. and Ava Ann Davis — December 23, 1841
DREW, John L. and Peggy McMurty — February 14, 1803
DUDLEY, George E. and Mary Gregory — July 12, 1804
DUFFIE, James and Vina Barnett — February 27, 1843
DUKE, Hardman and Sally Jordan — March 28, 1805
DUKE, Ransom and Janey Williams — May 20, 1798
DUKE, Robert and Betsey Cassell — January 5, 1811

DUKEN, Willis and Sarah Hopkins — October 9, 1824
DUNN, David and Mary P. Dunn — April 21, 1825
DUNN, Drury T. and Mary T. Howard — October 12, 1847
DUNN, Dr. Dudley and Eliza W. Cox — December 9, 1814
DUNN, Isham and Lucy G. Taliferro — February 21, 1825
DUNN, John and Janey Harris — November 6, 1796
DUNN, John W. and Dilenda Thornton — March 4, 1820
DUNN, Waters and Polly Dunn — February 19, 1806
DUNN, William and Sarah Anglin — November 24, 1828
DUNSTON, William and Rachel Walker — November 14, 1804
DUPREE, John and Polly Carter — September 20, 1806
DUPREE, Lewis J. and Kezziah Woody — February 24, 1815
DUPREE, William H. and Jane A. Goodrich — December 24, 1839
DURHAM, Lindsey and Martha Walker — June 26, 1822
DURHAM, Samuel and Patsey Reynolds — April 28, 1801
DYER, Micajah and Lucinda Haynie — January 2, 1817

E

EABRY, Enoch and (blank) — November 7, 1798
EADES, John H. and Martha Eades — December 14, 1835
EADS, John and Mary Smith — December 29, 1832
EADS, Tarlton M. and Elizabeth Pry (Cry) — August 2, 1834
EADSON, William and Judith Richardson — March 27, 1823
EARLY, Jacob and Milissa Hays — September 19, 1812
EASCO, George and Nancy Miller — January 3, 1829
EASLEY, Warham and Polly W. Strong — October 28, 1805
EASON, Elisha and Polly Donohoe — December 14, 1815
EASON, John and Nancy Arther — December 10, 1807
EASON, John G. and Martha G. Townsend — January 21, 1833
EASON, Thomas and Nancy Bryant — September 2, 1833
EASTON, Phillip and Sally Flint — February 14, 1811
EBERHART, Abel and Mary Sterling — September 25, 1835
EBERHART, Adam and Franky McElroy — May 11, 1809
EBERHART, Eli and Elizabeth Howard — September 13, 1841
EBERHART, Jacob and Caroline M. Beasley — December 18, 1841
EBERHART, John and Syntha Morgan — November 6, 1822
EBERHART, John and Sara Mattox — July 20, 1842
EBERHART, Martin and Catharine L. Johnson — October 25, 1841
EBERHART, Robert and Eliza H. Johnson — December 29, 1845
ECHOLS, James and Salley Rutledge — June 15, 1799
ECHOLS, James and Rebekah Barton — January 3, 1800
ECHOLS, John and Isabella Moon — September 14, 1807
ECHOLS, Joseph H. and Martha Eleanor Smith — January 31, 1844
ECHOLS, Obadiah and Betsey Strong — June 29, 1804
ECHOLS, Reubin and Betsey Owens — December 19, 1803
ECKLES, Edward and Nancy Rutledge — December 23, 1819
ECTOR, John and Jane Scott — April 12, 1803
ECTOR, John and Martha Pope — November 21, 1809
ECTOR, Joseph and Patsey Thurmon — May 31, 1803
EDMONDS, Wm. A. and Mary Frances Appling — November 2, 1840
EDMONDSON, Crawford and Hannah Reese — December 20, 1800

EDMONDSON, John and Mary Findley — July 6, 1819
EDMONDSON, Richard and Matilda Glaze — November 7, 1827
EDMONDSON, Samuel and Patsy Wilson — December 24, 1800
EDMONDSON, William and Matilda Rainey — January 4, 1832
EDSON, Lewis and Priscilla Jinnings — March 13, 1823
EDWARDS, Albert Henry and Louisa Elmira Hughes — December 20, 1850
EDWARDS, Benjamin and Amy Jones — April 12, 1818
EDWARDS, John and Polly Carin — December 21, 1801
EDWARDS, John and Malissa Stewart — October 25, 1821
EDWARDS, John G. M. and Ann Eliza Martin — June 26, 1852
EDWARDS, John M. and Polly Pass — January 15, 1818
EDWARDS, Lemual and Mary Johnson — August 8, 1820
EDWARDS, Lillte B. and Sally Whitsell — November 21, 1814
EDWARDS, Marshall W. and Jane Jewel — December 24, 1844
EDWARDS, Mordecai and Harriet Dillard — February 14, 1843
EDWARDS, Nathan and Dorcas Young — September 26, 1822
EDWARDS, Reubin and Nancy Bledsoe — November 5, 1808
EDWARDS, Simon and Mary Mikel — February 11, 1824
EDWARDS, Stephen W. and Louisa Glenn — October 3, 1827
EDWARDS, Thomas and Sally Pinson — November 6, 1820
EDWARDS, Thomas and Elizabeth Faust — April 2, 1829
EDWARDS, William and Betsy Bennett — November 17, 1804
EDWARDS, William and Frances Wright — March 26, 1810
EDWARDS, William and Catharine Martin — October 29, 1818
EDWARDS, Willis D. and Elizabeth Langford — September 20, 1816
EIDSON, Boss and Katharine Willard — December 2, 1812
EIDSON, Joseph and Elizabeth Richardson — October 4, 1827
ELDER, David and Isabella Mitchell — January 25, 1820
ELDER, John and Betsey (Elisabeth) Waters — March 31, 1816
ELEY, Bennett H. and Sarah Arnold — August 9, 1826
ELEY, Jesse and Nancy Shackleford — December 28, 1797
ELKINS, Erwin and Elizabeth Garrott — December 21, 1818
ELKINS, James and Diana Johnson — December 28, 1832
ELKINS, Joseph and Fanny Allen — February 4, 1812
ELKINS, Thomas and Ann Pope — March 13, 1809
ELKINS, William and Amelia Garrott — July 14, 1814
ELKINS, William and Martha Smith — April 17, 1839
ELLIOT, Cornelius and Frances Howel — June 9, 1834
ELLIOTT, George and Susannah Martin — November 7, 1815
ELLIS, Benjamin and Polly Burford — October 4, 1820
ELLIS, James and Olive Varner — March 12, 1816
ELLIS, John and Susan Varner — December 12, 1822
ELLIS, John and Dorothy Freeman — September 18, 1827
ELLIS, John and Mary E. Swanson — April 7, 1845
ELLIS, Nathan and Polly Phelps — December 7, 1820
ELLIS, William and Patsy Echols — December 3, 1795
ELLIS, Willis and Louisa Brooks — April 12, 1827
ELLIS, Willis and Elizabeth Stroud — October 3, 1826
ELSBERRY, Benjamin and Margaret Luckie — February 24, 1800
ELSBERRY, Joseph and Ann Smith — February 9, 1797
ELSBERRY, Michael and Eliza L. Ponder — December 26, 1827
ELY, Osbourn and Adgilene Birdsong — February 25, 1828

EMBRY, Brittain and Caty Elliott — March 10, 1804
EMBRY, Henry T. and Pauline A. Andrews — November 7, 1826
EMBRY, James and Frances P. O'Kelly — September 8, 1808
EMBRY, John M. and Jenny Mackleroy — November 30, 1809
EMBRY, John and Parthena Thomas — March 13, 1848
EMBRY, Joseph, Sr. and Polley Howard — February 2, 1809
EMBRY, Mene and Viney Howard — December 1, 1804
EMBRY, Murray and Betsey (or Patsey) Bridges — March 4, 1817
EMBRY, Thomas and Nancy McElroy — March 26, 1812
EMBRY, Wiley and Divina Howard — December 23, 1824
EMBRY, Wiley and Mary Ann Hawks — November 20, 1839
EMORY, Elijah and Frances Noell — May 16, 1816
EMORY, Joshua and Sally Banks — February 16, 1807
EMORY, Samuel and Anna Banks — November 18, 1806
ENGLAND, John and Nancy Woodruff — March 12, 1823
ENGLAND, Thomas and Susan A. Pinson — June 22, 1844
ENGLAND, William and Lucy Woodruff — June 6, 1817
ENGLAND, William and Mary Frances Sims — December 12, 1836
ENGLISH, George L. and Elizabeth Hudson — October 31, 1826
ENGLISH, Henry and Elizabeth Duke — August 24, 1822
ENGLISH, Parmenas and Nancy Starkey — November 21, 1814
EPPS, Marshall and Almarine L. Cramer — December 8, 1851
ERTS, Miles and Fredda Morris — August 29, 1801
ESCOE, John and Clarisa Hammonds — November 21, 1850
ESPY, Joseph and Martha Bog — February 28, 1796
ESTES, Colwell and Minervy Holifield — December 10, 1807
ESTES, George S. and Elizabeth Banks — December 9, 1852
ESTES, John L. and Rhoda Cunningham — December 31, 1826
EVANS, Davis T. and Mary Williamson — May 6, 1823
EVANS, John C. and Betsey Martin — December 30, 1801
EVERETT, Mathew and Elizabeth Thomas — September 29, 1815
EVERETT, Sideur and Tabitha Owen — June 13, 1801
EVERETT, William W. and Lucy H. Howard — December 20, 1842

F

FALL, John and Fidelia Newton — January 12, 1807
FAMBROUGH, Alexander and Elizabeth A. Michael — November 17, 1846
FAMBROUGH, Allen Loveless and Nancy Jane Noell — July 13, 1848
FAMBROUGH, Anderson and Delilah Maxey — September 4, 1810
FAMBROUGH, Doctor W. and Mary Ann McCarty — December 20, 1837
FAMBROUGH, John and Abey Walker — October 10, 1815/16
FAMBROUGH, John and Julitta Landrum — May 3, 1841
FAMBROUGH, Pendleton S. and Sarah A. Christopher — March 14, 1842
FAMBROUGH, Thomas and Kavenhapneck Maxey — November 8, 1816
FARMER, George and Nancy Bolling — April 7, 1798
FARMER, Henry and Elizabeth Carter — March 28, 1816
FARMER, Henry and Kissiah Jennings — December 22, 1825
FARMER, Thomas and Tempy Lee — May 24, 1817
FARMER, Thomas and Sally Hubbard — March 5, 1818
FARMER, Thomas and Elizabeth Watkins — April 25, 1838
FARRAR, John S. and Dorcas Barnett — March 7, 1799

FAULKNER, Thomas Jefferson and Mary B. Lessueur — December 23, 1848
FAULKNER, William O. and Susan T. Stephens — June 13, 1827
FAUST, Balsir B. and Sarah Ann Rains — February 7, 1838
FAVER, John and Sally Wynne — February 7, 1810
FAVOURS, John and Martha A. Lumpkin — January 15, 1839
FEARS, William and Polly Griffin — January 25, 1802
FEARS, William and Joyce Rainey — December 4, 1817
FELTON, James and Polley Espey — July 7, 1818
FELTON, John and Polly D. Smith — February 8, 1816
FERGUSON, James and Betsy Kitchens — September 15, 1804
FERGUSON, James and Salley Rolling — December 23, 1818
FEW, Clement and Salley Stephens — February 18, 1809
FIELDS, James and Holley Cooper — November 14, 1816
FINCH, Bird and Anna McLain — February 1, 1817
FINCH, Burdette and Polly Brown — December 30, 1802
FINCH, Burdette and Ann Thornton — August 21, 1841
FINCH, John and Eliza Green — January 24, 1811
FINCH, Lorenzo and Maryann Trible — January 2, 1844
FINCH, Sanford and Elizabeth Drake — August 25, 1827
FINCH, Thomas and Jane Price — October 17, 1820
FINCH, William and Polly Dunn — September 5, 1820
FINCH, William H. and Mary S. Barker — January 11, 1837
FINDLEY, C. H. and Elizabeth Smith — December 8, 1812
FINDLEY, Rainey and Nancy Martin — September 13, 1810
FINDLEY, Samuel P. and Sally Mitchell — February 17, 1817
FINLEY, James and Mary Wray — May 29, 1821
FINLEY, Oliver P. and Margaret J. Campbell — October 22, 1849
FLEEMAN, Henry and Nancy Farmer — May 19, 1832
FLEEMAN, John S. and Elizabeth Tucker — December 22, 1821
FLEEMAN, Thomas and Elizabeth Johnson — December 16, 1805
FLEMING, Thomas and Eliza Jane McWhorter — January 7, 1850
FLEMING, John and Milley Mann — June 30, 1797
FLEMING, Peter and Nancy Mann — June 9, 1795
FLEMING, Royal M. and Mary A. Echols — April 22, 1827
FLINT, William and Charlotte Tillery — December 15, 1814
FLOURNOY, Gent Thomas A. and C. A. Howell — October 7, 1834
FLOUGH'D, Robin and Nancy Hardman — December 27, 1799
FLOYD, Benjamin and Emily Stephens — July 29, 1824
FLOYD, John and Nancy Stewart — September 28, 1797
FLOYD, John and Barbary Black — November 27, 1817
FLOYD, John and Milley Stovall — May 30, 1822
FLOYD, John and Jane Vernon — April 19, 1824
FLOYD, William and Patsey O'Kelly — August 1, 1816
FLUKER, Subal O. and Rebecca N. Hawkins — December 10, 1840
FLUKER, Wm. N. and Jane H. Boswell — December 30, 1842
FORD, Ephraim and Betsy Elsberry — June 17, 1811
FORD, James and Harriet Harvel — September 5, 1836
FORD, John and Elisabeth Farrar — February 1, 1804
FOREMAN, James and Rebecca Rhines — January 20, 1817
FOREMAN, Martin B. and Susanah Stovall — November 20, 1817
FORTSON, Benjamin F. and Rebecca A. O'Gelvis — April 19, 1841
FOSTER, Arthur and Polly Potts — March 18, 1795

FRANKLIN, William and Polly B. Rainey — March 22, 1810
FREEMAN, Bailey and Polly Maxey — August 27, 1803
FREEMAN, Bozwell and Nancy Smith — February 18, 1808
FREEMAN, George and Polly Smith — August 11, 1809
FREEMAN, Hugh and Lucy Murray — December 30, 1800
FREEMAN, Jacob and Ann Clark — January 29, 1796
FREEMAN, Jacob and Elisabeth Ann Gillum — December 18, 1828
FREEMAN, James and Dorcas Johnson — January 11, 1802
FREEMAN, James and Patsey Lacy — December 22, 1808
FREEMAN, James and Sara Rowland — December 15, 1818
FREEMAN, John and Elisabeth Wilkes — June 20, 1803
FREEMAN, John and Elizabeth Goolsby — February 10, 1811
FREEMAN, Nathaniel A. and Sally Lacy — August 17, 1840
FREEMAN, Noah and Judy Rodgers — February 11, 1802
FREEMAN, Richard and Elizabeth Haygood — May 3, 1797
FREEMAN, Richard and Polly Knight — May 6, 1810
FREEMAN, Samuel and Jenny Foster — October 23, 1804
FREEMAN, Samuel B. and Elizabeth Ward — November 16, 1842
FREEMAN, William and Mary Lane — August 6, 1794
FRENCH, Hiram L. and Emeline Hurt — September 24, 1838
FROST, Johnson and Rebecca Hogue — October 1, 1812
FULLOLOVE, James G. and Tabitha Holmes — December 30, 1831
FURMAN, William and Lucinda Dillard — December 6, 1831
FUZELL, Edward and Peggy Glaze — September 14, 1815

G

GAGE, Matthew and Polly Eaton (Ector) — September 26, 1798
GAINES, William and Martha Smith — January 18, 1833
GAINS, Edward and Polly Moon — November 1, 1811
GALEY, Robert and Sally Hales — December 6, 1811
GALLAWAY, Anderson and Delilah Ponder — January 11, 1816
GALLAWAY, Isaac and Winnifred Ragan — November 29, 1796
GALLAWAY, Levi and Sinia Scogin — October 10, 1810
GALLAWAY, Thomas and Nancy Mathews — February 22, 1807
GALLOWAY, Britain and Ann Ponder — February 22, 1820
GAME, Abner and Betsy Anderson — April 1, 1807
GARLAND, Robert C. and Sarah McGewin — November 5, 1822
GARLINGTON, Christopher and Eliza Aycock — January 17, 1819
GARLINGTON, Edwin and Margaret Smith — October 21, 1807
GARNER, Charles and Jane B. Carter — December 21, 1826
GARNER, Samuel and Sarah Cooper — February 22, 1802
GARRETT, James and Margaret Welch — October 27, 1814
GARRETT, Jesse and Polly Tatum — December 15, 1797
GARRETT, Richard and Rachel Flint — April 12, 1814
GARRETT, William and Sarah Watkins — May 28, 1804
GATHRIGHT, Ausburn M. and Nancy Deupree — September 12, 1826
GAY, Gilbert and Polly Sams — August 27, 1818
GEAR, David and Helena McWhorter — July 26, 1833
GEE, Samuel and Elisabeth Jane Bryant — November 24, 1849
GEER, James M. and Frances S. Schles — August 12, 1834
GEORGE, William and Patsy Ector — February 22, 1800

GERARDIN, William L. and Lucy Lumpkin — March 27, 1839
GERDINE, John and Eliza Bass — November 11, 1817
GHOLSTON, Leonard N. and Nancy Howard — November 22, 1819
GIBSON, Hugh and Peggy Simmons — August 21, 1817
GIBSON, Jonathan and Susan Ann Glenn — November 22, 1826
GIBSON, Luke and Betsey Simmons — April 5, 1815
GIBSON, Michael and Polly Hales — November 24, 1814
GILBERT, John and Nancy Webb — October 5, 1815
GILBERT, John Henry and Eliza Germany — July 21, 1845
GILDERSHAM, Benjamin and Frances Langston — December 6, 1824
GILHAM, Ezekiel and Rebeckah Vint — April 16, 1799
GILHAM, Jacob and Frances Bowden — January 5, 1832
GILHAM, Robert S. and Jane Nicholson — September 28, 1833
GILHAM, Thomas and Martha Milligan — January 11, 1797
GILHAM, Thomas A. and Amanda J. Bugg — August 24, 1847
GILL, Benjamin and Polly Smith — November 22, 1808
GILL, Brand and Elizabeth Gill — August 21, 1817
GILL, Joseph and Sally Spears — November 10, 1808
GILLAN, Andrew and Eliza Tuggle — January 24, 1852
GILLIAM, Elijah and Mary Gunnels — June 27, 1816
GILLIAM, John and Patsy Link — September 13, 1817
GILLOM, Daniel and Sally Goode — December 2, 1805
GILMER, George and Martha Johnson — May 21, 1812
GILMER, James B. and Eligen L. Gilmer — July 10, 1834
GILMER, James J. and Elizabeth Jordan — January 21, 1828
GILMER, John and Lucy D. Johnson — December 7, 1814
GILMER, Nicholas M. and Amelia G. Clark — March 17, 1798
GILMER, William B. and Lucy E. Gilmer — July 24, 1834
GILMO, Peachy R. and Caroline M. Thomas — October 25, 1834
GLASS, George I. and Rebecca H. Smith — April 27, 1829
GLASS, James A. and Nancy Hales — September 1, 1819
GLASS, Joel and Jane Rutledge — April 3, 1805
GLASS, Joseph C. and Sarah Gresham — March 26, 1822
GLASS, Joshua and Mildred Hubbard — January 4, 1803
GLENN, Charles L. and Nancy Marks — August 3, 1824
GLENN, Charles T. and Sarah Cochran — September 7, 1840
GLENN, Erra and Sally Henderson — April 12, 1800
GLENN, James and Sally Noell — August 15, 1816
GLENN, Jesse and Nancy Goolsby — March 7, 1801
GLENN, John A. and Ann C. O'Kelly — January 10, 1850
GLENN, John A. and Elizabeth Kidd — April 12, 1852
GLENN, Joseph and Betsy Eades — October 2, 1805
GLENN, Mathew and Mary Floyd — January 17, 1826
GLENN, Radford M. and Narcis Thornton — January 28, 1842
GLENN, Thomas and Charlotta Meriwether — June 25, 1807
GLENN, Thomas J. and Lucinda M. Huff — May 29, 1848
GLENN, Thomas M. and Ann H. Roberts — December 25, 1827
GLENN, William and Nancy Meriwether — December 18, 1802
GLENN, William and Martha Glenn — December 24, 1823
GLENN, William and Mary Black — April 4, 1826
GLENN, William H. and Elizabeth Frances Huff — December 19, 1843
GLIDWELL, Archa (Archebold) and Betsy Jones — October 6, 1808

GLOON, Abner and Caroline Davis	February 23, 1817
GODFREY, William D. and Mary Smith	January 14, 1846
GOLDEN, Thomas W. and Susan Strong	February 5, 1818
GOLDSBY, James, Jr. and Betsy Cardin	January 2, 1797
GOLDSBY, Richard and Zillah Thornton	November 31, 1795
GOODE, James C. and Cornelia Ann Hopper	December 14, 1842
GOODMAN, John and Sally (blank)	January 21, 1806
GOOLSBE, Toliver B. and Martha Mann	December 1, 1833
GOOLSBY, Aaron and Ann Stewart	November 26, 1798
GOOLSBY, Allen and Summerville Haynie	July 17, 1824
GOOLSBY, Anson and Riah Osbourne	January 3, 1826
GOOLSBY, Fleming A. and Louisa J. Hammons	July 18, 1843
GOOLSBY, Floyd E. and Julian B. (Julia Ann) Wood	December 10, 1845
GOOLSBY, George and Barbara Webb	January 27, 1841
GOOLSBY, Hezekiah and Cassey Goolsby	March 21, 1821
GOOLSBY, Isaac and Elizabeth Mane	June 23, 1798
GOOLSBY, Isaiah and Genny Herring	August 31, 1808
GOOLSBY, Joshua and Elisabeth Hay	October 13, 1808
GOOLSBY, Micajah and Elisabeth Green	February 16, 1826
GOOLSBY, Miles W. and Mary Perry	December 19, 1817
GOOLSBY, Peter and Cealey Pye	June 2, 1801
GOOLSBY, Reubin and Nancy Fry	December 17, 1804
GOOLSBY, Samuel and Judith Stephens	June 17, 1799
GOOLSBY, Simeon and Cyntha Berry	April 25, 1826
GOOLSBY, Thomas and Delilah Green	December 11, 1839
GOOLSBY, Wade and Javal Lacy	December 9, 1811
GOOLSBY, William and Patsy Mathews	February 15, 1796
GOOLSBY, William and Letty Merritt	November 17, 1805
GOOLSBY, William and Anna Sorrow	October 25, 1812
GOOLSBY, William and Martha Wilson	June 3, 1821
GOOLSBY, Wm. P. and Barbara Fiquett (Fickett)	Sept. 30, 1837
GORDON, James F. and Sarah Ellis	April 22, 1817
GORDON, Thomas and Lydia Prestage	May 25, 1795
GORDON, William J. and Sally Lacy	July 2, 1838
GORDON, Wm. Judge and Rachael Chaplin	September 10, 1839
GORDON, Zekle (Ezekiel) and Nancy Smith	January 22, 1818
GORE, Nolley and Sally Patton	June 14, 1808
GORHAM, Jackson and Mary E. Penn	May 2, 1846
GORWIN, Henry and Clarissa Sims	April 10, 1818
GOSDEN, George A. and Susanah Bullock	April 11, 1811
GOSS, Ezekiel Fleming and Lucy Huddleston	December 18, 1810
GOSS, Isham and Rebecca Watson	July 18, 1822
GOSSETT, Jacob and Rebecca Morris	December 5, 1822
GOWER, Robert M. and Mildred T. Buford	March 6, 1826
GRAHAM, Armsted and Nutty Whitehead	January 9, 1820
GRAHAM, Hamilton S. and Althe Jane Weaver	January 7, 1833
GRANADE, Benjamin M. and Milley Bowling	March 8, 1824
GRANADE, Shephen and Sally Easter	July 24, 1799
GRAVES, Charles and Polly Taylor	June 3, 1817
GRAVES, David and Polly Russell	March 31, 1812
GRAVES, William and Polly Young	December 15, 1808
GRAY, Absolem and Sally Street	February 7, 1800

GRAY, George and Holley D. Carter — December 9, 1818
GRAY, John and Permelia Ward — November 15, 1814
GRAY, William G. and Mary A. Fleeman — September 27, 1849
GREEN, Augustin F. and Amanda J. Robertson — January 29, 1839
GREEN, George G. and Sarah Edmondson — July 28, 1851
GREEN, John and Elisabeth Goolsby — December 8, 1818
GREEN, William and Patsey Peters — December 31, 1800
GREEN, William and Polly Hodnett — May 7, 1805
GREEN, William and Martha Edmondson — January 30, 1821
GREENWOOD, Thos. B. and Ann Thornton Bass — April 7, 1817
GREER, Abraham and Betsey Beasley — January 22, 1798
GREER, Aquilla and Patsey Arnold — January 10, 1808
GREER, Aquilla and Mary Williams — February 26, 1818
GREER, Elisha and Hannah Cabiniss — December 16, 1797
GREER, Harry H. and Sarah Ann Nutt — November 6, 1828
GREER, Henry and Susan Tillery — December 14, 1795
GREER, Richard and Nancy Reynolds — March 14, 1798
GREER, William and Delilah Haynes — January 14, 1808
GRESHAM, Barnett and Lucy Powell — November 18, 1806
GRESHAM, Ferdinan and Sarah D. Hogue — July 18, 1816
GRESHAM, George W. and Amelia Hill — October 31, 1832
GRESHAM, James and Elisabeth Winfrey — December 29, 1812
GRESHAM, John and Nancy Callahan — January 15, 1823
GRESHAM, John and Susan Barnett — October 28, 1823
GRESHAM, Josiah and Peggy Riley — June 5, 1811
GRESHAM, Robert and Polly Mandley — April 17, 1800
GRESHAM, Thomas T. and Jane P. Smith — August 25, 1825
GRESHAM, William and Elisabeth Sutherlin — May 5, 1812
GRESHAM, William and Salley Glass — February 12, 1819
GREY, Absalom and Eliza Adams — October 28, 1837
GRIER, Ebeneza T. and Rebecca Wright — September 28, 1840
GRIER, Young H. and Almedy T. Beasley — September 3, 1835
GRIFFETH, James M. and Elizabeth H. Nicholson — July 25, 1849
GRIFFIN, Silas and Peggy Armstrong — February 16, 1814
GRIFFITH, Ezekiel and Polly Barber — November 28, 1816
GRIFFITH, John and Mahala Porter — March 1, 1821
GRIFFITH, John and Julia A. Embry — December 20, 1821
GRIFFITH, William and Sally Craws — October 22, 1821
GRIGSBY, James and Betsey Moody — January 7, 1808
GRILL, Joseph and Nancy Manley — November 10, 1802
GRIMES, Gabriel W. and Saleta Ann Mathews — May 1, 1848
GRIMES, William and Deanea Taylor — January 25, 1802
GUEREY, William and Martha G. Marke — October 3, 1798
GUILL, Augustus and Martha Milner — December 5, 1824
GUILL, Bluford and Mary Orr — April 2, 1825
GUNN, James R. and Elizabeth T. Morgan — February 27, 1832
GUNN, Radford and Peggy Roder — August 27, 1813
GUNTER, James M. and Louisa Hopper — March 25, 1850
GUTHREY, Nehemiah and Nancy B. Turner — January 24, 1828

H

HAIL, Josey and Sally Hill	November 19, 1807
HAILES, Obid and Milley Hailes	December 3, 1801
HAILEY, James and Betsey Hailey	August 13, 1802
HALE, Daniel and Frances McLaughlin	December 15, 1824
HALE, Moab and Fanny Whitehead	November 7, 1811
HALE, Thomas and Susanah Jennings	October 18, 1814
HALE, Thomas and Obedience Wise	January 16, 1825
HALE, John and Milly Rhodes	January 31, 1823
HALES, Samuel and Elizabeth Bradford	February 16, 1826
HALEY, Andrew and Cynthia Jinnings	July 3, 1823
HALL, Hillard S. and Nancy C. Crowder	December 7, 1841
HALL, Robert and Sintha Newton	March 28, 1809
HAM, Stephen and Lucy R. Glenn	January 4, 1817
HAMILTON, John and Rebecca Holoway	June 3, 1795
HAMILTON, Walter and Eliza J. Carrol	January 9, 1841
HAMLET, Hugh and Rhode Colley	November 17, 1800
HAMMIL, James and Sarah Lesly	July 11, 1824
HAMMOCK, John and Elizabeth Mealor	September 16, 1833
HAMMOND, Abram and Lilley Elsberry	November 2, 1808
HAMMOND, Jackson and Sarah Ann Bridges	April 17, 1847
HAMMOND, Jasper and Ann Hancock	September 17, 1845
HAMMOND, Jesse and Mary Lovron	December 19, 1839
HAMMOND, Samuel and Ann H. Glenn	October 2, 1835
HAMMOND, William and Susan Vaughn	January 31, 1822
HAMMONDS, Boswell and Nancy Miller	November 18, 1831
HAMMONDS, Samuel H. and Lilpha Wray	December 12, 1836
HAMNER, Mathew and Sally Spike	June 22, 1811
HAMNER, William and Elizabeth H. Hamner	June 9, 1804
HAMPTON, David and Reason Meadows	June 1, 1820
HANCOCK, Abraham and Mary Edes	November 12, 1835
HANCOCK, Absalom and Ann Wray	September 9, 1837
HANCOCK, Benjamin and Mary Porter	January 23, 1804
HANCOCK, Micajah and Mahuldah Cox	February 27, 1819
HANCOCK, Micajah and Fanny Hopper	November 8, 1822
HANCOCK, Phillip and Emelia Kent	January 1, 1828
HANCOCK, Simon and Rachel McLeroy	September 16, 1801
HANCOCK, William and Judith Wise	June 15, 1818
HAND, Christopher and Polly Turner	January 26, 1815
HAND, William and Malinda Finley	December 22, 1819
HANSON, Richard P. and Eliza Sophia Wray	July 4, 1810
HARDEMAN, Bibsey and Olly Watkins	January 23, 1834
HARDEMAN, Charles B. and Martha Whitehead	May 1, 1833
HARDEMAN, Robert S. and Sarah Eades	August —, 1832
HARDEMAN, William and Barbara Frances Crook	November 13, 1845
HARDEN, George and Clementine Floyd	March 16, 1832
HARDIN, Thomas J. and Sarah Jane Farmer	July 31, 1846
HARDMAN, Allan and Synthy Johnson	August 26, 1815
HARDMAN, Atha Elias and Elizabeth Smith	October 14, 1846
HARDMAN, Charles and Betsy Willingham	January 9, 1817
HARDMAN, Elbert and Charlotta Barnett	January 4, 1818

HARDMAN, Isaac and Elizabeth C. Hill — December 13, 1827
HARDMAN, Isaiah and Tabitha Ford — July 11, 1803
HARDMAN, Jesse and Almeda Ann Smith — July 15, 1846
HARDMAN, John and Nancy Smith — March 13, 1797
HARDMAN, John and Polly Cochran — November 25, 1815
HARDMAN, John and Paulina Hill — December 19, 1822
HARDMAN, Phelix and A. Jennings — April 16, 1820
HARDMAN, Samuel and Nancy Gower — August 26, 1803
HARDMAN, Samuel Z. and Amanda S. Rains — November 1, 1837
HARDMAN, William B. and Elizabeth Colquitt — January 2, 1851
HARDY, William W. and Mary J. Drake — May 4, 1846
HARGROVE, Charles and Mariah Smith — October 10, 1826
HARMON, Jabes and Jeanett Edwards — September 3, 1840
HARPER, Henry and Tempy Ray — May 7, 1822
HARPER, James and Patsey Southerland — February 13, 1812
HARRELL, Mark and Penelephy Johnson — November 3, 1804
HARRIMAN, Naman and Joyce Smith — December 22, 1809
HARRIS, Absolem and Mary Ann Latimore — December 6, 1825
HARRIS, Daniel and Martha Poss — August 20, 1832
HARRIS, David and Hannah Smith — October 20, 1801
HARRIS, Gillam and Zilpha Griffith — September 22, 1819
HARRIS, Jesse and Chanty Napp — May 3, 1804
HARRIS, John and Levina Thornton — July 4, 1816
HARRIS, John and Lucy Hawkins — December 21, 1824
HARRIS, John and Sydney Pye — December 27, 1837
HARRIS, Leonard and Amy Baughn — December 14, 1817
HARRIS, Nathan and Jane Poss — December 21, 1831
HARRIS, Nathan and Martha Pace — October 21, 1844
HARRIS, Samuel and Mary Norris — June 13, 1797
HARRIS, Thomas and Margaret Lawrence — October 13, 1801
HARRIS, Thomas and Jane McCord — July 4, 1798
HARRIS, Thomas E. R. and Emily Bowling — May 17, 1847
HARRIS, Tyre and Eliza Edwards — January 15, 1812
HARRIS, William and Madiah Northcutt — February 2, 1796
HARRIS, William F. and Mildred J. Howard — March 11, 1848
HARRIS, William P. and Sally Lorance — December 18, 1806
HARRISON, Jeremiah and Rebecca Ramsey — November 19, 1796
HARRISON, Robert and Mary Edwards — February 8, 1832
HART, Archabold and Polly Berry — November 26, 1802
HART, James R. and Harriet Lester — January 6, 1833
HART, James and Elizabeth Tiller — October 28, 1836
HARTLEY, John B. and Parthena Carter — August 21, 1838
HARTSFIELD, Andrew and Rebeckah McKelvy — April 1, 1797
HARTSFIELD, Andrew and Elizabeth Whitehead — December 24, 1816
HARTSFIELD, Andrew and Gaskey Hartsfield — July 24, 1817
HARTSFIELD, Godfrey and Sally Muckle — November 1, 1802
HARTSFIELD, Henry and Polly Olive — August 7, 1798
HARTSFIELD, Henry and Elizabeth Olive — January 1, 1829
HARTSFIELD, James and Nancy Oliver — April 15, 1812
HARVEY, Joseph A. and Martha England — August 10, 1825
HARVEY, William and J. M. Wynne — August 10, 1823
HARVILL, John and Betsey Davidson — December 20, 1801

HARWELL, Egbert M. and Martha Cochran — November 24, 1838
HARWELL, Mark and Betsey O'Kelly — March 12, 1816
HATCHETT, Edward and Harriet L. Ogden — July 28, 1828
HATCHETT, William and Mary Biggers — December 13, 1823
HAWKINS, Alexander and Betsey Williams — May 27, 1804
HAWKINS, John and Nancy Smith — March 2, 1801
HAWKINS, John and Elizabeth Elliott — July 5, 1825
HAWKINS, Thaddeus H. and Martha E. Johnson — January 13, 1852
HAWKINS, Thomas H. and Ammoretta Milner — January 13, 1839
HAWKINS, Wyatt and Nancy Allen — December 28, 1803
HAWKINS, Wyatt and Winney Ragan — December 17, 1812
HAWKS, Frederick and Nancy Adkins — January 19, 1807
HAWKS, Henry and Elisabeth Farmer — September 13, 1812
HAWKS, Henry and Elizabeth Johnson — October 6, 1840
HAWKS, Thomas D. and Frances R. Allen — January 10, 1839
HAWKS, William H. and Sarah J. A. Sims — February 1, 1849
HAY, Gilbert and Darney Goss — December 31, 1808
HAY, Gilbert and Laney Hales — March 6, 1814
HAY, Hugh and Polly Hailes — August 6, 1815
HAY, Hugh and Janey Strain — July 6, 1799
HAY, Samuel and Esther Brantley — October 24, 1800
HAY, William and Nancy Lumpkin — May 16, 1797
HAYES, Hiram and Elizabeth Jones — February 17, 1825
HAYNES, Henry S. and Martha Ann Gresham — February 7, 1842
HAYNES, Jasper and Lucy Slaton — May 17, 1820
HAYNES, Parmenas, Jr. and Genny Phillips — April 30, 1807
HAYNES, Richard and Abe Ragan — June 4, 1800
HAYNIE (Haney) Charles and Nancy Haney — August 23, 1802
HAYNIE, Francis and Martha E. Smith — July 15, 1816
HAYS, William and Crosha M. Barnett — October 25, 1815
HEAD, Daniel and Elizabeth Hannah — September 23, 1794
HEAD, James and Peggy Roberts — February 4, 1795
HEARD, B. U. and Mary G. Johnson — September 29, 1843
HEARD, George and Sally Bostwick — February 6, 1796
HEFLIN, Wiley and Hannah Boggs — November 3, 1800
HELTON, James and Anna Lawrence — August 20, 1803
HENDERSON, Felix G. and Flora Jackson — September 19, 1836
HENDERSON, Isaac P. and Lasy Bridges — April 4, 1814
HENDERSON, Miller and Nancy McCowen — November 11, 1824
HENDERSON, Samuel and Patsy Copland — August 26, 1803
HENDON, Andrew and Margaret Simmons — January 6, 1826
HENDON, Hartsfield and Elizabeth Olive — January 7, 1829
HENDON, Isham and Sally Murray — August 5, 1803
HENDON, Israel and Susannah Turner — August 22, 1803
HENDON, Johnston and Sally Scroggin — April 15, 1800
HENDRICK, Emanuel and Jane Wilson — January 10, 1821
HENDRICKS, John and Nancy Pamcoly — August 31, 1803
HENSON, John K. and Betsy Radford — July 17, 1804
HERNIE, Elisha and Sally Martin — September 22, 1800
HERRIN, Gresham and Elisabeth Hendricks — October 25, 1810
HERRING, Abner and Kisiah Hendon — August 16, 1802
HERRING, David and Elisabeth Viney — December 12, 1809

HERRING, Jonathan and Emily Buzbin	December 16, 1837
HERRING, Samuel and Mary Hendon	October 5, 1808
HESTER, James and Unisy Dunn	November 20, 1804
HEWELL, Jesse W. and Patsey Berry	May 17, 1814
HEWELL, William and Catherine Ficquet (Fickett)	March 17, 1832
HICKMAN, James and Elly Bowden	January 2, 1811
HICKMAN, William W. and Aunia Gann	October 7, 1834
HICKS, Thomas and Sarah Thomas	September 14, 1846
HIGGAMBOTHAM, Olliver and Nancy Doggett	January 31, 1797
HIGH, John and Nancy Garlington	December 4, 1827
HIGHTOWER, Phillip and Lotty House	December 21, 1815
HIGHTOWER, Rubin and Tempery House	January 25, 1812
HILL, Abram I. and Patsy Hardin	March 19, 1817
HILL, Abram W. and E. E. Hubbard	January 9, 1837
HILL, Blanton M. and Elisabeth Ann Hill	June 16, 1825
HILL, Carter and Nancy T. Mayes	September 26, 1839
HILL, James A. and Amelia W. Hill	October 9, 1818
HILL, Jeremiah and Peggy Allen	December 28, 1803
HILL, Miles and Tabitha Pope	January 26, 1795
HILL, Noah and Nancy Pope	September 28, 1796
HILL, Thomas and Sally McGehee	June 28, 1799
HILL, Wiley and Patsey Pope	March 29, 1799
HINTON, James and Dicey Hatley	October 19, 1808
HITCHCOCK, Jesse and Lucy Harris	June 20, 1803
HITCHCOCK, John and Julie Bridges	November 11, 1805
HITCHCOCK, John W. and Martha A. Howard	December 4, 1849
HITCHCOCK, Radford E. and Patsey Sims	July 31, 1826
HOBBS, Nathan A. and Harriet Tiller	December 28, 1852
HODGE, Archebold and Milley Bell	February 12, 1800
HODGE, Elliote and Milley Booth	October 5, 1801
HODGE, Elliotte and Polly Booth	September 17, 1808
HOLBROOK, Nathan and Ann Luckie	February 12, 1828
HOLEYFIELD, Algra and Milley Frey	January 7, 1799
HOLLAND, John and Peggy Gallaway	January 15, 1808
HOLLAND, Thomas A. and Ann Mann	December 22, 1834
HOLLAND, Thomas A. and Elizabeth C. Goolsby	June 28, 1839
HOLLIFIELD, Jesse and Pheriby Lacy	August 31, 1815
HOLLIFIELD, Willie and Polly Saffold	December 31, 1807
HOLLOWAY, Asa and Sally Moody	December 27, 1810
HOLLOWAY, Jesse and Mary Smith	August 8, 1800
HOLLOWAY, Vowel and Barbary Pace	November 24, 1816
HOLLOWAY, William and Sabara Baughn	November 28, 1811
HOLMES, Ben and Nancy Jenkins	January 21, 1811
HOLMES, Burwell and Sarah F. O'Gilvin	June 29, 1840
HOLMES, John and Nancy Smith	April 4, 1802
HOLMES, John and Polly Hall	June 20, 1815
HOLMES, John and Eliza T. O'Gilvin	December 26, 1840
HOLMES, Robert and Sally Pope	February 10, 1806
HOLMES, William and Nancy Eaton	February 25, 1805
HOLMES, William and Elisciss C. Wright	September 29, 1845
HOLMES, Willie and Sarah B. Richards	May 24, 1844
HOLT, Herman and Isabel Foster	October 27, 1801

HOLT, Thadeus and Anne Woodson	September 13, 1808
HOLTZCLAW, Horace and Mariah Willingham	December 30, 1824
HOLTZCLAW, Williford and Mary Edmonds	June 3, 1819
HOOD, Joel and Martha Dowdy	December 5, 1815
HOOPER, William and Milley Roberts	January 13, 1849
HOPKINS, Solomon A. and Nancy Howard	June 29, 1808
HOPPER, John and Elizabeth Ranchshaw	June 23, 1798
HOPPER, Jonathan and Sarah Vaughn	July 28, 1824
HOPPER, Rolley and Clasy Freeman	October 1, 1807
HOPPER, Samuel and Nancy Goolsby	December 25, 1798
HORNBUCKLE, Nathaniel and Elisabeth Cross	November 8, 1814
HORTON, Joel and Betsey Reynolds	November 12, 1796
HOUGHTON, Joshua and Nancy Bailey	August 28, 1815
HOUGHTON, Mathew and Nancy L. Lumpkin	September 13, 1820
HOUGHTON, Mathew and Jane Lumpkin	January 20, 1825
HOUSE, Burrel and Eadith Forester	December 26, 1797
HOUSE, James D. and Emily Buzby	November 12, 1838
HOUSE, Mark and Polly Maxey	July 4, 1816
HOUSE, Memorial (or Memory) and Susanah Gunnels	November 22, 1816
HOUSE, Richard and Anna Muckle	December 25, 1802
HOUSE, Wilie and Jane Grathouse	January 3, 1811
HOWARD, Asa J. and Elisabeth Glenn	November 22, 1822
HOWARD, Charles Henry and Sarah F. Johnson	January 4, 1842
HOWARD, Grover and Lucy Meriwether	December 27, 1802
HOWARD, Grover and Nancy W. Lee	January 20, 1825
HOWARD, Henry and Betsy Ann Collier	January 27, 1820
HOWARD, Isaac A. and Elisabeth H. Hawkins	April 27, 1825
HOWARD, Robert and Mary Glenn	December 22, 1822
HOWARD, Robert and Mary B. Glenn	June 28, 1828
HOWARD, Robert and Elizabeth Frances Robertson	January 31, 1842
HOWARD, Thomas and Polly Tarpley	December 17, 1806
HOWARD, William G. and Martha E. Barnett	December 9, 1851
HOWARD, William T. and Rebecca Milner	September 11, 1833
HOWELL, James and Franky Williams	December 15, 1808
HOWELL, Robert G. and Susan J. Fambrough	August 20, 1845
HUBBARD, Barnet and Susanna Griffin	November 7, 1796
HUBBARD, Creed and Camilla Barker	December 23, 1843
HUBBARD, Erwin and Lucky Jones	March 30, 1820
HUBBARD, John J. and Mary Ann Bowman (Brown)	March 4, 1834
HUBBARD, Joseph and Dosha Hudson	July 12, 1811
HUBBARD, Joseph and Elisabeth Wade	April 16, 1829
HUBBARD, Robert and Nancy Waters	January 27, 1812
HUCKABY, Samuel and Peggy Milliner	March 17, 1808
HUCKABY, William and Sally Bohannon	February 21, 1803
HUDDLESTON, Allen and Salina Hudspeth	October 12, 1820
HUDDLESTON, George and Susanah Jennings	July 8, 1818
HUDDLESTON, Joseph and Jeney Williams	September 9, 1809
HUDGENS, Starling and Betsy Hammett	February 1, 1802
HUDSON, John and Patsey Beasley	December 23, 1824
HUDSON, Robert and Lucinda Beadles Stewart	December 19, 1827
HUDSON, Robert and Nancy Ward	November 4, 1834
HUDSON, Ward and Demaris Goolsby	December 10, 1828

HUDSON, William and Nancy Collier — October 26, 1835
HUDSON, William and Eliza Johnson — August 8, 1850
HUDSPETH, Curtis and Nancy Patman — January 1, 1829
HUDSPETH, George and Annie Jennings — February 10, 1796
HUDSPETH, Richard and Polly Sims — March 19, 1800
HUFF, James and Mary Brown — April 21, 1841
HUFF, James R. and Martha Stephens — December 16, 1839
HUFF, John P. and Nancy H. Martin — April 7, 1838
HUFF, Robert and Sally Hardman — June 30, 1814
HUFF, William B. and Barbara W. Anthony — December 23, 1839
HUGHES, Embray B. and Elizabeth Michael — December 23, 1831
HUGHES, Joseph and Viney Powell — April 26, 1845
HUGHEY, John and Dorcas Young — January 31, 1806
HUMPHRIES, George W. and Sarah S. Gee — October 16, 1817
HUNT, Mr. and Ether Martin — June 23, 1798
HUNTER, Ephraim and Margaret McCannon — February 20, 1797
HUNTER, Nathan and Anna Smith — December 17, 1839
HURT, Joel and Eliza Edmondson — December 19, 1814
HUTCHESON, P. W. and Mary A. E. Smith — September 30, 1846
HUTCHINSON, Thos. D. and Arabella J. Jones — March 7, 1846

I

IRWIN, Christopher and Martha Moore — April 6, 1810
IRWIN, John and Polly Moore — October 28, 1807

J

JACKS, John and Jane Maxey — July 15, 1817
JACKSON, Ephraim and Louisana Baugham — January 25, 1834
JACKSON, Joel and Holly Ann Wilson — November 21, 1812
JACKSON, John B. and Mary Colquitt — May 4, 1836
JACKSON, Johnson W. and Ann Baughn — March 3, 1839
JACKSON, Joseph and Anna Rainey — January 18, 1804
JACKSON, Mathew and Exey Sims — August 30, 1839
JACKSON, Mercer and Elizabeth Stephens — March 21, 1838
JACKSON, Owen F. and Polly Jones — December 12, 1820
JACKSON, Pyent E. and Irena McLane — January 2, 1836
JACKSON, Shadrack and Abagail Grimes — October 3, 1809
JACKSON, William and Agnes Stiles — December 16, 1808
JACKSON, William and Susan Martindale — August 2, 1822
JACKSON, Woody and Sally Haynes — September 2, 1807
JAMES, Abner and Sally Green — March 1, 1796
JAMES, Casey and Jemima Rainey — April 11, 1815
JAMES, John and Sally Joiner — March 10, 1810
JAMES, Sherwood and Ruth Gilham — January 7, 1808
JARRETT, Jacob and Caty Nowell — September 20, 1810
JARRETT, Nicholas and Elizabeth Johnson — February 16, 1800
JARRETT, Tos. K. and Harriet McGehee — August 5, 1823
JARROTT, Patterson and Elizabeth Hudspeth — May 2, 1815
JARVEL, William and Elizabeth Bell — May 15, 1827
JARVIS, James and Susan Burt — December 31, 1840

JARVIS, Jesse and Polley Harris   January 8, 1816
JASMON, Lewis and Nancy Brown   October 5, 1835
JEFFORS, George and Catherine Tuggle   December 18, 1798
JENKINS, Daniel and Salley Rainey   May 5, 1814
JENKINS, Francis M. and Margaret Elizabeth Ogden November 2, 1846
JENKINS, James and Nancy Kene   June 26, 1802
JENKINS, James and Betsey James   February 16, 1809
JENKINS, Jesse and Hannah Suddath   February 10, 1817
JENKINS, Joab J. and Elizabeth A. Holloway   December 11, 1837
JENNINGS, Allen and Cintha Varner   January 17, 1822
JENNINGS, Boswell and Nancy Crowley   December 30, 1823
JENNINGS, David and Lucky Bailey (Susanah)   November 27, 1808
JENNINGS, Edgar and Susannah M. Dodd   December 18, 1821
JENNINGS, Henry and Nancy Landrum   April 1, 1820
JENNINGS, Jonathan and Ann Goolsby   January 10, 1837
JENNINGS, Jonathan L. and Elizabeth Smith   April 15, 1839
JENNINGS, Levi and Rhoda Harrison   August 29, 1803
JENNINGS, Levi and Nelly Barker   December 24, 1835
JENNINGS, Mathew and Betsy Wray   November 23, 1807
JENNINGS, Miles and Sarah Mattox   December 25, 1838
JENNINGS, Robert M. and Louisa Brown   December 8, 1831
JENNINGS, Solomon and Nancy Smith   January 20, 1800
JENNINGS, Solomon, Jr. and Martha Goolsby   November 21, 1839
JENNINGS, William and Rhoda Hill   November 11, 1809
JENNINGS, William and Mary Baber   October 23, 1811
JENNINGS, William G. and Mary Bush   March 24, 1835
JEWELL, James and Rebecca Bell   February 3, 1819
JINKS, Abner and Sintha Anderson   March 20, 1805
JINKS, Abner and Chanty King   January 23, 1812
JINKS, William and Betsy King   August 23, 1805
JINKINS, Obadiah and Abagail Smith   April 6, 1803
JOHNS, Ines and Polly Eads   November 20, 1825
JOHNSON, Alfred and Sina Ford   October 6, 1816
JOHNSON, Cary W. and Ann E. Jordan   September 18, 1850
JOHNSON, Daniel D. and Gloriannah Wood   January 1, 1845
JOHNSON, David and Elizabeth Nunnally   February 28, 1809
JOHNSON, David and Lucy Ann Moore   February 19, 1818
JOHNSON, David and Polly Nay   June 21, 1800
JOHNSON, David and Susan Ann Dowdy   December 10, 1833
JOHNSON, Dempsey and Harriet S. Andrews   January 6, 1825
JOHNSON, Drury and Nancy Stovall   January 10, 1811
JOHNSON, Edwin and Rebecca Edwards   December 7, 1832
JOHNSON, Elijah W. and Mary E. Clark   July 10, 1848
JOHNSON, Francis M. and Nancy Carter   January 11, 1837
JOHNSON, Green and Rhoda Goolsby   October 28, 1817
JOHNSON, Grover W. and Susannah Thornton   February 13, 1818
JOHNSON, Henry and Nancy Penington   May 12, 1794
JOHNSON, Isaac W. and Martha Goolsby   July 30, 1818
JOHNSON, Issac and Susana Embry   February 1, 1821
JOHNSON, Isaac W. and Judith J. Howard   April 21, 1821
JOHNSON, Isaac W. and Sarah Ann Glenn   June 8, 1826
JOHNSON, James and Polly George   February 21, 1798

JOHNSON, James and Lucy Duepree — May 13, 1817
JOHNSON, James C. and M— Goss — January 26, 1824
JOHNSON, James E. and Susan Wise — February 16, 1844
JOHNSON, James Shelton and Tracey Hammond — December 24, 1851
JOHNSON, James T. and Sarah Jennings — December 11, 1840
JOHNSON, James W. and Elizabeth Ann Moody — May 18, 1836
JOHNSON, Jeremiah and Sally Bradley — December 7, 1805
JOHNSON, Joel and Matilda Williamson — January 10, 1822
JOHNSON, John and Polly Dotson — December 26, 1808
JOHNSON, John and Elizabeth Edwards — April 2, 1814
JOHNSON, John and Salley Starkey — November, 1814
JOHNSON, John and Elizabeth Avant — June 6, 1827
JOHNSON, John R. and Mary Eads — June 24, 1837
JOHNSON, Jonathan and Elizabeth Brown — March 30, 1826
JOHNSON, Joseph and Sidney Johnson — January 7, 1846
JOHNSON, Josiah and Sally Turner — September 16, 1819
JOHNSON, Langford and Clarisa Eades — November 18, 1840
JOHNSON, Larkin and Henrietta Davenport — December 27, 1802
JOHNSON, Leander Martin and Mary P. Hunt — December 5, 1845
JOHNSON, Luke and Elizabeth Elsberry — March 24, 1800
JOHNSON, Luke and Elizabeth B. Cochran — August 16, 1828
JOHNSON, Luke D. and Nancy F. Brown — October 7, 1848
JOHNSON, Luke G. and Mary A. E. Hutcheson — December 6, 1847
JOHNSON, Martin and Polly Murray — February 4, 1812
JOHNSON, Michael A. and Rebecca Barnett — December 18, 1827
JOHNSON, Nathan and Zellia Smith — December 11, 1823
JOHNSON, Nathan and Jane S. Carlton — January 8, 1833
JOHNSON, Neal and Susan Hammonds — September 29, 1845
JOHNSON, Nicholas and Nancy Taylor — January 20, 1806
JOHNSON, Noel and Tempey Stamps — August 31, 1802
JOHNSON, Rayborn H. and Margaret Wood — March 21, —
JOHNSON, Reuben and Mary Sorrow — December 9, 1840
JOHNSON, Robert and Milley Maxey — October 18, 1821
JOHNSON, Robert G. and Mrs. Harriet Ann Kidd — February 16, 1852
JOHNSON, Robert T. and Nancy E. Jackson — May 17, 1851
JOHNSON, Rubin and Sarah Murry — February 23, 1812
JOHNSON, Samuel and Polly Simmons — March 20, 1806
JOHNSON, Samuel and Susannah Edwards — July 27, 1815
JOHNSON, Sandford and Eliza Lester — December 30, 1833
JOHNSON, Sankey and Ave P. Andrews — October 2, 1821
JOHNSON, Scott A. and Jane Zuber — May 28, 1850
JOHNSON, Sherwood B. and Elizabeth Campbell — March 1, 1817
JOHNSON, Thomas and Mary Griffie — November 2, 1796
JOHNSON, Thomas M. and Jane M. Gilmer — January 7, 1816
JOHNSON, Thomas W. and Margaret L. Bledsoe — August 16, 1821
JOHNSON, Thomas and Peninah Gillespie — January 19, 1837
JOHNSON, Thomas and Mary Ponder — October 28, 1799
JOHNSON, Washington and Ruth Canteberry — September 28, 1805
JOHNSON, Whitson G. and Mary E. Meriwether — August 7, 1826
JOHNSON, William and Elizabeth Groove — December 8, 1809
JOHNSON, William and Leathy Hardman — May, 9, 1811
JOHNSON, William and Jane D. Gresham — October 9, 1823

JOHNSON, William and Henrietta Andrews — January 13, 1828
JOHNSON, William and Malinda Rhodes — September 30, 1828
JOHNSON, William and Louisa W. Stamps — December 2, 1828
JOHNSON, William R. and Sarah W. Varner — May 12, 1825
JOINER, John and Annis Tiller — September 4, 1841
JONES, Aaron and Sarah Jones — March 28, 1822
JONES, Alexander and Susannah Gresham — October 23, 1823
JONES, Alexander and Louisiana Lumpkin — February 4, 1824
JONES, Barrington and Rebecca Davis — December 25, 1817
JONES, Brewington and Rebecca Carter — February 16, 1852
JONES, Claiborn and Sarah Powers — March 14, 1826
JONES, Henry P. and Nancy Carter — August 2, 1827
JONES, James and Sally Spears — August 16, 1803
JONES, James M. and Elizabeth A. Mercer — September 12, 1850
JONES, Joab and Ann Wilkerson — August 19, 1824
JONES, John and Rebecca Johnson — July 22, 1806
JONES, Isaac W. and Mary E. Jones — January 13, 1851
JONES, Leroy and Milley Taylor — January 1, 1800
JONES, Miles and Patsey Williams — December 20, 1810
JONES, Moses and Martha Mathews — February 10, 1829
JONES, Pleasant and Martha W. Bowling — December 20, 1824
JONES, Robert and Betsy Halchite — January 22, 1805
JONES, Robert and Polly Thomas — October 12, 1820
JONES, Russell and Susannah Martin — December 22, 1827
JONES, Seaborn and Edy Herring — May 4, 1818
JONES, Dr. Thomas W. and Mrs. Margaret Graves — December 8, 1849
JONES, Wiley and Sally Walker — November 15, 1806
JONES, William and Frances Mathews — January 21, 1832
JONES, William and Elizabeth Merritt — December 18, 1845
JORDAN, Burwell and Sarah T. Blake — May 3, 1827
JORDAN, Charles T. and Rebecca Johnson — July 13, 1825
JORDAN, Eldred T. and Joanah D. Haynie — May 28, 1827
JORDAN, Fleming and Ann Meriwether — March 30, 1811
JORDAN, Henry and Elizabeth P. Applewhite — December 23, 1822
JORDAN, James and Mary Blake — December 14, 1803
JORDAN, James E. and Sarah Freeman — August 5, 1824
JORDAN, John M. and Nancy Woodruff — December 11, 1832
JORDAN, Josiah and Zilly Parks — March 17, 1795
JORDAN, Josiah and Patsey Taylor — September 17, 1816
JORDAN, Reuben and Ann M. Johnson — May 21, 1809
JORDAN, Thomas D. and Jonah Hains — March 20, 1805
JORDAN, Willis A. and Sarah W. Dunn — September 10, 1822

K

KEAN, Josiah and Nancy Slaton — March 6, 1802
KEEN, John and Betsey Jenkins — August 18, 1803
KEER, William and Nancy Jones — April 21, 1818
KELLER, David Cincinnatus and Sarah Frances Clark — October 8, 1850
KELLEY, Shadwick and Patia Nuwbit — May 4, 1814
KELLUM, John and Elizabeth Bridges — September 27, 1823
KELLUM, Samuel and Polly Stephens — March 31, 1827

KENNEY, James and Sarah Alexander — ———, 1796
KENT, Allen and Dicy Turner — December 24, 1812
KENT, Allison and Drury Turner — December 24, 1812
KENT, Daniel and Sally Broughton — January 15, 1816
KENT, David and Nancy Brown — November 19, 1809
KENT, Elijah and Sally Finch — December 18, 1813
KENT, Francis M. and Louisa Price — September 21, 1847
KENT, Hardin and Louisa Bailey — February 14, 1822
KENT, Jesse and Polly Bradford — January 30, 1821
KENT, John and Danah English — July 28, 1811
KENT, Larkin T. and Mary F. Edwards — April 17, 1849
KENT, Lewis and Polly Kent — December 20, 1810
KENT, Sampson and Anna Turner — April 3, 1803
KENT, Thomas and Francis Turner — January 25, 1816
KENT, Thompson and Fanny Walker — August 27, 1818
KERLIN, John and Ann Lesky — December 26, 1810
KERLIN, Peter and Polley Lesley — December 15, 1820
KEY, George and Madaline C. Stephens — October 21, 1833
KEY, Jasper N. and Mary E. Howard — October 21, 1844
KIDD, Abraham and Deborah Wilson — September 30, 1810
KIDD, Abraham and Mary Antionett Kidd — January 21, 1836
KIDD, Absolem and Betsy Callaway — January 7, 1807
KIDD, Anderson and Polly Perkins — November 21, 1811
KIDD, James and Elizabeth Andrews — December 20, 1827
KIDD, James and Harriett Ann Collier — August 4, 1834
KIDD, John and Rachael Smith — December 17, 1799
KIDD, John M. and Susan Frances Fleeman — July 17, 1850
KIDD, Josiah and Eliza Johnson — July 31, 1846
KIDD, Nicodemus R. and Sarah Ann Carter — December 18, 1850
KIDD, Peyton T. and Mary E. Thompson — December 13, 1845
KIDD, Richard and Elizabeth Gillespie — December 4, 1817
KIDD, Robert M. and Polly Graham — May 24, 1827
KIDD, Webb and Malinda Kidd — March 16, 1825
KIDD, William and Nancy Carter — December 27, 1813
KIDD, Zachariah and Frances Carter — September 23, 1802
KIDD, Zachariah and Sally Sorrow — June 25, 1795
KIDD, Zacharias and Nancy Bradberry — October 6, 1800
KILGOE, Willis and Susan Harris — November 11, 1833
KILGORE, Allen and Harriott Bush — December 26, 1815
KILGORE, Benjamin S. and Julia Bush — November 7, 1823
KILGORE, John L. and Nancy Harris — December 14, 1814
KILLIAN, William and Nancy Busbin — December 21, 1822
KIMBELL, Christopher and Polly Waters — October 23, 1819
KIMBELL, John T. and Mary Lumpkin — March 24, 1834
KIMBELL, Joseph W. and Harriet Bryant — January 1, 1840
KIMBRELL, Joseph W. and Martha Lumpkin — October 20, 1841
KIMBLE, Ransom and Martha Harris — July 18, 1823
KIMBLE, Thomas and Nancy Thompson — February 8, 1815
KING, Ezekiel and Louisa Caroline Landrum — July 21, 1847
KING, Jaby and Nancy Cochran — January 12, 1818
KING, James C. and Adeline E. Jacks — August 2, 1852
KING, John and Lucy Jordan — February 15, 1817

KING, Jesse and Susan Dillard	—— 13, 1825
KINNEBREW, Columbus D. and Salina A. Briks	November 12, 1834
KINNEBREW, Columbus D. and Nancy H. Young	December 17, 1851
KINNEBREW, Henry and Nancy Jane Huff	January 14, 1852
KINNEBREW, Littleberry and Sally Denson	April 11, 1807
KINNEBREW, Madison and Eliza Dunn	October 7, 1834
KINNEBREW, Newton and Mary E. Pinson	October 28, 1839
KINNEY, John and Tibatha Patton	March 4, 1799
KIRK, John F. and Eliza Busbin	November 16, 1839
KNAPP, Justus and Charity Webb	July 24, 1795
KNAPP, Robert and Polly McVay	March 19, 1805
KNOX, Benjamin and Winfred Simmons	March 20, 1794
KNOX, Thomas and Betsy Arnold	March 8, 1806

L

LACY, John and Anna Davis	July 14, 1815
LACY, Stephen and Sally Freeman	June 13, 1803
LACY, William and Peggy Wise	November 22, 1810
LANDERS, Humphrey D. and Sally Oraweiner	February 10, 1815
LANDERS, Thos. B. and Polly Berry	March 14, 1810
LANDRUM, Burton and Miss Glass	February 26, 1799
LANDRUM, Columbus J. and Elizabeth Barker	November 29, 1848
LANDRUM, Elisha and Elisabeth Deupree	December 5, 1826
LANDRUM, Francis M. and E. E. Durby	August 2, 1852
LANDRUM, James B. and Annis Young	June 28, 1808
LANDRUM, James B. and Susan Ann Stroud	July 16, 1838
LANDRUM, James M. and Mary Bryant	November 24, 1835
LANDRUM, John and Betty Ann Young	January 8, 1807
LANDRUM, John L. and Jennett H. Birdsong	April 24, 1837
LANDRUM, Joseph and Susannah Powell	January 21, 1819
LANDRUM, *Bishop* Sylvanus and Naomi Lumpkin	December 1, 1846
LANDRUM, Thomas and Nancy Watkins	December 29, 1825
LANDRUM, Thos. B. and Minerva Tarpley	August 5, 1828
LANDRUM, William and Jane Bledsoe	January 5, 1820
LANDRUM, Wm. M. and Rebecca Ann Fluker	December 11, 1848
LANDRUM, Wm. T. and Sarah Milner	December 23, 1852
LANE, Joel and Susana Leggett	December 31, 1809
LANE, Jonathan and Polley Golley	December 27, 1804
LANFORD, Thos. G. and Sarah B. Jordan	January 5, 1825
LANGSTON, James and Margaret Bradford	November 7, 1848
LANIER, James and Susannah Young	January 22, 1818
LANKFORD, William and Ester Thompson	January 14, 1802
LANMAN, Travis and Barbara Mattox	October 14, 1797
LANSFORD, Henry and Judith Rainey	November 29, 1804
LANSFORD, Samuel and Nancy Britain	November 12, 1806
LATIMER, James W. and Hannah W. Davis	October 1, 1845
LATIMER, John P. and Martha Jordan	January 31, 1826
LATIMER, Thos. and Elizabeth Gordon	March 4, 1835
LAVOUNE, John and Charlotta Perkins	December 11, 1804
LAW, John and Salley Lacy	July 18, 1804
LAWLER, Thomas and Polly Glidewell	July 28, 1814

LAWLESS, George W. and Eliza Busbin — December 13, 1837
LAWLESS, James and Permelia Argle — February 4, 1835
LAWLESS, Jacob and Frances Leggett — July 31, 1823
LAWRENCE, Zachariah and Judah Berry — September 19, 1809
LAWRENCE, Zachariah and Temperance Lee — January 2, 1823
LAWS, Joseph and Frances Barrett — October 21, 1816
LAY, Elijah and Patsey Richardson — September 21, 1815
LAY, William and Edith Gilham — January 24, 1803
LEE, Charles B. and Sally Young — December 12, 1803
LEE, Charles H. and Eliza Anderson — February 16, 1825
LEE, Charles H. and Ann A. Arnold — February 5, 1839
LEE, George H. and Mary Ann Hawkins — November 13, 1828
LEE, Joseph D. and Frances Taylor — December 16, 1812
LEE, William and Mary L. Smith — December 12, 1809
LEGERY, Ira and Mary Bradberry — November 5, 1820
LEGGETT, Alexander and Elizabeth Glass — March 16, 1815
LEMON, Angus and Mary Martha Edwards — October 12, 1848
LEONARD, Wm. P. W. and Elizabeth Taylor — September 13, 1820
LESTER, George and Patsey Standfield — November 16, 1807
LESTER, George and Eliza Harriet Goss — November 20, 1828
LESTER, George H. and Martha E. Gresham — January 9, 1843
LESTER, Jacob and Nancy Smith — November 4, 1824
LESTER, John and Nancy Lumpkin — November 25, 1803
LESTER, Lewis and Elizabeth Patman — May 7, 1812
LESTER, Robert and Betsy Nash — February 16, 1810
LESTER, Robert and Fanny Elkins — August 14, 1822
LESTER, Robert and Martha Daniel — April 16, 1851
LESTER, William and Sarah Brown — December 8, 1826
LESSUEUR, John C. and Viney Weaver — December 26, 1839
LESSUEUR, Joseph A. and Elizabeth Curtis — November 4, 1831
LEVERET, Absolom and Polly McElroy — January 7, 1799
LEVERETT, Robert and Sydney Bailey — December 15, 1815*
LEVERETT, Absolem and Anna McLeroy — November 8, 1802
LEVERITT, Robert L. and Sydney Bailey — December 15, 1817*
LEWIS, David and Lucy Clement — November 21, 1839
LINSEY, Benjamin F. and Elizabeth Hunter — September 14, 1819
LIONS, Norris and Betsy Tarpley — April 21, 1808
LITTLE, James J. and Lena A. Matthews — December 7, 1852
LITTLETON, John and Nancy Farmer — August 10, 1814
LIVELY, Crawford and Melitta Sorrow — February 8, 1843
LIVELY, John and Fanny Jones — September 15, 1794
LIVELY, Samuel and Nancy Kent — January 2, 1832
LIVELY, Terry and Mary Ann Jones — March 21, 1798
LOCKLIN, Samuel G. and Rebecca Stephens — January 18, 1832
LOGAN, David and Sephey Leftwich — February 21, 1799
LOW, Isaiah and Drucillah Starkey — March 22, 1796
LOW, William and Jane Scroggins — March 26, 1826
LOWE, Isaac and Amanda Mickelborough — September 18, 1823
LOWRY, John and Dicy Kunt — September 27, 1805
LUCAS, James H. and Sophia Mitchell — July 20, 1825
LUCK, Joseph and Sarah Embry — November 18, 1826
LUCKIE, David and Mary Burgers — March 10, 1794

LUCKIE, James and Nancy Mitchell	February 28, 1821
LUMPKIN, A. J. and Nancy Pittard	May 3, 1848
LUMPKIN, Elijah and Barbary Ann Brown	September 14, 1823
LUMPKIN, Giles and Sary Adams	June 10, 1805
LUMPKIN, Henry H. and Lucy L. Milner	August 17, 18—
LUMPKIN, Henry M. and Elizabeth Pittard	December 18, 1850
LUMPKIN, John B. H. and Penelope Bowling	October 3, 1848
LUMPKIN, Joseph and Anna Bullock	March 7, 1804
LUMPKIN, Joseph J. and Martha W. Hawkins	November 10, 1841
LUMPKIN, Joseph N. and Sarah E. Johnson	October 14, 1847
LUMPKIN, Joseph N. and Martha E. Pittard	January 27, 1849
LUMPKIN, Nevil M. and Mary Beasley	May 25, 1841
LUMPKIN, Pittman and Nancy Hendricks	January 24, 1802
LUMPKIN, Samuel and Mary Arnold	June 21, 1815
LUMPKIN, Samuel, Sr. and Lucy Johnson	December 4, 1844
LUMPKIN, William and Betsey Ragan	January 29, 1801
LUMPKIN, William and Patsy Mickelborough	November 29, 1803
LUMPKIN, William and Susannah Edwards	June 6, 1815
LUMPKIN, William W. and Elizabeth B. Lumpkin	October 19, 1840
LUNSFORD, Hayes and Lucindy Evans	October 26, 1821
LUNSFORD, Henry and Elizabeth Edwards	December 6, 1818
LUNSFORD, Henry H. and Mary Bennett	January 1, 1824
LUNSFORD, Jacob and Martha P. Birdsong	September 25, 1827
LUNSFORD, Moses and Patsey Jonson	December 24, 1805

M

McCANDLESS, John and Elizabeth Thompson	October 10, 1827
McCANE, William and Peggy Bohannon	April 16, 1807
McCARTY, John Daniel and Sarah A. Maxwell	August 3, 1844
McCARTY, John and Polly Walker	December 13, 1808
McCARTY, John and Patsy O'Kelly	January 20, 1820
McCARTY, Sherrod and Sally Finn	January 10, 1801
McCARTY, Sherwood and Martha Wise	October 7, 1839
McCLAIN, Thomas and Judith Willingham	January 13, 1805
McCLAIN, Thomas and Nancy Carter	June 19, 1827
McCLUSTER, Gray and Kitty Oliver	July 27, 1841
McCOLLUM, George W. and Magery R. Thompson	October 1, 1832
McCOMMONS, Abraham and Rebecca C. Young	January 14, 1839
McCOMMONS, James and Susannah McCree	October 6, 1794
McCOMMONS, James and Frances Stewart	January 6, 1813
McCORD, John and Betsey Short	February 16, 1799
McCOWAN, James and Nancy Goolsby	April 30, 1823
McCOWAN, James and Emaline Mosely	August 30, 1845
McCOY, Alexander and Polly Hodge	February 12, 1800
McCOY, Henry K. and Catherine E. Hanson	December 7, 1841
McCREE, William B. and Frances A. Moore	November 7, 1836
McCOY, Jeremiah and Nancy Dickins	March 28, 1808
McDANIEL, Eli and Louisa Davis	April 15, 1819
McELROY, Anderson and Nancy Whitehead	January 18, 1826
McELROY, Andrew and Phebe Meadows	June 5, 1817
McELROY, Chas. G. and Susan Frances Barnett	December 13, 1851

McELROY, John and Tabitha Buckhanon — January 15, 1816
McELROY, Thomas and Curasa Meadows — April 14, 1819
McEWEN, John W. and Mary Hartley — December 22, 1825
McEWIN, Robert and Rachel Hawkins — January 27, 1801
McGAFFEY, James and Mary H. Gordon — September 12, 1820
McGAUGHEY, Thomas I. and Margaret Walker — September 29, 1825
McGEE, William and Mary Spicer — December 25, 1797
McGEHEE, Abner and Jane M. Johnson — May 11, 1824
McGEHEE, Abraham and Harriet A. Hill — June 27, 1817
McGEHEE, Abraham and Catharine Pennington — December 28, 1826
McGEHEE, Edward and Sally Penn — September 16, 1805
McGEHEE, John G. and Sarah M. Hill — March 4, 1828
McGEHEE, John S. and Malina Hill — October 28, 1811
McGEHEE, Madison T. and Lucy C. Meriwether — May 11, 1835
McGEHEE, Thomas and Eliza Gilmer — October 8, 1798
McGEHEE, Thomas and Mildred Cumming — December 21, 1809
McGLOCKLAND, John and Anna Harrison — August 5, 1799
McGUIER, William F. and Nancy L. Brown — December 15, 1843
McGWIER, Sherwood B. and Nancy Zuber — December 9, 1845
McHENRY, James and Miriam Grimes — December 23, 1816
McKEE, Jacob and Nancy Peacock — August 27, 1805
McKEE, Samuel and Elizabeth Manship, or Maurhiss, or Winship — January 19, 1803
McKGRAD, Robert and (blank) — February 19, 1799
McLAUGHLIN, George and Elizabeth Hall — September 24, 1818
McLAUGHLIN, John and Sally Gurings — October 21, 1805
McLAUGHLIN, John C. and Peggy Farr — February 14, 1814
McLAIN, Samuel and Susanah Hill — August 8, 1798
McLEROY, Andrew and Polly Shropshire — March 1, 1811
McLEROY, Billy and Nancy Johnson — May 24, 1800
McLEROY, Charles and Mary Luckie — December 13, 1800
McLEROY, David and Lucy Booth — December 21, 1803
McLEROY, Jacob and Polley Horn — June 18, 1799
McLEROY, Mark and Lucy Briant — April 26, 1809
McLEROY, William and Mary Arnold — January 14, 1801
McLOCKLIN, William and Susannah Tuck — March 23, 1809
McMURRAY, Andrew and Eliza Callahan — March 23, 1799
McMURRAY, James and Rebecca Callahan — November 15, 1800
McNEDY, Robert and Nelley A. Moon — February 8, 1803
McWHORTER, Moses H. and Eliza B. Williams — July 10, 1837
MAGBY, Wm. T. and Martha Ann Willingham — December 31, 1844
MALONE, Doctor R. and Celestial A. Williams — November 15, 1836
MALONE, William and Betty Cole — September 3, 1796
MAN, Joseph T. and Malinda Fullilove — September 10, 1842
MANLY, Joseph and Eliza Bailey — May 2, 1814
MANLY, Lafayette Y. and Susan C. Scogins — July 2, 1849
MANN, John and Elizabeth Hanner — May 4, 1806
MANN, Shimie and Susannah Bush — October 6, 1814
MANSFIELD, George and Peney House — February 12, 1800
MANTOOCH, Robert and Lucinda Simms — January 13, 1829
MARABLE, George and Sarah Ann Early — September 22, 1824
MARABLE, Robert and Elizabeth B. Campbell — November 23, 1841

MARCOM, George R. and Mary Elizabeth Radin	August 14, 1849
MARKS, John and Susannah Tompkins	June 11, 1794
MARKS, Wm. M. and Ann M. Oliver	August 6, 1828
MARR, John and Delana Bailey	December 7, 1816
MARSHALL, Samuel and Sarah Echols	November 14, 1826
MARTEN, John and Betsey Walker	November 1, 1796
MARTIN, Benjamin W. C. and Malissa Dowdy	January 15, 1818
MARTIN, Bennett and Polly Bailey	February 15, 1826
MARTIN, Charles and Caroline Macklin	December 27, 1827
MARTIN, Charles and Lucy Hopper	June 13, 1798
MARTIN, Cornelius G. and Susannah Jennings	March 5, 1832
MARTIN, Elijah and Amanda Amis	April 1, 1832
MARTIN, Gibson and Sally Buckley	September 22, 1800
MARTIN, Hobson and Susan Harrison	February 20, 1850
MARTIN, James and Sarah Buzbin	January 22, 1839
MARTIN, John and Betsy Robertson	November 10, 1797
MARTIN, John and Ann L. Sims	March 13, 1832
MARTIN, John M. and Mary Ann Nowell	January 29, 1834
MARTIN, John W. and Susan Ann Little	November 24, 1852
MARTIN, Richard and Susannah Stephens	June 23, 1798
MARTIN, Smithfield and Elizabeth Martin	January 5, 1825
MARTIN, Thompson and Salley Morris	December 5, 1822
MARTIN, Woodbury and Elizabeth Gallaway	April 23, 1822
MATHEWS, Abraham M. and Elizabeth Burrough	December 15, 1813
MATHEWS, Cary J. and Sally Smith	May 19, 1820
MATHEWS, Coleman and Sarah Ann Griffith	April 12, 1825
MATHEWS, Fleming J. and Saletha Ann Bridges	November 14, 1843
MATHEWS, Isaac and Sarah E. Collier	December 21, 1835
MATHEWS, Jacob E. and Winney Jordan	April 20, 1814
MATHEWS, James and Magdalin Lay	December 21, 1806
MATHEWS, Littleberry and Jerusha Hopper	April 6, 1807
MATHEWS, Little Berry and Salina Meartin	September 9, 1840
MATHEWS, Rolley and Mary Ann Dowdy	October 26, 1835
MATHEWS, Ted M. and Martha E. Chandler	August 2, 1838
MATHEWS, Thomas and Sally Smith	February 11, 1807
MATHEWS, William, Jr. and Polly Herring	August 12, 1818
MATTHEWS, James and Elizabeth Patman	November 17, 1841
MATTOCKS, John and Betsey Knight	May 9, 1808
MATTOX, A. W. and Margaret Jewell	October 30, 1810
MAXEY, Augustus R. and Frances Susan Brown	January 5, 1847
MAXEY, Barnabas and Dinah Wells	December 16, 1831
MAXEY, Bennett H. and Frances Eason	October 3, 1836
MAXEY, Booze and Syntha Varner	April 20, 1818
MAXEY, Garland and Betsy Swanson	November 19, 1796
MAXEY, Jesse and Elizabeth Arthur	September 21, 1847
MAXEY, John and Sally Brooks	September 9, 1806
MAXEY, James and Sally Traylor	April 9, 1818
MAXEY, Jeremiah and Polly Allen	February 13, 1808
MAXEY, Jesse and Anna Eason	January 6, 1835
MAXEY, John H. and Mary Frances Campbell	September 19, 1843
MAXEY, Yeltervon and Jennie Penn	August 2, 1797
MAXWELL, James and Rachel Phillips	August 17, 1803

MAXWELL, James and Kitty Gilbert — February 18, 1810
MAXWELL, Richard and Elizabeth Hardman — January 11, 1804
MAXWELL, Robert and Barbary Roland — February 11, 1802
MAXWELL, Thos. (?) R. and Susan A. Smith — January 1, 1849
MAXWELL, William and Sarah Hancock — June 1, 1833
MAY, Richard and Hannah Dotson — April 29, 1825
MAY, Samuel and Polly Rafferty — February 22, 1800
MAY, Samuel and Betsy Rhodes — February 28, 1805
MAYES, Wm. A. and Martha H. Swanson — December 17, 1847
MAYES, Andrew and Nancy Oakes — October 6, 1806
MAYES, Bird and Cela Thornton — April 13, 1814
MAYS, Bird and Cealey Thaxton — April 14, 1814
MAYS, James and Penny Rowlin — April 30, 1814
MAYS, Levi and Eliza Jentry — December 17, 1828
MAYS, Robert and Pricilla Parker — November 27, 1806
MAYS, Samuel and Polly Read — September 1, 1801
MEADOWS, Abram and Peggy Simmons — January 26, 1804
MEADOWS, Bailey H. and Mary Petty — January 18, 1826
MEADOWS, Bailey H. and Elizabeth Britten — August 16, 1837
MEADOWS, Enoch and Leviena G. Kidd — March 9, 1852
MEADOWS, Isaac and Nancy Bridges — December 10, 1805
MEADOWS, James W. and Nancy E. Sims — December 31, 1844
MEADOWS, Noah W. and Sarah Elizabeth Brooks — July 15, 1850
MEALEE, George and Sally Rains — August 10, 1807
MEALER, James R. and Lucy Jane Murphy — November 23, 1839
MEALER, Richard and Elizabeth Miller — November 21, 1815
MEDDERS, Rowan and Catharine Petty — November 5, 1852
MEGAN, James and Sarah Bankson — September 5, 1797
MEGEE, Thomas and Lary Mitchell — December 22, 1796
MENEFEE, George and Nancy Hardeman — July 27, 1807
MERCER, Dr. Wm. S. and Emily Jewel — December 25, 1849
MERIWETHER, James O. and Lucy M. Johnson — October 2, 1851
MERIWETHER, Nicholas and Mary Davenport — February 28, 1805
MERIWETHER, William and Sarah S. Molloy — November 11, 1817
MERRITT, Benjamin G. and Sally Davis — July 22, 1823
MICHAEL, John and Nancy Moseman — February 10, 1822
MICHAEL, Thos. J. and Sarah Ann Tarpley — July 6, 1850
MICHAEL, William and Delaney Cannon — October 25, 1818
MICHAEL, William and Mary Catharine Nowel — October 15, 1844
MICHAEL, Wm. L. and Lucinda M. Fambrough — October 23, 1849
MICKELBERRY, Alden and Betsey Young — December 13, 1807
MICKELBOROUGH, James and Polly Powell — January 4, 1809
MILES, John and Rebecca Warnock — October 13, 1808
MILLER, Henry and Ritter D. Fleeman — June 15, 1843
MILLER, Preston and Anna Simmons — March 16, 1795
MILLER, Thomas and Elizabeth Leggett — November 29, 1821
MILLIGAN, William and Betsy Bowden — February 17, 1806
MILLS, Augustus L. and Susan A. Peterman — December 5, 1849
MILLS, Charles C. and Sally L. Stokes — July 5, 1813
MILLS, William H. and Susannah Nash — January 8, 1816
MILNER, Jonathan and Rebecca Dunn — December 11, 1805
MILNER, Jonathan G. and Susan Robertson — April 5, 1841

MILNER, John D. and Matilda Lumpkin	September 11, 1833
MINES, John and Frances Naomi Chancey	August 10, 1852
MINGUS, John A. and Sarah Jane Cramer	January 19, 1848
MITCHELL, Augustus G. C. and Elizabeth W. Hill	January 5, 1814
MITCHELL, Britton and Nancy Kimbrell	August 3, 1826
MITCHELL, Hartwell and Patsy Jordan	August 21, 1806
MITCHELL, Henry and Sophia Hill	January 7, 1811
MITCHELL, James and Eliza Jordan	August 2, 1798
MITCHELL, John and Chuleanna Flint	April 9, 1800
MITCHELL, John and Matilda Denson	June 7, 1806
MITCHELL, Nathaniel R. and Temperance Jordan	October 6, 1806
MITCHELL, Robert and Elizabeth Garrott	August 28, 1814
MITCHELL, Thomas and Ruth Tillery	September 18, 1814
MITCHELL, William and Martha Hill	November 22, 1808
MOBLEY, Alexander and Elender Meadows	June 15, 1833
MOBLEY, John and Pheby Meadows	January 5, 1826
MONTCRIEF, Caleb and Sally Ann Short	July 17, 1807
MONTCRIEF, William and Sally Nickerson	November 19, 1807
MONTGOMERY, John and Nancy Johnson	May 20, 1799
MOODY, Avel and Hixey Drake	December 23, 1836
MOODY, James W. and Judith L. Holloway	August 23, 1836
MOODY, Joseph and Sally Hubbard	May 7, 1829
MOON, Isaac M. and Nancy P. Paul	September 29, 1850
MOON, Isral and Sally Phonsby	December 26, 1807
MOON, John and Sally Hannah	September 21, 1809
MOON, John and Nancy Findley	August 29, (?)
MOON, John and Patsy Webb	May 6, 1811
MOON, John and Sally Thornton	August 1, 1812
MOON, Joseph J. and Polley Thomas	September 2, 1808
MOON, Joseph J. and Eliza W. Gregory	December 7, 1815
MOON, Thomas and Polly Willingham	January 18, 1802
MOON, William and Polly Day	September 23, 1805
MOORE, Barnard D. and Sarah J. Moore	April 15, 1844
MOORE (or Mooretin) Burnett and Martha Lumpkin	February 14, 1842
MOORE, Daniel and Caty Swanson	February 1, 1804
MOORE, Francis and Sara Grimes	May 17, 1806
MOORE, Francis and Priscilla Holmes	January 24, 1828
MOORE, George and Aley Moore	December 12, 1797
MOORE, George W. and Ann Elizabeth Armstrong	August 14, 1847
MOORE, John and Polly Varner	March 30, 1807
MOORE, John and Charlotta Pate	May 7, 1809
MOORE, Joseph J. and Mary C. Baldwin	October 29, 1806
MOORE, Joseph and Arianna Collier	March 13, 1828
MOORE, Joshua and Polly Vinson	March 17, 1806
MOORE, Joshua G. and Mary Early	December 9, 1819
MOORE, Seaborn and Elizabeth Colley	December 16, 1811
MOORE, William and Nancy Roan	December 12, 1810
MOORE, Wm. A. and Elizabeth Cramer	December 15, 1849
MORGAN, Charles and Polly Osburn	April 18, 1800
MORGAN, Daniel and Gracy Rhodes	January 14, 1805
MORGAN, Hardy and Nancy Odom	April 19, 1804
MORGAN, Henry and Henrietta Berry	January 24, 1803

MORGAN, Jesse and Elizabeth Arnold   January 12, 1807
MORGAN, John and Betsey Stiles   July 2, 1794
MORGAN, John and Anna Watson   September 7, 1808
MORGAN, Joshua and Rachel Bane   November 8, 1813
MORGAN, Thomas and Mary Stiles   April 7, 1794
MORGAN, William and Agnes Smith   December 10, 1807*
MORLEY, Stephen and Polly Davis   January 5, 1810
MORRIS, James and Nancy Strain   July 9, 1799
MORRIS, Samuel and Peggy Hill   June 29, 1811
MORROW, Thomas and Elizabeth Callahan   May 3, 1843
MORTON, Major John and Eunis Elizabeth Landrum June 23, 1851
MORTON, Joseph, Jr. and Martha Manley   June 20, 1804
MORTON, Thomas R. and Elizabeth Fullelove   October 25, 1823
MORTON, Thomas R. and Cynthia Edwards   October 14, 1841
MORTON, William T. and Lucy Duke   April 23, 1798
MOSELY, Thomas M. and Elizabeth Ann Smith   April 22, 1846
MOSS, John and Elender Hall   April 29, 1819
MOSS, John D. and Martha Strong   March 16, 1824
MOSS, Johnson and Nancy Smith   December 10, 1812
MOSS, Stephen and Charity Anderson   December 5, 1798
MOSS, Thomas B. and Parmelia A. Hanson   December 4, 1849
MOSS, William and Sally Wood   September 30, 1819
MUCKLEREATH, John and Polly Davis   November 3, 1816
MUCKELROY, William and Lucyann S. Birdsong   May 4, 1836
MURPHEY, Joseph and Nancy Richardson   February 29, 1824
MURPHEY, Paschal and Sally Howard   January 22, 1815
MURPHY, Martin M. and Polly Traylor   March 17, 1807
MURRAY, James M. and Elizabeth Ogilvie   December 10, 1844
MURRAY, John and Patsy O'Kelly   June 9, 1817
MURRAY, John B. and Elizabeth Ann Eartey   December 14, 1840
MURRAY, Thomas and Holley Carter   August 4, 1817
MURRAY, Thomas and Sally Fleeman   September 8, 1817
MURRAY, William and Aley Sims   July 6, 1804
MURRAY, William and Margaret Lawrence   May 11, 1819
MURRAY, Wm. T. and Sarah Emaline S. Barnett   December 9, 1846

N

NAPIER, Skelton and Jane E. Gage   November 6, 1820
NEAL, James and Susannah Varner   November 29, 1810
NEAL, Thomas and Elizabeth Varner   March 16, 1812
NELSON, Silvester and Margaret Wiley   November 27, 1800
NESBIT, John and Nancy Phinizy   April 23, 1818
NEWELL, William and Mary Tuck (Thursday Eve)   February 14, 1822
NEWTON, Ebenezer and Ann L. Strong   December 1, 1819
NEWTON, Col. Josiah and Penena Strong   April 9, 1821
NICHOLS, Christopher and Martha Davis   January 4, 1825
NICHOLS, Henry and Prudence Farresby   December 6, 1820
NICHOLS, William and Rebecca Ogletree   April 10, 1843
NICHOLDS, William and Viena Porter   December 26, 1837
NICHOLSON, George W. and Martha H. Hale   November 1, 1836
*Foot Note: "They were married May 1807"

NICHOLSON, Joseph M. and Elizabeth Ann Meddows January 5, 1847
NICHOLSON, William and Martha Moore — October 10, 1816
NICKELSON, George and Betsey Walker — November 6, 1802
NICKS, David and Mary Cox — September 7, 1804
NICKS, Edward and Milley Akens — June 28, 1797
NICKS, Edward and Sintha Patton — July 24, 1808
NICKS, Robert and Susana Nicks — January 28, 1804
NOELL, Beverly and Avy Anderson — November 2, 1820
NOELL, James and Hulda W. Lee — August 30, 1813
NOELL, James S. and Sarah Cunningham — October 10, 1849
NOELL, John and Sophia Dowdy — November 15, 1817
NOELL, Thomas and Elizabeth G. Andrews — September 1, 1814
NOELL, William A. and Mary Ann Frances Ellis — December 13, 1842
NORRIS, John W. and Frankey Belk — February 10, 1814
NORRIS, Needham and Polly Elsberry — February 16, 1796
NORTH, Abraham and Elizabeth Holmes — August 12, 1823
NORTH, Anthony and Polly Hubbard — January 26, 1815
NORTH, William and Frances Arnold — August 23, 1820
NORTHCUT, Alexander and Lucy Roberson — October 17, 1806
NORTON, James and Julia (or Judie) Edwards — December 18, 1838
NORTON, William and Polly Landrum — January 3, 1810
NOWELL, James T. and Susan A. Kent — December 21, 1839
NUNALLY, Jacob G. and Elizabeth F. Noell — March 21, 1846
NUNNALLY, Josiah E. and Nancy Anderson — January 1, 1818
NUNALY, John A. and Elizabeth Philips — May 8, 1833
NIXON, James and Polly Ward — January 11, 1809

O

OAKES, Reubin and Rebecca Williams — December 24, 1817
OAKS, Thomas and Mary Warten — December 31, 1808
OAKS, Thomas and Hanner Martin — February 22, 1816
OGDEN, Elijah and Cordelia A. Landrum — November 7, 1844
OGLETREE, John and Polley Chessire — November 25, 1815
OGLETREE, Micajah and Sally Nichols — October 22, 1838
OGILVY (Ogilvie), Benj. W. and Darilly Jordan — January 4, 1826
OGILVIE (Ogilvy), John and Eliza Eason — December 20, 1810
O'KELLY, Benjamin and Winney Hendon — October 26, 1809
O'KELLY, Chas. D. and Polly Stamps — October 12, 1820
O'KELLY, James and Eady Trible — June 19, 1812
O'KELLY, James and Frankey Harwell — November 10, 1814
O'KELLY, James and Dicey (Dilley) Stamps — March 3, 1817
O'KELLY, Thomas D. and Sally Stamps — November 8, 1826
OLIVE, Anthony and Harriet Carithers — December 6, 1845
OLIVE, Hendon and Sally Hartsfield — December 3, 1806
OLIVE, Jesse and Arian Collier — October 29, 1851
OLIVE, Samuel C. and Mildred S. McGhee — January 5, 1826
OLIVER, Dronysius and Lucinda McLynn — December 27, 1810
OLIVER, Dronysius and Sarah Hill — December 14, 1839
OLIVER, James and Sara Meriwether — December 25, 1808
OLIVER, Peter and Cordelia A. Hill — December 26, 1840
ORMOND, James and Margaret Martin — March 22, 1811

Georgia Society, Daughters of the American Revolution

ORR, Durham and Lidie McKee	December 29, 1808
ORR, Jesse and Betsey Ragan	August 4, 1801
ORR, Jonathan and Sarah Glenn	October 18, 1822
ORR, Mathew and Nancy Sims	December 21, 1822
ORR, Robert and Polly Howard	December 13, 1813
OSBORN, William and Mary Tiller	July 23, 1828
OSBORNE, Nicholas and Nancy Wood	October 2, 1832
OWEN, Ben and Ruth Riley	November 27, 1810
OWEN, Davis and Salley Arnold	March 9, 1814
OWEN, George and Catherine Parks	November 21, 1797
OWEN, Jacob J. and Frances E. Wilson	May 11, 1843
OWEN, Mr. and Amy Powell	December 12, 1799
OWIN, Robert and Polly Kinnebrew	March 11, 1805
OWING, John and Polly Collier	December 19, 1803

P

PACE, Ensil and Georgiana Goolsby	March 23, 1851
PACE, James and Mary Ann Lovett	November 2, 1796
PACE, James and Nancy Duffee	February 4, 1824
PACE, Paris and Mary Kitchens	August 31, 1815
PAINE, Abner and Elizabeth Colwell	January 4, 1813
PARKS, Bird and Watty Smith	February 18, 1803
PARKS, George and Margaret Townsend	February 7, 1826
PARKS, Thomas and Mary Hill	December 21, 1828
PARKS, Welcom and Betsy Duke	October 2, 1801
PARKS, Welcome and Sandal Ann Smith	February 28, 1828
PARR, John and Margaret Bolton	August 22, 1816
PARR, John and Martha Latimore	December 14, 1819
PARRIS, Nathan K. and Sally Jewell	December 11, 1819
PASCHAL, George and Agnis Brewer	November 23, 1802
PASCHAL, John and Betsy Brewer	November 27, 1804
PASS, Adam and Nancy Curry	December 28, 1826
PASS, John and Charloty Huell	November 25, 1806
PASS, John and Dicy Simmons	July 23, 1807
PASS, Mathew J. and Dicy Eberhart	March 16, 1820
PATMAN, David W. and Elizabeth Collins	December 18, 1828
PATMAN, Elias and Lucinda Peterman	March 5, 1838
PATMAN, Isham W. and Lonna Carter	March 9, 1838
PATMAN, James and Elizabeth Nicholson	March 24, 1816
PATMAN, James and Elizabeth Baty	January 2, 1822
PATMAN, James P. and Lucy A. Yarbrough	March 5, 1845
PATMAN, John and Polly Weaver	May 14, 1809
PATMAN, John and Sarah Wright	May 2, 1822
PATMAN, Watson and Polly Leggett	June 11, 1815
PATMAN, William and Nancy Leggett	September 13, 1812
PATMAN, Wm. B. and Charlotte C. Faust	July 12, 1834
PATRICK, John and Peggy Nickolson	November 2, 1801
PATRICK, Joseph and Polly Batey	January 20, 1800
PATRICK, Lewis and Nancy Waters	March 26, 1802
PATRICK, Miliken and Polly Duke	March 23, 1799
PATRICK, Samuel and Betsy Williams	September 16, 1802

PATRICK, Samuel and Doratha Alexander — December 22, 1795
PATRICK, William and (blank) — November 5, 1821
PATTERSON, David and Mary Hart — January 4, 1821
PATTERSON, David and Eliza P. Farmer — December 15, 1841
PATTILLO, Lewis A. and Sarah Powers — February 6, 1850
PATTON, Allen D. and Zilliann E. Barnett — November 18, 1852
PATTON, Benjamin and Anna Goolsby — December 30, 1819
PATTON, George B. and Polley E. Brown — March 26, 1815
PATTON, Jacob and Elizabeth Cox — December 27, 1834
PATTON, John and Ferribah Harris — January 13, 1796
PATTON, Mathew S. and Lucy Barnett — October 6, 1845
PATTON, Peter B. and Elizabeth Bridges — November 10, 1848
PATTON, Robert and Sally Murray — January 30, 1823
PATTON, Samuel and Polly Pye — January 21, 1805
PATTON, Samuel and Lydia Holmes — April 2, 1807
PATTON, Samuel and Kezziah Herring — August 4, 1821
PATTON, Solomon and Lucinda Wright — March 18, 1819
PATTON, Solomon C. and Lilly P. Thornton — December 1, 1831
PATTON, William and Sally Miller — October 18, 1797
PATTON, Williford and Sarah Barker — December 21, 1836
PAUL, Archibold M. and Caroline C. Scroggins — December 27, 1847
PAUL, Henry and Nancy Hopper — December 20, 1837
PAULETT, Jesse C. and Hariett Barnett — March 28, 1821
PAYNE, Flail and Doratha Colwell — January 24, 1815
PAYNE, Thomas and Jane Nichols — December 21, 1825
PEACOCK, John and Susannah Bohannon — December 29, 1800
PEACOCK, William and Rachel McGree — December 25, 1803
PEARCE, Stephen and Sarah Ann Rhymes — July 27, 1812
PEARMAN, Robert and Elizabeth Northington — June 22, 1818
PEDDIGREW, Ebinezer and Lucinda Smith — March 27, 1816
PEMBERTON, Selam H. and Ann Mosely — September 26, 1845
PENDERGRASS, Simeon and Mary S. Andrews — December 11, 1832
PENN, Edmond and Phebe Moore — December 20, 1798
PEOPLE, Isham and Jane Crowley — June 23, 1824
PERCE, Jeremiah and Nancy McClain — November 20, 1805
PERRY, Alfred G. and Mary Drake — November 14, 1821
PERRY, Alfred G. and Sarah Eidson — December 10, 1827
PERRY, Green and Elizabeth Blake — November 29, 1827
PERSON, Francis and Betsey Dunn — March 13, 1800
PETERMAN, Benjamin and Matilda Dowdy — January 23, 1812
PETERMAN, Columbus and Martha Patman — June 18, 1839
PETERMAN, Henry and Malissa Norble — September 11, 1833
PETERMAN, James M. and Mary J. Armstrong — March 12, 1851
PETERMAN, John F. and Nancy Yarbrough — September 23, 1846
PETERMAN, Newton J. and Martha Bonds — December 22, 1846
PETERS, Jesse and Rebekah M. Boon — December 8, 1814
PETERS, John and Rhoda Watson — December 20, 1815
PETTETT, John G. and Melissa A. Johnson — December 27, 1837
PETTY, James T. and Mary Ann Nicholson — July 10, 1847
PHARR, Alexander and Permelia Hardin — August 24, 1820
PHELPS, Overton and Mary Barkwell — September 6, 1813
PHILIPS, George and Jemima Pope — December 9, 1799

PHILLIPS, Dr. George and Polly Morton — February 22, 1812
PHILLIPS, Hardy and Delilah Phillips — June 1, 1824
PHILLIPS, James and Polly Harris — December 3, 1804
PHILLIPS, John and Martha Tiller — June 4, 1833
PHILLIPS, Richard R. and Eliza Wilson — December 26, 1828
PHILLIPS, Samuel and Dicey Jenkins — June 3, 1810
PHILLIPS, Thomas and Elizabeth Bellough — August 7, 1800
PHINIZY, Jack and Sarah T. Merawether — November 28, 1836
PHINIZY, Jacob and Matilda Stewart — May 17, 18—
PHINIZY, John F. and Martha Dillard — April 2, 1832
PHINIZY, Marco and Nancy Baldwin — September 6, 1813
PINCKARD, John and Sarah Edmonds — February 12, 1809
PINSON, David R. and Eliza Carter — January 23, 1839
PINSON, James and Jenny Hughes — March 24, 1804
PINSON, James and Edny Carter — November 8, 1824
PINSON, Jesse and Mary T. Johnson — December 19, 1849
PINSON, Joseph J. and Elizabeth Johnson — January 22, 1828
PINSON, Thomas B. and Nancy Patman — January 28, 1819
PITTARD, Archabel S. and Mary E. Wooten — June 10, 1851
PITTARD, Davis and Eliza M. Hart — December 22, 1833
PITTARD, Humphrey and Sarah Hall — December 26, 1826
PITTARD, James and Althetha Wood — January 22, 1838
PITTARD, John and Lucy Glenn — February 6, 1824
PITTARD, John and Mary Patterson — February 21, 1833
PITTARD, Thompson and Clarey Hails — June 19, 1799
PITTARD, William and Nancy O'Kelly — March 16, 1815
PITTARD, Wm. and Curacy McKelvey — March 28, 1828
PITTARD, William and Mary Glenn — May 22, 1829
PITTARD, Wm. S. and Mrs. Salina F. Simmons — June 13, 1846
PITTMAN, Daniel N. and Assineth Baber — March 17, 1826
PLATT, Edwin and Susan A. Smith — April 10, 1850
PLATT, Ephraim H. and Harriet B. Hawkins — April 20, 1839
PLATT, George F. and Mary Elizabeth Smith — November 15, 1836
POLK, Charles and Betsey Roland — January 2, 1810
POLK, Ezekiel and Betsy Phillips — July 14, 1804
POLLARD, William and Polly Allen — May 30, 1803
PONA, Asa and Lucy Ann Goulding — April 13, 1826
PONDER, James H. and Elizabeth E. Barnett — June 8, 1809
PONDER, John and Synthia Johnson — September 19, 1816
PONDER, John M. and Mourning H. Wade — July 2, 1824
PONDER, John M. and Sarah Edwards — November 27, 1827
PONDER, Wm. L. and Elizabeth Johnson — January 19, 1801
PONDERS, Abner and Jane Knox — October 3, 1802
POOL, Benjamin and Martha Barnett — March 6, 1823
POOL, Sylvanus P. and Mazy Pace — May 6, 1852
POPE, Archelus and Nancy Eason — December 30, 1797
POPE, Augustus B. and Mary Gillespie — October 9, 1822
POPE, Burwell and Sarah K. Strong — December 11, 1815
POPE, Benjamin and Eliza Rountree — November 15, 1827
POPE, Henry and Mary Davis — May 27, 1799
POPE, Josiah and Frances Compton — June 16, 1808

POPE, Middleton and Lucy Lumpkin   November 27, 1820
POPE, Nicholas and Sarah Miller   December 27, 1822
POPE, Wiley and Polly Hill   March 20, 1794
POPE, Wilie and Sally Davis   February 11, 1807
PORTER, James T. and Sarah A. Brown   April 20, 1846
PORTER, John and Elizabeth Glenn   June 7, 1825
PORTER, Johnson and Anna Hogue   January 14, 1801
PORTER, Natt and E. Kinnebrew   May 15, 1805
PORTER, Wm. and Betsy Elliott   November 27, 1805
PORTER, Wm. T. and Elizabeth Thaxton   October 22, 1845
POSS, Andy and Jinney Tiller   November 18, 1813
POSS, Jackson and Martha Ann Martin   March 27, 1841
POSS, John D. and Mary E. Carlton   December 22, 1845
POSS, Usiah and Alis Ann Black   February 24, 1838
POTTS, Samuel and Sally Brown   March 8, 1802
POTTS, Stephen and Ann Tiller   December 14, 1795
POTTS, Stephen and Jane Potts   January 18, 1798
POULLAIN, Thomas N. and Harriet B. Wray November 16, 1814
POULNOTT, John B. and Mary Elliott   April 28, 1826
POUND, Daniel J. and Malissa Short   October 18, 1831
POUNDS, Isham J. and Martha W. Ogden   November 27, 1833
POWELL, Chapman and Elizabeth Hardman   April 7, 1824
POWELL, Drewry and Nancy Dunn   February 7, 1815
POWELL, Edward W. and Polly Hardin   July 23, 1812
POWELL, Edward and Susan Landrum   December 27, 1836
POWELL, John and Viney Williams   February 25, 1799
POWELL, Johnson and Rhoda Webb   September 1, 1808
POWELL, Thomas and Sally Milner   October 12, 1804
POWERS, James B. and Tabitha Harriet Hays December 27, 1848
POWERS, Michal and Jane Tobair   August 18, 1803
POWERS, William G. and Nancy Barnett   July 4, 1821
PRATT, Barbel and Caty Silvey   March 23, 1814
PRICE, George and Tabitha Acock   December 3, 1807
PRICE, Joseph and Betsey Phillips   December 2, 1795
PRICE, Joseph and Betsey Wyatt   November 26, 1798
PRICE, Thomas and Milley Bolling   November 31, 1796
PULLEN, Thomas Y. and Mary M. Britain   September 19, 1843
PURSELL, David and Adaline Willis   July 4, 1824
PURYEAR, William H. and Lucy A. Christopher July 3, 1848
PUTNAM, John J. and Permelia Bledsoe   May 11, 1833
PYE, Allen and Peggy Pye   November 19, 1817
PYE, Andrew and Peggy Hopper   November 22, 1810
PYE, James and Agnes Herring   October 14, 1810
  (License issued February 3, 1810)
PYE, Jesse and Polly Freeman   February 11, 1810
PYE, Theophilus and Elizabeth Patton   October 26, 1815

R

RADEN, William and Mary Bowden   September 30, 1827
RADEN, Thomas and Nancy Thompson   December 22, 1801
RADFORD, William and Nancy James   July 17, 1804

RAGAN, Jonathan and Susan Walker — December 21, 1808
RAGIN, Asa and Syntha Ector — February 23, 1803
RAGIN, David and Betty Simmons — September 17, 1805
RAGIN, Hamilton and Kezziah Hendon — August 13, 1812
RAGIN, John and Polly M. Granger — October 24, 1816
RAINEY, Josiah and Elizabeth Dupree — March 9, 1815
RAINEY, Thomas F. and Mary E. Taliferro — June 9, 1818
RAINEY, William and Betsey Morgan — April 1, 1799
RAINEY, William and Eliza Bell — January 18, 1824
RAINEY, William B. and Matilda Penn — November 17, 1823
RAINEY, Woodson and Hetty Williams — January 29, 1822
RAINS, David B. and Nancy Stewart — February 3, 1816
RAINS, Henry and Mary Smith — November 7, 1816
RAINS, Henry and Susan Mann — February 13, 1826
RAINS, Ignatius and Rody Hubbard — May 31, 1821
RAINS, Thomas and Gusey Simmons — July 25, 1800
RAKESTRAW, Robert G. and Martha Smith — December 31, 1811
RAMSAY, William and Margaret Woodside — December 15, 1802
RAMSEY, James and Cathy Moore — June 16, 1806
RAMSEY, James and Jane Reese — August 14, 1820
RAMSEY, John and Margaret Read — January 27, 1798
RAMEY, John B. and Fanny Penn — August 20, 1817
RATCHFORD, William and Martha Espey — September 6, 1802
RAY, Elisha and Nancy Prince — June 1, 1818
RAY, Ephraim and Harriot Reed — January 15, 1842
RAY, Isaac and Polly Starkey — November 12, 1806
RAY, John and Margaret Griffith — September 5, 1816
RAY, John and Viana Mays — March 16, 1826
RAY, Joseph and Polly Orr — August 26, 1803
READ, Anderson and Lucky Mays — November 3, 1804
RAY, Moses and Polly Wilson — January 6, 1804
RAY, Thomas and Hannah Bentley — July 25, 1816
READ, George and Anna Vinson — August 21, 1813
READ, Hugh and Leanah Griffin — March 25, 1805
READ, Joseph and Peggy Temple — January 4, 1802
READY, Richard and Elizabeth P. Lee — March 28, 1822
REDING, Wiley and Caroline Boaden — December 19, 1836
REED, John and Mary Mays — October 11, 1800
REED, Wiley and Margaret Brockman — September 18, 1831
REED, William and Susanah Hales — April 1, 1820
REESE, David A. and Mary G. Meriwether — November 9, 1819
REESE, Thomas and Jane Brown — March 10, 1820
REID, Marquis DeLaffayette and Nancy Ramsey — December 21, 1850
REMBERT, Wm. P. and Sarah Jane Abbot — March 25, 1835
REMBERT, Wm. P. and Victoria L. Cox — December 9, 1841
RENEAU, William and Genny Scroggins — December 29, 1807
REYNOLDS, James and Nancy Edwards — September 18, 1827
REYNOLDS, John and Elizabeth Stephens — August 29, 1821
REYNOLDS, John and Nancy C. Brooks — December 16, 1845
RHODA, William and Salley Peters — December 30, 1805
RHODES, Isaac and Prudence Lyde — January 17, 1820
RHODES, John and Lucinda Garvin — February 17, 1825

RICE, Thomas and Julia Russell — October 16, 1837
RICH, Charles and Milley Bailey — November 12, 1806
RICHARDS, Stephen and Annie Watley — December 9, 1794
RICHARDSON, Allen and Salley Olive — June 26, 1811
RICHARDSON, Morgan and Eady Ward — May 31, 1827
RICHEY, Joseph and Jenny Moon — November 13, 1801
RICKEL, John and Sally Huckaby — July 27, 1803
RICKLES, William and Nancy Loving — October 2, 1814
RICKS, Anthony and Betsey Pate — June 24, 1811
RIDDLE, Thomas and Rebecca Goolsby — August 16, 1802
RIGHT, William and Minney Jones — December 17, 1805
RILEY, John C. and Cloey Ann Kent — August 2, 1838
RINGS, Nathaniel and Polly Dill — December 16, 1810
ROADER, Richard and Charlot Bentley — January 25, 1800
ROADS, James and Elizabeth Jennings — October 30, 1802
ROBERTS, Henry W. and Sarah G. Power — November 14, 1848
ROBERTS, Lindsey and Betsy Meadows — June 17, 1833
ROBERTS, Oziah and Elizabeth Webb — January 27, 1844
ROBERTS, Richard and Polly Base — April 2, 1794
ROBERTS, William and Mary Jackson — January 8, 1819
ROBERTSON, Alvin M. and Nancy Kidd — February 20, 1833
ROBERTSON, Charles and Mary D. Trammel — December 22, 1847
ROBERTSON, David and Betsey Leggett — December 6, 1812
ROBERTSON, Elijah D. and Sarah Ann Miller — October 8, 1834
ROBERTSON, Isham and Jane Leavens — April 17, 1808
ROBERTSON, James H. and Mary Robertson — April 14, 1822
ROBERTSON, Pleasant and Clasy Purkins — November 29, 1808
ROBERTSON, Thos. L. and Mary Ann Carter — November 26, 1849
ROBERTSON, Wm. H. and Elizabeth Hardman — February 7, 1828
ROBINS, William and Levinia Stratten — October 6, 1799
ROBINSON, Francis J. and Lucinda E. McKinley — March 9, 1843
RODDAM, Robert and Sarah Law — October 31, 1801
ROGERS, David and Mary Stubblefield — January 19, 1801
ROLAND, —— and Rhoda Adkins — September 27, 1794
ROLAND, Hosea and Fanny Roland — September 30, 1810
ROLAND, John and Milley Hendley — July 2, 1799
ROSEBERRY, Richard and Frances J. Hewell — June 20, 1811
ROUSEY, Simson and Mada Gaines — December 3, 1834
ROWE, Jesse L. and Nancy C. Dorough — October 23, 1850
ROWLAND, James and Martha Newel Holtzclaw — May 10, 1842
ROYAL, Samuel and Racy Scott — December 18, 1804
RUCKER, Gideon and Nancy Freeman — February 26, 1822
RUMLEY, John and Jane Austen — April 16, 1796
RUPERT, John and Nancy Young — June 14, 1810
RUSSELL, William R. and Maza Colton — December 20, 1819
RUTLEDGE, Dudley and Rachel Glass — December 29, 1801
RUTLEDGE, Thomas and Nancy Echols — October 3, 1799

S

SACKWELL, Benjamin and Jane Allen — March 21, 1819
SAFFOLD, Daniel and Genny Hemphill — August 7, 1802

Georgia Society, Daughters of the American Revolution 197

SAFFOLD, Isham and Genny Waters	June 26, 1808
SALLY, Obadeah M. and Rachel Hanner	June 17, 1805
SANDERS, Argalus and Susan Johnson	January 8, 1824
SANDERS, James and Sally Johnson	August 4, 1797
SANDERS, James and Syntha Hubbard	September 26, 1833
SANDERS, Peyton D. and Parmelia Davis	February 2, 1826
SANDERS, Seaborn and Alpha Jane Patton	February 4, 1852
SANDERS, Wm. J. and Maryann Black	December 11, 1850
SANFORD, Josiah and Edith Oglee	June 22, 1801
SAPPINGTON, Henry L. and Sarah S. Owen	August 2, 1826
SATTERWHITE, Charles and Lettie Mathews	May 10, 1812
SATTERWHITE, Stephen and Nancy Raffity	February 12, 1812
SAUNDERS, James M. and Saphronia J. Bush	October 29, 1851
SAVIN, Richard and Sarah Bacon	October 23, 1841
SCOGAN, Gresham and Winney Watson	June 10, 1800
SCOGGIN, Humphrey and Lydia Rafferty	January 13, 1805
SCOGGINS, Wm. Jasper and Maryann Butler	June 10, 1848
SCOGGINS, Wylie and Polly Elsberry	April 25, 1821
SCOGGINS, Young and Sarah McElroy	November 29, 1827
SCOTT, Daniel and Jemima Walker	October 5, 1812
SCOTT, George and Maryann B. Moore	April 9, 1828
SCOTT, James and Patsey Barber	June 29, 1797
SCOTT, John and Martha Ann Daniel	November 11, 1845
SCOVILLE, Wm. H. and Mary Jane Swanson	May 24, 1849
SCROGANS, Chatten and Disie Johnson	January 24, 1798
SCROGIN, Thomas and Nancy Birdsong	November 7, 1808
SCROGGINS, Hudson and Mrs. Sophia Cunningham	March 22, 1845
SCROGGINS, James and Judith Raffity	July 10, 1810
SCROGGINS, Michael H. and Sarah Busbin	October 7, 1844
SCROGGINS, Millinton and Sally Henson	January 18, 1800
SCROGGINS, Robert and Martha Landrum	July 28, 1836
SELF, Elijah and Patsy Beavers	November 11, 1805
SETTLE, John and Mary Bridges	December 28, 1824
SHANKS, John and Mary Jennings	December 18, 1821
SHANNON, Samuel and Sally Kennedy	August 8, 1796
SHARP, Francis J. and Elizabeth Sims	September 21, 1821
SHAW, Amos and Sarah Maxey	June 25, 1812
SHAW, Jonah W. and Sarah E. Carlton	March 26, 1811
SHEPPERD, Alfred and Isabella Northington	January 6, 1829
SHEPPARD, William and Alce Crittenton	August 16, 1806
SHIELDS, Samuel and Fanny Edmondson	November 18, 1808
SHIELDS, William G. and Lucinda Short	December 3, 1847
SHORT, Archibald and Mary Ann Allen	November 24, 1834
SHORT, Barber and Polly Hancock	December 2, 1819
SHORT, Pleasant W. and Susan Crowley	December 28, 1826
SHORTER, Henry and Dorothy Collier	October 8, 1831
SHROPSHIRE, Joshua and Sally Maxey	October 11, 1821
SILON, Drewry and Margaret Warnock	February 16, 1807
SILVEY, Abraham and Temperance Knap	November 29, 1815
SIMMONS, Asa and Fannie Sims	April 1, 1822
SIMMONS, Asa B. and Temp Sterling	December 24, 1838
SIMMONS, Charles and Mary Hardman	December 3, 1824

SIMMONS, David and Caty Simmons — May 25, 1805
SIMMONS, Jesse and Frances S. Pittard — January 19, 1835
SIMMONS, John and Polly Whitsel — December 22, 1807
SIMMONS, John and Elisabeth Harrison — April 11, 1814
SIMMONS, John and Malinda Echols — March 5, 1816
SIMMONS, Richard and Sally Huckaby — March 14, 1794
SIMMONS, Seaborn and Sally Patman — January 30, 1839
SIMMONS, Turner and Nicey E. Barnett — August 31, 1845
SIMMONS, Vinson and Lucy Simmons — December 2, 1818
SIMMONS, William and Biddey Sims — March 15, 1810
SIMMONS, William and Jane Martin — August 2, 1813
SIMON, Thomas and Jenney Wilson — March 10, 1800
SIMONS, Addam and Betsy Muckleberry — December 19, 1803
SIMONS, John C. and Elizabeth Smith — November 25, 1834
SIMONTON, Theophilius and Mary Potts — September 8, 1836
SIMPSON, Malisa and Alice Williams — November 30, 1805
SIMPSON, Robert and Sarah Cowen — December 9, 1795
SIMPSON, William and Sally Wallace — December 8, 1800
SIMS, Allen and Tempy Hartsfield — August 14, 1797
SIMS, Allen and Polly Lawrence — May 16, 1809
SIMS, Andrew J. and Mary Jennings — November 31, 1842
SIMS, Gresham and Micha Davis — January 7, 1826
SIMS, James S. and Amanda B. Moore — May 24, 1832
SIMS, John and Fanney Gar (blank) — October 10, 1805
SIMS, John and Mrs. Martha Spratling — June 28, 1852
SIMS, Lewis and Nancy Anderson — February 10, 1820
SIMS, Little Berry and Frankey Lacy — June 25, 1803
SIMS, Martin and Elisabeth Hartsfield — January 29, 1807
SIMS, Warren and Lucy Scroggins — October 12, 1801
SIMS, Wiley and Mary Hartsfield — May 24, 1796
SIMS, Wm. G. and Parmelia Cheatam — December 9, 1836
SIMS, Wm. P. and Patsy Tarpley — September 17, 1805
SIMSON, Buc and Rachel Williams — February 7, 1800
SINETH, John and Beddy Spicer — January 11, 1802
SINETH, James L. and Frances Brooks — June 26, 1806
SIPPER, Willie and Nancy Cleaton — January 6, 1812
SKINNER, James and Susannah Smith — July 4, 1814
SKINNER, Livingston and Ideda E. Hughes — July 4, 1824
SLATEN, Isaac D. and Susan B. Baughn — June 8, 1842
SLATON, Rembret and Becky Jenkins — April 12, 1800
SLATON, Rubin and Sally Stemmons — January 20, 1802
SLATON, William and Nelly Knowles — November 22, 1803
SLEDGE, Wiley and Martha Lyon — September 20, 1827
SLOATE, Edward R. and Cornelia Virginia Lessueur — April 4, 1843
SMITH, Adam and Elizabeth Smith — December 31, 1841
SMITH, Adam and Martha M. Moseley — April 28, 1842
SMITH, Andrew and Betsy Hammonds — June 26, 1832
SMITH, Arthur W. and Annie Findley — December 20, 1809
SMITH, Arthur W. and Frances N. Moore — January 28, 1837
SMITH, Benjamin and Martha Moody — July 14, 1817
SMITH, Brinkley and Susana Tiller — January 1, 1807
SMITH, Brittain and Nancy Carden — December 24, 1803

SMITH, C. H. and Ann T. Finch — April 10, 1837
SMITH, Charles F. and Catherine Hudson — January 4, 1833
SMITH, Cladius D. and Martha Goolsby — January 21, 1851
SMITH, Coleman and Nancy Thornton — April 19, 1821
SMITH, David and Winney Helton — November 16, 1809
SMITH, Davis and Nancy Heard — October 20, 1801
SMITH, DeWit C. and Caroline Rains — December 17, 1849
SMITH, Drury L. and Rebecca Jane Mosely — September 11, 1837
SMITH, Edward and Julia H. Arnold — November 16, 1826
SMITH, Edward and Dorothy Owen — May 29, 1828
SMITH, Francis M. and Jechia Ann Murphy — September 2, 1837
SMITH, George E. and Urania L. Langston — November 30, 1844
SMITH, George M. and Rebecca Bradshaw — June 15, 1823
SMITH, Hardaway and Sarah Amis — November 2, 1843
SMITH, Harrison K. and Rebecca H. Smith — January 30, 1817
SMITH, Henderson and Frances Fequitt — December 19, 1822
SMITH, Henry and Malissa Davis — October 25, 1827
SMITH, Henry and Elvina Ann Johnson — August 18, 1846
SMITH, Hill and Elizabeth Barbee — March 6, 1832
SMITH, Isaiah and Martha L. Brown — December 22, 1827
SMITH, Jackson and Martha Crowley — November 1, 1827
SMITH, Jacob and Louisa Hammons — October 22, 1835
SMITH, James and Patsy Thornton — January 7, 1824
SMITH, James B. and Martha F. Collins — December 23, 1841
SMITH, James E. and Martha Jane Campbell — July 21, 1845
SMITH, J. B. and Harriet N. McLaughlin — March 29, 1837
SMITH, Jeremiah and Fanney Penn — October 23, 1799
SMITH, John and Pracilla Autry — January 23, 1797
SMITH, John and Nancy Stephens — December 19, 1798
SMITH, John and Patsey Bradford — February 7, 1801
SMITH, John and Fanny Martin — April 2, 1814
SMITH, John C. and Penelope P. Haynes — July 27, 1847
SMITH, John J. and Elizabeth Saffold — March 23, 1809
SMITH, Joseph and Sarah Black — October 26, 1799
SMITH, Joseph and Elizabeth Poss — January 25, 1837
SMITH, Joseph and Martha Crook — January 1, 1839
SMITH, Kilpatrick and Frances E. I. Smith — March 18, 1828
SMITH, Leon and Rebecca Robertson — June 26, 1810
SMITH, Mark and Nancy Gilham — November 29, 1814
SMITH, Marion and Sally Collier — June 25, 1807
SMITH, Montgomery and M. D. Howard — December 24, 1834
SMITH, Moses and Frances Sims — May 8, 1810
SMITH, Nathaniel C. and Sally Murphy — May 19, 1828
SMITH, Parker and Caroline Garrott — November 20, 1822
SMITH, Paschal and Polly Jewel — December 21, 1809
SMITH, Paschal and Elizabeth Ann Haynes — March 27, 1841
SMITH, Peter and Hannah Elsbury — March 25, 1794
SMITH, Peter and Polly Bridges — February 11, 1813
SMITH, Peterson and Sally Owen — September 18, 1810
SMITH, Robert B. and Matilda A. Dunn — November 24, 1841
SMITH, Robert L. and Lucinda D. Gresham — November 24, 1814
SMITH, Robin and Ginney Slaton — April 20, 1799

SMITH, Roddey and Sally Simmons — February 6, 1811
SMITH, Samuel and Martha Carter — December 16, 1845
SMITH, Thomas and Polley Barnes — January 28, 1801
SMITH, Thomas and Polly Goolsby — November 6, 1802
SMITH, Thomas M. and Margaret Gillespie — January 28, 1828
SMITH, Vines and Rebeckah Powell — September 13, 1810
SMITH, William and Isabel Foster — January 16, 1796
SMITH, William and Elizabeth Elder — December 24, 1813
SMITH, William E. and Lucy Amis — September 13, 1836
SMITH, Wm. G. and Alice Hardman — November 30, 1815
SMITH, William H. and Mary Ann Pittard — September 15, 1838
SMITH, Wm. P. and Mary Ann Berry — November 11, 1839
SMITH, Wm. P. and Camilla Jewel — February 13, 1850
SOME, Etheldnd and Sally Walker — April 7, 1810
SORRELL, Green and Susannah Barnett — June 2, 1808
SORRELL, Grine and Polly Diggins — March 17, 1808
SORRELL, Needdom and Polley Sims — August 17, 1801
SORRELLS, Wiley J. and Aby Varner — January 9, 1817
SORRELL, William and Dorcas Sanders — October 20, 1797
SORROW, Elias and Letty Bell — October 10, 1840
SORROW, Elijah and Nancy Nash — December 6, 1805
SORROW, George and Susannah Hardman — March 26, 1818
SORROW, George P. and Martha Ann Barnett — September 27, 1843
SORROW, George W. and Mary Elizabeth Davis — January 10, 1850
SORROW, Harris and Adaline Kidd — March 3, 1837
SORROW, James and Sally Hudson — June 5, 1814
SORROW, John and Priscilla Eads — June 27, 1795
SORROW, John and Sarah Johnson — April 28, 1822
SORROW, John S. and Sarah Sorrow — January 3, 1839
SORROW, Joshua and Sally Stephens — March 12, 1807
SORROW, Nicholas and Frances Smith — September 30, 1840
SORROW, William and Priclah Eads — January 14, 1805
SORROW, William and Lucy Johnson — November 14, 1815
SOUTH, John and Penelope Howell — December 29, 1825
SPARKS, Nathan and Sally Elsberry — May 10, 1800
SPRATLIN, James A. and Elizabeth Britain — December 12, 1844
SPRATLIN, James A. and Louisa Edwards — January 1, 1852
SPRATLIN, Jesse M. and Elizabeth J. Dupree — October 26, 1839
SPRATLIN, Johnson and Betsy Eberhart — December 10, 1828
SPRATLIN, Joseph and Patsey Bridges — May 5, 1829
SPRATLING, James and Lysetha Johnson — January 24, 1803
SPRATLING, William and Mary Edwards — February 1, 1823
SPRINGFIELD, Aaron and Betsy Potts — November 2, 1796
STALLINGS, Silas S. and Mandy Jackson — September 17, 1838
STAMPS, Henry and Fanny Roberts — July 4, 1832
STAMPS, James and Anna Davis Hendrick — January 7, 1818
STAMPS, John I. and Nancy Lester — June 12, 1817
STAMPS, Thomas and Polly Hendon — February 27, 1817
STANDARD, John and Patsey Turner — November 24, 1810
STANDERFORD, Benjamin and Nancy Echols — December 29, 1802
STANFIELD, Wm. B. and Elizabeth Johnson — March 16, 1820
STANFORD, Joseph and Elisabeth Reynolds — February 16, 1822

STAPLES, Thomas and Nancy England — December 20, 1834
ST. JOHN, John and Polly Dickins — April 12, 1809
STARETT, Alexander and Sarah Strong — June 8, 1820
STARKEY, Gidion and Sally Beavers — June 10, 1806
STARKS, Jesse and Nancy Short — January 12, 1819
STATEANS, Moses and Polly Moody — January 6, 1829
STEPHENS, Obediah and Martha Watkins — July 18, 1832
STEPHENS, Alexander and Elizabeth Edwards — January 3, 1825
STEPHENS, Allen and Martha Watkins — December 19, 1832
STEPHENS, David and Frances Harris — November 17, 1796
STEPHENS, George W. and Elizabeth Jane Wilson — September 31, 1850
STEPHENS, Haley and Catharine Brewer — August 4, 1812
STEPHENS, James and Sally Sorrow — July 26, 1815, or June 1, 1816
STEPHENS, John and Sarah Stewart — December 11, 1815
STEPHENS, John C. and Elizabeth Loyd — February 1, 1842
STEPHENS, Joseph and Patsey Carter — August 3, 1808
STEPHENS, Joseph and Mahala Smith — January 13, 1835
STEPHENS, Joseph and Celestia McWhorter — November 21, 1842
STEPHENS, Minor M. and Mildred L. Glenn — August 2, 1852
STEPHENS, Newton and Elizabeth Butler — November 29, 1851
STEPHENS, Thomas and Sarah Baughn — March 3, 1839
STEPHENS, Thomas P. G. and Mary A. J. Taylor — June 19, 1826
STEPHENS, William and Elizabeth Goolsby — June 23, 1798
STEPHENS, William and Susan Sorrow — August 19, 1806
STEPHENS, William and Polly Sorrow — October 16, 1809
STEP, John and Genny Diggans — June 2, 1806
STEPP, Stephen and Rosey Price — July 1, 1807
STERLING, Isaac and Sarah Lester — November 26, 1844
STERLING, Josiah and Elizabeth Muckleroy — March 31, 1814
STEVENS, Patrick M. and Sarah C. Wynn — November 21, 1848
STEVENS, Silas and Sarah P. Ogilvie — August 20, 1846
STEWART, Alfred and Hannah Phillips — November 6, 1800
STEWART, Charley and Rachel Freeman — June 2, 1801
STEWART, Floyd and Sara Williams — December 30, 1824
STEWART, George W. and Sara B. Brooks — June 10, 1829
STEWART, Gresham and Sally Ragin — October 26, 1804
STEWART, James and Jane Russell — June 12, 1822
STEWART, John B. and Parmelia Ann Wray — July 20, 1826
STEWART, John M. and Nancy Willingham — December 20, 1809
STEWART, John M. and Elizabeth J. Eason — June 3, 1839
STEWART, Thomas and Nancy Russell — December 21, 1812
STILES, Ephraim and Parmelia Ann Hopping — December 18, 1827
STILES, Joseph and Betsey Barber — March 13, 1799
STILES, Joseph and Salley Davis — July 9, 1807
STINSON, Burwell and Patsey Jones — June 13, 1806
STOKER, Arnold and Rebecca Jones — January 31, 1836
STONE, Thomas and Milley Hay — June 27, 1801
STOVALL, Isham and Emily Wright — December 8, 1835
STOVALL, Marshall K. and Angeline Bugg — January 19, 1841
STOVALL, Wm. W. and Ann Goolsby — May 1, 1850
STOVALL, Wm. Y. and Martha C. Dillard — December 18, 1849

STRAUGHN, James and Dorcas Ward — November 28, 1809
STRICKLAND, Jacob and Widow Sanders — February 22, 1798
STRICKLAND, Tilman and Rebecca House — May 6, 1822
STRINGFELLOW, Henry and Polly Moore — January 11, 1797
STRONG, Elisha and Ann Scott Hill — September 18, 1821
STRONG, John B. and Polly Wilks — September 18, 1816
STRONG, Mumford and Nancy Thomas — April 23, 1824
STRONG, Samuel and Caty Dunn — July 29, 1810
STRONG, Samuel and Oney Martin — June 12, 1818
STROUD, Sherwood and Susanah McCarty — July 17, 1810
STUBBLEFIELD, Jeremiah and Sally Nicks — December 5, 1806
STUBBLEFIELD, Joe and Polly Nicks — September 21, 1801
STUBBLEFIELD, John and Elisabeth Wooten — February 12, 1812
SUDDATH, Charles A. and Mary M. Birdsong — October 22, 1828
SUDDATH, Warren A. and Dilly Calender Whitehead — April 4, 1843
SUDDETH, Jarratt and Elizabeth Martin — December 3, 1809
SUDUTH, Seaborn M. and Martha Ann Whitehead — November 21, 1840
SUMER, Kimbrel and Martha Glenn Guthrey — February 20, 1822
SUTHERLAND, William and Ann W. Kendricks — April 28, 1825
SUTHERLIN, Edward and Casandra Varner — April 26, 1813
SWAN, Henry and Rebecca Davis — December 29, 1803
SWANSON, Andrew and Catey Smith — November 29, 1796
SWANSON, John and Anna Russell — December 12, 1803
SWANSON, William M. and Julia Hays — January 25, 1842
SWANSON, Lemnes and Polly Bledsoe — December 9, 1805

T

TALAFERRO, Warren and Polly Glenn — April 30, 1803
TALIAFERRO, Lewis B. and Elizabeth Johnson — August 10, 1809
TALLIFERRO, Nicholas M. and Ann Hill — February 8, 1824
TANNER, Archabald and Peggy Smith — December 4, 1797
TARPLEY, Archibold and Sarah B. Crowder — November 6, 1848
TARPLEY, Joel and Rachel Bradshaw — November 14, 1825
TARPLEY, John and Polly Johnson — July 15, 1810
TARPLEY, John C. and Elizabeth Jenkins — December 17, 1826
TARPLEY, Joseph and Emeline Stewart — October 28, 1817
TATE, Samuel and Polly England — January 12, 1797
TATE, William and Nancy McDaniel — January 5, 1809
TATEM, Howell and Rebecca Pearce — July 27, 1812
TAYLOR, Clark and Elizabeth Eades — September 27, 1821
TAYLOR, Clark and Elizabeth J. Smith — December 21, 1825
TAYLOR, Clark and Phoebe Calvary — May 24, 1829
TAYLOR, George and Polly House — September 9, 1808
TAYLOR, John and Tempey Fullelove — January 20, 1801
TAYLOR, John and Elizabeth Ellison — January 5, 1847
TAYLOR, John and Eliza Stubbfield — January 19, 1801
TAYLOR, John and Sally Stiles — November 17, 1802
TAYLOR, Lewis and Dorothy Ann Reed Carter — December 25, 1825
TAYLOR, William and Betsey Goolsby — March 10, 1804
TAYLOR, William and Anne McGehee — May 24, 1824
TEMPERANCE, John Oliver and R. Ogilive — December 11, 1848

TERRELL, Joseph and Nolley Powers — March 20, 1811
TERRELL, Joseph R. and Elizabeth Hood — July 1, 1816
TERRELL, Thos. H. and Sarah H. Arnold — January 29, 1826
TERRY, Orin T. and Nancy L. Patman — June 16, 1852
TERRY, Samuel and Louisa Elizabeth Simmons — April 21, 1837
THACKER, Sheldon P. and Gabriella M. Hale — February 21, 1842
THAXTON, Peter and Rhoda Nichols — November 22, 1822
THOMAS, Caleb and Sally Cutchings — July 5, 1806
THOMAS, David and Susannah Ann Mobley — December 7, 1825
THOMAS, Edward L. and Polly Hogue — August 1, 1806
THOMAS, James G. and Mary Antionett Kidd — October 8, 1846
THOMAS, Jett and Susan Cox — December 23, 1805
THOMAS, John and Martha Gregory — August 8, 1808
THOMAS, Joseph T. and Mary Ann McLaughlin — April 23, 1849
THOMAS, Solomon H. and Sarah Smith — September 21, 1846
THOMAS, Stephen and Peninnah W. Jordan — March 12, 1822
THOMAS, Stephen and Lucinda Mobley — December 20, 1832
THOMAS, William and Malinda Echols — February 28, 1815
THOMAS, William and Cleo Bentley — August 22, 1816
THOMAS, William and Polly Wright — December 27, 1817
THOMAS, William G. and Mary Short — April 3, 1843
THOMPSON, Alexander and Winney Carrington — July 15, 1810
THOMPSON, James and Elizabeth Sorrow — February 6, 1823
THOMPSON, John and Jane Mayes — March 19, 1799
THOMPSON, John and Rebeckah Simmons — October 17, 1804
THOMPSON, John and Elizabeth Short — May 7, 1817
THOMPSON, Robert and Mary Lay — October 24, 1797
THOMPSON, Samuel and Sarah Williams — June 18, 1821
THOMPSON, Thomas and Emila A. Marable — September 2, 1840
THOMPSON, Thos. P. and Susie A. Strong — July 29, 1845
THOMPSON, William and Polly Garrott — March 31, 1810
THOMPSON, William and Sally Harris — August 28, 1817
THRELKELD, Thos. J. and Elizabeth Ann Sims — October 3, 1833
THORNTON, Blanton F. and Rebecca Harris — February 11, 1832
THORNTON, Howard and Nancy Wise — April 7, 1826
THORNTON, Isaac and Jane Goolsbee — March 15, 1833
THORNTON, Isaac N. and Louisa Tiller — November 30, 1852
THORNTON, John and Polly Haynes — April 7, 1812
THORNTON, John B. and Sarah Wise — January 14, 1846
THORNTON, Peter and Rhoda Nickols — November 22, 1821
THORNTON, Richard and Viney Jennings — September 13, 1794
THORNTON, Wiley and H. H. Hardin — April 26, 1821
THORNTON, Wood and Sally Smith — March 17, 1800
THORNTON, Wyatt and Margaret Pye — March 29, 1833
THURMOND, Harris and Katharine Greenwood — February 11, 1812
THURMOND, Harris and Martha F. Oglesby — May 15, 1828
TILLER, Burwell and Nancy Green — April 9, 1817
TILLER, Elijah and Fanny Pass — December 18, 1823
TILLER, Elisha and Viney Johnson — July 19, 1824
TILLER, James R. and Elizabeth Wood — December 15, 1851
TILLER, Jasper M. and Sarah Jane Crook — September 18, 1844
TILLER, John and Mary Ann Pass — February 9, 1817

TILLER, John and Judith Hopper — August 30, 1824
TILLER, John P. and Martha A. Martin — September 13, 1838
TILLER, Marshall and Edney J. Johnson — January 30, 1839
TILLER, Martin and Leala Robertson — December 29, 1824
TILLER, Martin and Sidney M. Martin — March 6, 1843
TILLER, Mitchell D. and Elizabeth Martin — December 17, 1835
TILLER, Randal and Jane Lacy — December 26, 1811
TILLER, Robert M. and Mary Ann Patman — November 18, 1852
TILLER, Shimme J. and Nancy Jane Crooks — January 4, 1842
TILLER, Thomas P. and Elizabeth H. Howell — December 18, 1841
TILLER, William and Ritter Pass — November 22, 1810
TILLER, William and Barbara Ann Crook — December 19, 1837
TILLERY, Henry and Ruth Brown — December 28, 1795
TILLMAN, Asa and Aley Williams — June 7, 1825
TIPPER, James and Creasy McKelvay — January 10, 1811
TOMLIN, Jonathan and Rosannah Hyett — September 21, 1839
TORBET, George T. and Anna Hardman — January 16, 1825
TORBET, James and Catharine J. Smith — June 24, 1819
TOTTEN, C. W. and Emily Barnett — October 10, 1832
TOWNS, John G. and Cinthy Walker — June 18, 1814
TRAMMEL, Robert and Elizabeth Amis — May 17, 1826
TRAYLOR, John and Nancy Hales — December 17, 1808
TRAYLOR, Paschal and Milly Angle — July 6, 1795
TRAYLOR, Thomas and Betsy W. Powell — June 4, 1802
TRAYLOR, Tilmon and Lucy Walker — February 7, 1828
TRENCHARD, John A. and Frances Armstrong — May 12, 1846
TRIBBLE, Benjamin H. and Elizabeth Pinson — December 4, 1818
TRIBBLE, Joel and Sarah Phillips — March 6, 1823
TRIBLE, Bery and Elizabeth Trible — October 19, 1808
TRIBLE, Richard T. and Jane E. Crowley — November 18, 1844
TRIBLE, Thomas and Susannah Anderson — October 1, 1810
TRIPLETT, William P. and Mary Cone — December 18, 1817
TUCK, Robert and Louisa Disey O'Kelly — January 6, 1844
TUCK, Wm. and Lucy J. Pinson — December 30, 1834
TUCK, Wm. S. and Elizabeth A. E. Buzbin — January 12, 1841
TUCKER, Brinkley A. and Margaret P. Power — October 30, 1848
TUCKER, Dean and Elizabeth Kidd — October 2, 1823
TUCKER, James D. and Cynthia C. Fleeman — November 29, 1851
TUCKER, Tarpley and Elizabeth Fleeman — November 9, 1842
TUCKER, Travis and Nancy A. Carter — December 18, 1849
TUCKER, Wm. T. and Jane W. Carter — December 22, 1847
TURNER, Andrew and Betsy J. Guthrey — April 12, 1816
TURNER, Benjamin and Betsy Murray — March 4, 1799
TURNER, Benjamin and Charlotta Pass — March 5, 1811
TURNER, Benjamin and Rebecca Everhart — April 6, 1819
TURNER, Henry and Mary Patton — April 30, 1823
TURNER, John and Susannah Glenn — November 22, 1809
TURNER, Mathew and Frances Blackney — March 15, 1815
TURNER, Robert and Margaret Ector — June 18, 1805
TURNER, Robert H. and Martha A. Tiller — December 11, 1841
TUGGLE, George and Polly Swanson — December 5, 1796
TUGGLE, Robert and Eliza Jeffries — April 5, 1799

TUGGLE, William and Anna Dunn — December 9, 1797
TYE, Henry and Sally Radford — May 30, 1807
TYE, Job and Nancy McCarty — January 26, 1826
TYE, Perry and Mary Harris — December 23, 1836
TYE, Samuel and Elizabeth Jones — May 15, 1829

U

UPSON, Francis L. and Sarah S. McKinley — October 21, 1836
UPSHAW, Horton and Claresy Whitsel — November 23, 1817
UPSHAW, Tinsley and Martha L. Phillips — January 2, 1823

V

VANDIVERE, Albert T. and Mary A. Bond — January 11, 1845
VAN LANDINGHAM, Dosson and Elizabeth Smith — December 8, 1819
VARNER, Early and Lucy Callaway — January 30, 1838
VARNER, Edward and Betsy Young — December 20, 1806
VARNER, Fellereck and Sally Graves — June 27, 1808
VARNER, George and Patience Jackson — December 17, 1805
VARNER, John and Nancy Powell — January 10, 1807
VARNER, John and Mary Campbell — July 27, 1824
VARNER, Marcus and Mary A. Bradford — January 19, 1823
VARNER, Mathew and Elizabeth Hawkins — June 30, 1825
VARNER, Mathew and Sarah Lumpkin — May 4, 1833
VARNER, Robert and Martha Hudson — October 11, 1820
VARNON, John and Aley Norton — January 18, 1819
VAUGHN, Abel and Aleys Goolsby — December 26, 1835
VAUGHN, James A. and Catharine Goolsby — April 15, 1842
VAUGHN, Jonathan and Emeline Eades — November 19, 1835
VAUGHN, Jonathan C. and Martha M. Goode — December 22, 1846
VAUGHN, Miles and Susan Ann Bridges — December 30, 1850
VAUGHN, Perkins and Sarah Mathews — August 5, 1819
VAUGHN, William and Sarah Colley — October 29, 1797
VAUGHN, William and Kizziah David — December 19, 1827
VAUGHN, William and Nancy Cox — January 22, 1839
VICKERS, James and Elizabeth Martin — March 3, 1794
VINES, William and Winney Mayfield — January 29, 1811
VINTS, William and Elizabeth Hutson — May 22, 1798

W

WADDELL, Charles and Elizabeth Morton — July 11, 1826
WADE, William and Saphrona Bolton — September 11, 1837
WAGGONER, David and Frances Burford — February 7, 1824
WAGGONER, Phillip and Caly Bradley — December 28, 1803
WAGNER (Waggoner) Seaborn and Creasy McCarty — December 6, 1822
WAGNOR (Waggoner) Daniel and Nancy J. Lumpkin — December 1, 1832
WALKER, Alpha and Martha Lawrence — September 4, 1823
WALKER, Benjamin and Mahalah W. Vaughn — October 17, 1832
WALKER, Elijah and Fanny Hardman — January 15, 1822
WALKER, Elisha and Cyntha Harrell — February 23, 1826

WALKER, James V. and Mary Ann Eliza Young	July 13, 1832
WALKER, Joseph and Jane Holmes	February 3, 1800
WALKER, Joseph and Nancy Moore	October 29, 1818
WALKER, Lee and Sarah Waters	June 7, 1821
WALKER, Simeon and Polly Walker	January 23, 1799
WALLER, Benjamin B. and Eliza Raines	December 15, 1840
WALLIS, John F. and Sarah Kerr	November 21, 1818
WALLIS, Newton and Mary Higgins	December 10, 1851
WALTERS, William and Betsy Hinton	April 7, 1805
WALTON, John and Nancy H. Scott	October 22, 1807
WALTON, P. R. and E. S. Tuggle	January 4, 1836
WALTON, Thomas and Celia Bridges	December 6, 1804
WALTON, Thomas L. and Ann E. Callaway	December 21, 1836
WANE, William and Betsey Andrews	May 15, 1809
WARD, Abner and Judith Young	July 17, 1822
WARD, John and Susan Pinson	April 30, 1818
WARD, John L. and Sarah Rowland	January 24, 1822
WARD, Richard and Emily Hancock	January 4, 1842
WARD, Robert and Martha G. Bradley	May 6, 1824
WARD, William and Peggy Campbell	November 28, 1811
WARD, William and Lucy Kimbell	December 22, 1846
WARNOCK, John and Martha O'Briant	May 30, 1817
WARNOCK, Thomas and Charity Peters	January 19, 1807
WARRANT, Jeremiah and Eliza J. Caduhead	August 15, 1800
WARTEN, Anthony and Mary Bennett	December 31, 1808
WATERS, Joseph and Eliza J. Aycock	October 2, 1815
WATERS, Samuel and Anna Bradford	February 21, 1803
WATKINS, Benjamin T. and Elizabeth Center	November 19, 1820
WATKINS, Leban and Polly Jones	November 18, 1819
WATKINS, Reace and Willy Traylor	December 15, 1800
WATKINS, Thadeus R. and Mary H. Colquitt	July 19, 1852
WATLEY, Willis and Kitty Ray	August 21, 1803
WATSON, Elisha and Christina Morgan	August 28, 1810
WATSON, Gro. and Betsy Bledsoe	February 1, 1806
WATSON, Jacob and Susan Willingham	January 5, 1838
WATSON, John and Mary Eberhart	December 13, 1810
WATSON, Marion and Emily Ann Norton	April 4, 1849
WATTS, Charles and Jenny Watson	October 1, 1798
WATTS, Harrison and Mary Biddle	December 5, 1797
WATTS, Littleberry and Polly Bailey	August 16, 1810
WATTS, Pleasant and Elizabeth Bailey	March 23, 1808
WATTS, Thomas and Peggy Morton	April 14, 1796
WAYNE, William and Gilley Smith	May 13, 1807
WAYNE, William and Judith Lawrence	December 7, 1811
WEATHERFORD, Josiah and Mary Bondurant	February 4, 1824
WEAVER, Andrew and Nancy Stephens	January 25, 1815
WEAVER, Andrew B. and Nancy J. Lester	August 8, 1837
WEAVER, Edward and Dorcas Rafferty	January 25, 1809
WEAVER, Isham and Mary A. Bradley	April 5, 1820
WEAVER, John P. and Priscilla Howard	February 1, 1810
WEAVER, Reuben and Fanny Willingham	February 27, 1802
WEAVER, Samuel and Polly Patman	December 4, 1800

WEAVER, William B. and Susannah Pye — January 28, 1813
WEAVER, William B. and Lurena Wray — January 22, 1834
WEBB, Gaines and Rebecca Mahuldy Goolsby — January 3, 1842
WEBB, Henry and Susan Bellima — January 10, 1807
WEBB, Jesse and Susana Bellamy — November 29, 1809
WELLBORN, James and Mary Walton — August 24, 1828
WELLS, James and Sally Liggett — June 17, 1802
WELLS, Mathew and Eliza Moore — October 3, 1821
WELUGHY, Thomas and Polly Harrison — March 10, 1804
WHATLEY, Archibald and Fanney Sorrel — December 15, 1797
WHATLEY, Robert and Polly Martin — November 25, 1796
WHELEM, Michel and Aggy Thornton — December 10, 1802
WHEELAS, Elisha and Creasy Garrett — August 10, 1801
WHEELOUS, Miles and Ann Griffith — September 17, 1825
WHITAKER, John and Frances Hornby — November 28, 1815
WHITE, Alex and Eliza Simmons — November 5, 1799
WHITE, Anderson and Saphroney Arnold — December 7, 1836
WHITE, David and Peggy Foster — September 16, 1799
WHITE, Isiah and Sarah A. O'Kelly — August 18, 1841
WHITE, Thos. L. and Rebecca M. Meriwether — July 15, 1828
WHITE, Thomas and Barbara Nina C. Meriwether — August 22, 1850
WHITEHEAD, Joel and Polly O'Kelly — November 21, 1816
WHITEHEAD, Samuel and Rebecca Patton — May 21, 1820
WHITEHEAD, Samuel and Anna Hardman — January 5, 1841
WHITEHEAD, Wiley S. and Polly Smith — December 25, 1828
WHITFIELD, George and Sally Varner — October 4, 1820
WHITLOCK, Beasley and Betsey Bell — February 17, 1812
WHITSELL, George and Elizabeth Meadows — February 9, 1801
WHITSELL, George and Betsy Lester — August 23, 1820
WIGGLEY, Joseph and Sally Brown — February 28, 1815
WILBANKS, Elam and Rebecca Glass — June 14, 1824
WILBANKS, Elam and Mary Edmondson — December 12, 1831
WILDER, Levi and Lucy Bailey — December 22, 1818
WILDER, Seaborn and Avis Adkins — December 3, 1825
WILEY, James and Elizabeth Payton — July 19, 1809
WILEY, Mathew and Betsey Shields — December 6, 1799
WILHITE, John and Lucy Martin — December 29, 1808
WILHITE, Phillip and Mooring Latimore — April 3, 1811
WILKES, Aaron H. and Martha Connell — May 14, 1846
WILKES, Osborn and Nancy Latimore — November 30, 1809
WILKES, William and Edny Ballard — December 4, 1816
WILKINS, David and Nancy Selancy — January 15, 1822
WILKS, Amos and Betsey Kilgough (Kilgore) — September 30, 1796
WILKS, Aron and Susannah Bradley — August 21, 1806
WILKS, John and Lydia Strong — December 26, 1815
WILKS, Osborne and Matilda M. Maxey — October 26, 1825
WILKS, William and Rebecca Strong — October 4, 1820
WILLIAMS, Arrington and Elizabeth Thornton — October 23, 1797
WILLIAMS, Henry E. and Caroline V. Bailey — March 9, 1819
WILLIAMS, Hugh and Salley Moore — July 28, 1807
WILLIAMS, James and Sarah Beasley — December 18, 1817
WILLIAMS, Joshua and Elizabeth Woodal — January 8, 1810

WILLIAMS, Matthew and Frances (blank)   October 29, 1809
WILLIAMS, Nathan and Elizabeth Adkins   January 6, 1823
WILLIAMS, Thomas and Susan H. Hill   January 6, 1819
WILLIAMS, Thomas and Nancy B. Landrum   January 6, 1835
WILLIAMS, William and Polly Weaver   January 26, 1802
WILLIAMS, William and Patsey Peters   October 18, 1802
WILLIAMS, William and Sally Mitchell   December 22, 1797
WILLIAMS, Wm. F. and Emily Allen   July 13, 1850
WILLIAMS, Wm. K. and Elizabeth Sappington   June 12, 1828
WILLIAMS, Wm. T. and Mary C. Towns   October 29, 1841
WILLIAMSON, John and Polly Arther   December 31, 1828
WILLIAMSON, Thos. W. and Elizabeth J. Townsend   December 31, 1826
WILLIAMSON, William and Tracy Wheeless   March 19, 1829
WILLIAMSON, Wm. F. and Charlotte M. Brown   November 15, 1836
WILLIFORD, John and Lucy Wright   January 20, 1807
WILLINGHAM, Alban and Bedea Herring   March 28, 1815
WILLINGHAM, Benjamin V. and Sarah Jane Smith   September 4, 1837
WILLINGHAM, Geo. W. and Mary Ann Patton   November 24, 1842
WILLINGHAM, Jesse and Judith Goolsby   June 30, 1803
WILLINGHAM, Jesse and Polly Zuber   February 25, 1804
WILLINGHAM, Jesse and Linda Floyd   January 1, 1828
WILLINGHAM, Joel A. and Susan Betsy Ann Walker   December 5, 1842
WILLINGHAM, Joseph and Mary Eason   September 16, 1831
WILLINGHAM, Troy and Elizabeth Bradley   November 20, 1816
WILLINGHAM, Willis and Susan Gillespie   August 31, 1841
WILSON, Benjamin H. and Lucinda E. Hopper   March 23, 1850
WILSON, Elijah and Fanny Ellis   November 16, 1822
WILSON, Hiram and Patsey Lowry   April 18, 1821
WILSON, James J. W. and Sarah A. Johnson   August 22, 1848
WILSON, James T. and Emily Barker   August 30, 1845
WILSON, John L. and Catherine Woodruff   May 13, 1829
WILSON, Joseph and Sally Pennington   July 4, 1798
WILSON, Joseph L. and Jane Barber   November 17, 1841
WILSON, Nelson and Susannah Woodruff   March 6, 1797
WILSON, Nicholas H. and Mertriss F. Wright   August 27, 1842
WILSON, Oliver P. and Jane Elizabeth Johnson   November 25, 1844
WILSON, Richard and Margaret Calhoun   November 30, 1803
WILSON, Washington and (blank)   October 12, 1798
WILSON, William and Martha Wright   September 29, 1814
WILSON, William S. and Delilah McCannon   December 25, 1835
WIMBISH, John and Ana Jane Bridges   April 4, 1809
WIMPEE, Tyro and Mary Bangan   September 7, 1799
WIMPEY, Mathew and Holley Ragan   June 25, 1807
WINFREY, Francis W. and Virginia Louisa Nunnally Nov. 18, 1846
WINFREY, William and Judith Wayne   October 7, 1819
WINGFIELD, Nathan and Elizabeth Thompson   November 28, 1797
WINN, David H. and Susan Farmer   October 27, 1838
WINN, Thomas B. and Caroline C. Hurt   January 13, 1836
WINTER, John W. and Permelia Edwards   April 4, 1845
WISE, Abner and Sarah Gilham   October 21, 1824
WISE, Jacob and Elizabeth Hubbard   December 18, 1797
WISE, Joel and Jane Steward   July 26, 1802

WISE, John and Judith Lacy — July 16, 1800
WISE, John and Martha Fanning — August 18, 1818
WISE, Patterson and Polly Lacy — September 14, 1802
WISE, Robert and Sarah Holt — October 21, 1800
WISE, Sherrod and Cyntha Colquitt — January 18, 1821
WISE, Zachariah and Catharine S. Glenn — December 18, 1821
WISE, Walen and Edna Wish (or Wise) — April 10, 1826
WITCHER, Ambrose and Mary Olive — November 6, 1837
WITT, David and Nancy George — July 22, 1801
WOOD, Fountain and Nancy Barnett — February 24, 1825
WOOD, Henry and Nancy Sorrow — May 29, 1794
WOOD, John and Nancy Vaughn — November 21, 1839
WOOD, Richard and Nancy Washburn — January 1, 1815
WOOD, Wm. B. J. and Martha Jane Davis — December 19, 1848
WOOD, Zachariah and Polly Wood — December 8, 1794
WOODALL, Tolbut (Tolbert) and Lydia Stubblefield — January 4, 1827
WOODROOF, Elijah and Polly Hill — December 4, 1802
WOODROOF, Clifford and Delina Perkins — November 21, 1804
WOODRUFF, Benjamin and Sally O'Kelly — September 21, 1820
WOODRUFF, Reubin and Frances F. Rosenberry — January 15, 1818
WOODS, John and Pincy Eads — August 29, 1850
WOODS, Samuel and Mary Johnson — April 17, 1819
WOODS, Samuel J. and Emily Tiller — December 16, 1852
WOODY, Samuel and Lorene J. Stamps — December 19, 1827
WOOTEN, John and Betsey Anderson — August 30, 1796
WOOTEN, John and Mary E. Goolsby — February 23, 1850
WORRAL, John and Patsey Young — October 11, 1797
WRAY, Albert G. and Susan M. Coxe — November 5, 1833
WRAY, William and Nancy Elliott — June 21, 1810
WRAY, Wiley and Margaret Johnson — December 26, 1816
WRIGHT, Asa and Jane Jones — April 10, 1823
WRIGHT, David and Elizabeth Hubbard — December 10, 1828
WRIGHT, George and Sarah Bridges — October 24, 1794
WRIGHT, James B. and Lucy Waters — August 28, 1815
WRIGHT, James T. and Eliza Yancey — September 30, 1836
WRIGHT, Johnson and Lucy Kidd — October 30, 1815
WRIGHT, Michal and Marion Clay — December 9, 1794
WRIGHT, Michael and Elizabeth Ann Sams — June 28, 1825
WRIGHT, Milton and Mary Ann Lumpkin — August 12, 1822
WRIGHT, Niling J. and Sarah Yancey — November 28, 1838
WRIGHT, Reubin and Sophah Ellis — October 12, 1816
WRIGHT, William and Jemima Smith — November 17, 1807
WRIGHT, Willie and Betsey Jones — January 18, 1810
WRIGHT, Winfield Jett and Mary Ann Aycock — December 22, 1813
WRIGLEY, John and Jane Crowder — October 12, 1809
WYATT, James and Eliza Ellis — November 5, 1798
WYNN, James and Hannah Thompson — January 22, 1812
WYNN, John L. and Maniva Thornton — June 1, 1835
WYNN, William and Frances Latimer — November 21, 1848
WYNNE, Asel and Sarah Ann Brooks — August 3, 1841
WYNNE, James and Peggy Step — May 7, 1806
WYNNE, John and Susannah Owen — October 30, 1809

Y

YANCEY, Thomas E. and E. Floyd	June 8, 1843
YARBROUGH, John and Nancy Raven	February 14, 1807
YARBROUGH, Wiley and Elizabeth Ferguson	May 1, 1823
YATES, Ervin and Agnes Hough	November 4, 1810
YORENCE, James and Rachael Hughey	November 13, 1799
YOUNG, Exum and Margaret S. Young	August 18, 1807
YOUNG, Frederick and Margaret Tanner	July 16, 1807
YOUNG, Henry and Polly Ward	January 2, 1812
YOUNG, James and Caroline Pace	November 15, 1849
YOUNG, James M. and Ann Young	December 22, 1841
YOUNG, John R. and Perrina Jane Goolsby	November 11, 1847
YOUNG, John T. and Elizabeth T. Glass	October 8, 1822
YOUNG, John T. and May Leftwich	July 25, 1828
YOUNG, Mack H. and Margaret Patrick	May 1, 1843
YOUNG, Moses and Polly Fair	December 15, 1798
YOUNG, Robert N. and Rebecca Brooks	February 14, 1833
YOUNG, Sanford W. and Nancy McElroy	February 10, 1820
YOUNG, Thomas N. and Jane Gresham	February 15, 1811
YOUNG, Wilie and Samuel Elizabeth Young	November 29, 1847

Z

ZUBER, Daniel and Nancy Finch	February 6, 1805
ZUBER, Emanuel and Nancy Anderson	September 10, 1807
ZUBER, Isaac and Rebecca Willingham	July 18, 1795
ZUBER, Joshua and Martha O. Brooks	October 24, 1838
ZUBER, Thomas E. and Martha Ann McElroy	December 21, 1840
ZUBER, William and Elizabeth Arthur	January 10, 1828
ZUBER, William M. and Mariah H. Brooks	February 13, 1838